Changing Europe

'The authors are to be congratulated for the production of a volume that combines clarity of thought with clarity of expression. *Changing Europe: Identities, Nations and Citizens* is prescient, topical and deals squarely with the main issues that face Europe at this decisive time in the continent's political development. It will engage the interest of a wide range of scholars and students of Europe.'

Dr Karl Cordell, *Principal Lecturer in Politics, University of Plymouth*

'This book offers an admirably clear and coherent introduction to many of the major issues confronting Europe at the start of the twenty-first century, and to the changing agenda of European governance and integration'.

Robert Bideleux, *University of Wales, Swansea*

What does 'Europe' mean and how is it changing?

Is there a European identity?

What are the main issues facing Europe in the twenty-first century?

Europe has changed significantly and is now facing even more dramatic transformations with the enlargement of the European Union, the introduction of the euro and its increased role as a global actor in world affairs. This clear and accessible textbook provides an introduction to the key issues now shaping the new Europe and its citizens.
The book features:

- A history of the idea of 'Europe' and the development of the European nation state
- Analysis of European identity and the challenges posed by citizenship, migration, human rights, regionalism and nationalism
- Examination of the enlargement process and the impact of globalisation
- Key learning points, text boxes and guides for further reading to help students

Changing Europe: Identities, Nations and Citizens is an essential user-friendly textbook for students of European politics and European societies.

David Dunkerley, Lesley Hodgson and **Andrew Thompson** teach at the University of Glamorgan, Wales. **Stanisław Konopacki** is a lecturer at the University of Łodz, Poland. **Tony Spybey** is Professor of Sociology at Staffordshire University and Visiting Professor of Sociology at Glamorgan University.

EUROPEAN POLITICS
Please visit our European Politics Arena at www.politicsarena.com/euro

Changing Europe

Identities, nations and citizens

David Dunkerley, Lesley Hodgson,
Stanisław Konopacki, Tony Spybey
and Andrew Thompson

London and New York

First published 2002 by Routledge
11 New Fetter Lane, London EC4P 4EE

Simultaneously published in the USA and
Canada
by Routledge
29 West 35th Street, New York, NY 10001

*Routledge is an imprint of the Taylor & Francis
Group*

© 2002 David Dunkerley, Lesley Hodgson,
Stanisław Konopacki, Tony Spybey and
Andrew Thompson

Typeset in Century Old Style by Keystroke,
Jacaranda Lodge, Wolverhampton
Printed and bound in Great Britain by
TJ International Ltd, Padstow, Cornwall

British Library Cataloguing in Publication Data
A catalogue record for this book is available
from the British Library

*Library of Congress Cataloging in Publication
Data*
A catalog record for this book has been
requested

ISBN 0–415–26777–3 (hbk)
ISBN 0–415–26778–1 (pbk)

For Abigail, Daniel, Elżbieta, Harriet, Hugh, Llewellyn, Mateusz and Natalie, whose lives will be so different as Europe changes.

Contents

CONTENTS

Tables

Chapter 1

Introduction

'Europe' is changing. While this may seem a statement of the obvious, it is nevertheless one that arguably more accurately applies to the present state of affairs in the European Union than to any time since the 1957 Treaty of Rome established the European Economic Community. Since the 1951 Treaty of Paris created the European Coal and Steel Community, the first step in the process of European integration, the membership of what we now recognise as the EU has expanded in size from its original six founding countries to its current fifteen member states. The scope of the EU has changed too during this period; from the original, limited concerns relating to the coal and steel industries to the broad, and expanding, portfolio that includes, among other areas, environmental policy, transport, regional development, education and training, cultural affairs, and significantly enhanced control over economic matters. Almost daily, new policies and directives are emerging from Brussels in areas as diverse as the environment, crime, justice systems, transport and consumer issues. Today, however, the EU is on the threshold of some of the most dramatic changes in the history of European integration.

At the time of submitting this manuscript, for example, the European Council in Laeken is about to debate 'the future of Europe' with a view to generating a common foreign and security policy. Moreover, the European Union was within days of introducing a European currency – the euro – to be used by the majority of its member states. With an eye on the very near future, the European Commission was making considerable progress in the negotiations to admit possibly ten new member states by 2004. The process of eastward enlargement holds numerous serious implications for the EU, not least that its institutions will have to undergo substantial restructuring in order to cope with the pressures of expanded membership (this matter was addressed in the 2001 Treaty of Nice).

The enlargement of the EU also raises issues relating to the meaning of 'Europe'. As we show in this book, in the post-1945 era what 'Europe' symbolises has become increasingly linked to the EU. During this period many of the countries currently applying to join the EU were on the other side of the 'Iron Curtain', allied with the USSR. Enlargement has therefore prompted discussion of what the common bonds between Europeans in an expanded Union are, as well as of where the external borders of 'Europe' now lie. Enlargement, and more particularly the possibility that increased size might mean increased distance from EU citizens, has also given rise to calls to reform not just the institutions of the EU, but also how the EU links with its citizens. The White Paper on *European Governance*, released in July 2001, notes that the 'Union is often seen as remote and at the same time too intrusive', and advocates a process of wide-ranging reform – including linking with citizens via local and regional democracy -- in order to connect EU citizens better to the EU. Change, then, refers not just to the mechanics of the processes driving the EU forward but also to the way in which what 'Europe' – as represented by the EU – means is evolving.

A changing 'Europe' therefore has a bearing on, and raises issues relating to, the identities of the inhabitants of the EU and the applicant countries. This volume addresses these issues at various levels – the region, the nation, the state, and the EU itself. How identities, as much as government, operate at different levels is a key concern for politicians and public alike as 'Europe' evolves.

Extracts from Tony Blair's speech to the European Research Institute, University of Birmingham, 23 November 2001

The instability of the world today makes a successful Europe more necessary than ever . . . The benefits delivered by the European Union and its forerunners have been enormous. The network of interdependence has helped countries across the continent develop stable and prosperous democracies . . . Europe has enlarged to include new democracies and now is opening to the former Communist bloc. We have a common foreign and security policy which offers hope to troubled regions like the Balkans and Afghanistan . . . Europe is in the forefront of world trade liberalisation and better help for developing countries. And now most of this new market of 380m people has a common currency. Yet Europe now faces huge challenges as it integrates and expands: how to make the single currency work well; economic reform; development of a common defence policy; and fundamental reform of its institutions . . . we must be whole-hearted, not half-hearted, partners in Europe . . . as a union of nations working more closely together, not a federal superstate submerging national identity . . . I want a sovereignty rooted in democratic consent. Rooted in being, in this century, not just a national power in shifting alliances, but a great European power in a lasting Union. A Union of nations, of democracies with shared goals, delivering shared peace and prosperity for our citizens.

The extract from the UK Prime Minister's speech encapsulates many of the changes and challenges currently confronting the EU, including the perennial matter of the relationship between national identities and European integration. While Tony Blair's vision is a positive one, it is not as committed as those of many other European leaders who would argue for more fundamental changes of both the Union itself and its institutions. The President of the European Commission, Romano Prodi, speaking two weeks earlier at the College of Europe in Bruges, argued forcefully for an enlarged and more united Europe.

Extracts from Romano Prodi's speech to the College of Europe, Bruges, 12 November 2001

We have the recipe for a form of integration which is both supranational and also respectful of the nations and states that it is composed of, however large or small: the Community method. Only this method, based on common institutions, allows member countries, large and small to contribute on an equal footing to carry out a joint project. We shall shortly have a Convention that will bring together the representatives of the European and national institutions to prepare the future of the Union . . . From the very beginning, this Commission's priority has been enlargement. We have already made extraordinary progress along the road . . . In a year's time, we shall be giving our assessment of each country's ability to take on the rights and obligations of membership of the Union. We are confident that at that time we will be able to conclude the negotiations with the countries that have complied with the accession criteria. In line with the objectives set by Parliament and the European Council, the necessary ratifications can be completed and these countries can enter the Union before the elections in June 2004. The determination with which we work for enlargement must not, however, make us blind or deaf to the fears that accompany this process. The foremost preoccupation is security. This is a legitimate concern to which we must give concrete answers. With enlargement, the European Union is faced with the problem of controls at its own external borders. Europe does not consider itself a fortress under siege, nor does it want to erect new walls . . . However, at this particular moment in time effective border controls are essential to internal security and public confidence . . . Europeans have constructed an area of wellbeing, development, stability and social justice and have achieved economic and monetary union . . . Europe has the resources and capacity to become a global player in the search for a new multipolar balance in the new century. An enlarged Europe working with the Euro will, above all, have the size and demographic, economic and financial weight to constitute a fundamental component in world equilibriums . . . Although each country has its own particular characteristics, European societies share a vision of human rights and the rights and duties of citizens and institutions that is based on a sense of solidarity . . . What does it mean to be European today, in Europe and the world? Trying to answer that question in practical deeds and proposals has been the guiding principle of our work . . . Europe is at a turning point in its history.

Both speeches address issues of central concern to this book, namely enlargement, the nation-state, integration, identity, sovereignty, immigration, human rights, citizenship, globalisation and so on. These are the issues confronting Europe at its 'turning point in history'. How the EU should proceed from this point is the subject of considerable debate. European politicians themselves appear as unsure as anyone, with Tony Blair calling for a 'superpower not a superstate', Jacques Chirac wanting 'not a United States of Europe but a United Europe of States', and Joschka Fischer supporting the idea of a 'European Federation'.

At the same time, it is questionable whether the citizens of Europe are actually welcoming these changes whatever and wherever they may be. A situation has developed where fewer people have been known to vote in European elections than in television game shows, where European-wide opinion polls show apathy if not outright opposition, where citizens express their feelings of alienation, exclusion and powerlessness to changes at the European level and where results of recent referenda (for example, in Ireland and Denmark) show citizens expressing their hostility to proposed changes. The European Commission is aware of the need to harness support at the grass-roots level and, indeed, the 2001 *Governance* White Paper is one such attempt to alleviate the 'democratic deficit' and the *grand ennui* especially in relation to European Union policy-making.

Against this backdrop, this volume addresses both the changes within institutions and developments relating to the identities of the citizens of the expanding

EU. The structure of the book has a clear pattern in addressing change at different levels, starting with past changes that explain the present, examining the issue of contemporary change at the national and sub-national level, moving to the impact of change on the individual whether as a citizen or a migrant or an asylum-seeker, and then broadening out to understand the institutions of the EU, including just what is being proposed with the candidate countries and, finally, to recognise that the EU is a player on the global stage, influencing and being influenced by global forces.

Our discussion of these issues begins with a consideration of an issue that is central to the debate on the future of Europe: citizenship. Within western Europe the growing interest in the idea of citizenship has been a result of the increased 'power gap' between governed and governments, raising in turn the question of rights and the potential for subjects to become 'citizens'. Furthermore, the deficiencies of welfare states and their questionable continuing ability to provide citizens with social conditions that have been enjoyed for the past fifty years have become more poignant in recent years.

Chapter 2 examines the idea of citizenship within the context of the tradition of European political thought. The starting point is Aristotle, where, in his *Politics*, 'man' is treated as a political animal whose identity is determined by participation in the *polis*. From here, the development of the idea of citizenship is briefly discussed within the traditions of the Roman Empire, the Middle Ages and the Renaissance. Special attention is given to the notion of 'modernity', starting with Marshall's ideas as an important reference point for all contemporary discussions of the problem. The four modern philosophical doctrines that focus on the idea of citizenship – liberalism, republicanism, communitarianism, neo-republicanism – are also discussed.

Chapter 2 also addresses the issue of European citizenship. There has been a growing interest in the idea of European citizenship over the past decade largely as a result of four political developments. First, the liberation of east central Europe and German reunification; second, the issue of European integration marked by the Maastricht Treaty and the Treaty of Amsterdam; third, the increasing number of immigrants coming to Europe from different parts of the world; and fourth, the challenge of further EU enlargement. The discussion therefore examines the objectives behind EU citizenship, the main purposes of which are to enhance the rights and freedoms of member states' nationals, to reduce the so-called democratic deficit, to create a European identity and to delimit those belonging to the EU. The provisions regarding European citizenship within the Maastricht Treaty, the Treaty of Amsterdam and the Treaty of Nice are central here.

The development of a transnational form of citizenship holds implications for the relationship between citizens and their national states, as modern citizenship rights have developed within the framework of the nation-state. Across the world there is speculation about the future of the nation-state; in the EU, and for those states which are in the process of applying to join the EU, this is an issue that is arguably of greater significance than for states elsewhere in the world. As most commentators, and even national politicians, recognise, membership of the EU comes at some cost with respect to the degree of control that national governments may exert over affairs within the territory over which they have *de jure* control. The introduction of the single currency zone for some member states has advanced this process qualitativel Chapter 3 therefore discusses the changing fortunes of the nation-state in Europe asks what is meant by 'nation-state' before exploring the development of the idea of the nation-state from the late eighteenth century to the contemporary period. The overall aim here is to consider why people have to position themselves as 'belonging' to a national community and assess whether there is any likelihood that this identification is likely to diminish in the future.

Chapter 4 continues this discussion of national identity. Political developments unfolding across Europe in recent years testify to the continuing salience of nationalism and national identity as major political forces. From the war in Kosovo and more recent disputes in Macedonia to the ongoing disputes about the implications of European integration for national identity, it is evident that nationalism remains a powerful force in European societies. Chapter 4 begins by examining how we can define 'nation' and 'nationalism', before moving on to discuss what factors have contributed to the rise and development of nationalism in Europe. The chapter finishes by evaluating some of the strategies employed to resolve conflict between nation-states, as well as between national groups.

Chapter 5 moves the discussion away from nations and nation-states to a more local form of attachment: the region. Over the course of the post-1945 period, and particularly since the late 1970s, a number of those states now incorporated within the EU have sponsored processes of regionalisation. There are nevertheless considerable disparities between the powers exercised by regions across the EU and the applicant countries. At one end of the scale, the federal systems in Belgium and Germany, for example, give elected regional politicians the right directly to participate in the EU policy-making process. At the other end, the Republic of Ireland, Greece, and many of the countries of central and eastern Europe do not possess a regional tier of government. Pressures to devolve more executive and legislative powers to regions are growing, however. In part, these pressures come from domestic political movements, as was the case in the reforms that led to the creation of a new constitution in Spain in 1978 and the changes in the UK in the late 1990s. The EU has also been a major influence in bringing regions more firmly into the limelight. From the beginning of EU regional policy in the 1970s to the European Commission's recent calls for greater involvement of regional governments in developing and implementing EU policy, the EU has helped the region to step out of the shadow of the nation-state.

Chapters 6 and 7 discuss the complementary issues of migration, asylum-seeking and human rights in Europe. Although migration to many European countries has occurred consistently since the end of the Second World War, it now has a changed and changing face. Economic migration has given way to political migration; the source countries of migrants have shifted from former colonial countries to a more global setting but especially from eastern and central Europe and North Africa; the sheer numbers have become almost overwhelming for some countries. In view of the changing nature of immigration, Chapter 6 looks specifically at how the situation has unfolded in France, Germany, the United Kingdom, Sweden and some Mediterranean countries. No consistent picture emerges given that national rather than European policy has tended to prevail. This is as true for asylum-seekers, although a clearer European strategy is beginning to emerge.

Chapter 7 argues that human rights have traditionally been bound up with national sovereignty, and that moves to internationalise rights have largely been hampered by a lack of commitment and implementation at nation-state level. The wide disparity between proclaimed ideals, expressed intentions and the actual situation is therefore emphasised. The role of the nation-state in the implementation of human rights treaties is analysed, as is the growth, in the post-1945 era, of various supranational mechanisms in Europe for advancing human rights.

Chapter 8 continues the focus on Europe as a transnational space, although here the focus is on the broader issue of a European identity. As this chapter argues, 'Europe' and 'European' are *ideas*, and as such the manner in which they have been defined has altered since the Middle Ages, when, as we will show, interest began to grow in them. How these ideas have been given form has always held important implications both for those who have been defined as belonging to 'Europe' and those defined as non-'European', and have been informed by changing political currents. In exploring the idea of 'Europe' and, more particularly, 'European identity', this chapter addresses three main issues. First, it considers the development of the idea of 'Europe' in order to demonstrate how the borders of this entity, and the cultural substance it supposedly embodies, have altered since the Middle Ages. Second, it examines the efforts of the EU, and the European Commission in particular, to give form to the idea of European identity. The final concern of the chapter is to point to the diversity within 'Europe'.

Part of the concern in Chapter 8 is the extent to which EU citizens identify with EU institutions. In recent years, and most recently within the 2001 *Governance* White Paper, concern has grown within the European Commission that EU citizens are unclear about the functions of the main institutions of the EU. Chapter 9 discusses the role of these institutions along with the process of European integration. Of the main institutions, arguably the most powerful is the intergovernmental institution of the Council of Ministers. By contrast the supranational bodies of the European Commission, the European Parliament and the European Court of Justice, while crucial to the principles of union, have yet to achieve the power to overrule the Council of Ministers and its nation-state government participants.

As has already been noted, enlargement, the subject of Chapter 10, will bring reform to these institutions. The chapter begins by addressing enlargement in an historical context, briefly outlining the processes undergone through previous enlargements, the rapid political/social changes in central and east European countries after 1989 and the strategy used by the Commission to assess whether a *prima facie* case existed for exploring further which countries might gain entry and which, in the first wave, might not. There are clear problems associated with enlargement. There has never been such an ambitious programme of enlargement. Never has there been entry of countries with such low relative incomes and the consequent problem of how to address the commitment to income redistribution. Enlargement is taking place in the wider context of increased economic globalisation. Euroscepticism within existing EU countries cannot be ignored. Further, there is the issue of how the enlarged EU will be seen by those countries at its new borders, especially Russia. Chapter 10 looks specifically at these problems and in so doing also examines the EU's *political* role, its *economic* role, and the impact of enlargement on the net budget contributors to the EU such as Germany, the UK and the Netherlands and aspects of European *social policy*.

Chapter 11 concludes the discussion of a changing Europe by looking at the place of an expanding EU within a global context. One of the earliest texts (Robertson 1992) contains the proposition that globalisation has existed for 2000 years – in other words, for the same period as Christianity. Globalisation also figures strongly in the work of Giddens (1990) who affirms that European (or Western) culture is the world's first truly global culture but that true globalisation has occurred only with the electronic communications revolution of the past two decades or so. The spatial dimension of globalisation is explicit in the term itself but the effects are unevenly distributed and the old inequalities remain or else are replaced by new ones. Ohmae (1996) describes a 'global triad' in which the full benefits of globalisation are concentrated in three geographic areas: North America, Europe and East Asia, especially Japan. By 'Europe' is meant the European Union, the existence of which may in large part be explained in terms of the growth of the other two parts of this 'triad'.

With the introduction of the euro and the possibility of increased responsibilities in the field of defence and security, the role of the EU as a key player on the global stage looks set to grow. The extent to which the EU is capable of acting as the voice of its member states on the world stage, however, let alone its citizens, remains to be seen. As the discussion in the following chapters suggests, for the near future it is difficult to imagine the EU emerging as a contender to nations and nation-states for the loyalties of EU citizens. The EU has undoubtedly succeeded in creating awareness of 'Europe', although not necessarily in a positive sense, and the changes mentioned at the outset may well enhance attachments to 'Europe'. The challenge will be to find ways of embracing the various levels of European identities in a changing Europe.

European citizenship

Key concepts

- Citizenship
- Nationality
- EU Citizenship
- Rights

Introduction

Within western Europe the growing interest in the idea of citizenship over the past ten years is mainly the result of three political developments. First, the liberation of central-east Europe and German unification; second, the issue of European integration marked by the Maastricht Treaty, the Amsterdam Treaty, and, finally, the challenge of further enlargement of the EU and the increasing number of immigrants coming to Europe from different parts of the world. The accession negotiations with the central-east European countries, which started in 1998, show that the prospect of their membership in the European Union poses the most important challenge to the privileges and rights of Western societies acquired and preserved so far by the concept of European citizenship. This process exacerbates the conflict between the universalistic principles of constitutional democracies, on the one hand, and the particularistic claims of communities to preserve the integrity of their habitual ways of life, on the other (see Habermas 1994: 255–256).

These three European phenomena are accompanied by some internal developments (visible at the national level) that somehow undermine the traditional idea of citizenship. Mass unemployment provides the gloomiest perspective for millions of people, excluding them from a sense of full participation in the civic society. Another issue is the conflict between the rights of the citizen and the overwhelming power of the contemporary state and private corporations. The issues at stake here include the rights to privacy in the context of accumulation of electronic data on individuals and the right to employment in a situation when a growing number of sectors of the economy are dependent on international financial markets. Interest in citizenship has also been heightened by the rising profile of 'new social movements', such as the feminist and gay rights movements and those groups representing ethnic minority groups. These movements problematise our ideas of identity and rights, as they are defined within traditional political settings. National citizenship, it seems, is being undermined by globalising developments as well as by local forces. These two opposing pressures, however, are intertwined. Local groups express their identity most forcefully as global developments tend to threaten them. It is no coincidence, for example, that the process of European integration is accompanied by a growth in support for nationalistic movements opposed to the idea of unification (for example, Le Pen's National Front and Haider's Freedom Party). The two developments undermine the stability of the state and thereby the civic dimension it determines.

The concept of citizenship

Usually the concept of citizenship involves both formal and substantive dimensions. Formally understood, citizenship refers to a status legally ascribed to a certain group of individuals that binds them together and distinguishes them from other individuals of the same or a different citizenship status. This status is conferred (or not) on an individual by the political community that constitutes the sovereign power (Sorensen 1996: 14). Thus, citizenship simultaneously excludes certain groups of people who are defined legally as not part of the political community. Throughout European history, among those excluded were the slaves in ancient Greece, women, children, workers, the poor, criminals and non-nationals in modern nation-states.

> The Greek word denoting the citizen – *polity* – comes from the term *polis* and means the rule of an individual (*polity*) by the community (*polis*), i.e. city-state. In the Roman tradition, on the other hand, the relationship between a citizen (*civis*) and the group (*civitas*) denotes a situation in which an individual plays a superior role to the state. Therefore, citizenship generally denotes a special kind of direct relationship (usually characterised by certain rights and obligations) between an individual and a political community (Barbalet 1988: 15). The status of citizenship refers only to individuals and not to any group of people like classes, minorities and organisations. On the other hand, a political community should be conceived in a very broad sense as an entity rooted in different geo-political and historical environments. Typical examples of these various polities are the Greek city-state, the Roman Empire, Feudal Europe, the modern nation-state, regional polities such as the European Union and *cosmopolis*.

The substantive dimension of citizenship involves rights and duties conferred upon individuals of a particular political community. These rights and duties may be seen as instruments of the political community in its effort to create internal security, stability and identity. Citizenship provides a sense of loyalty and belonging as well as (through, for example, military service and taxes) the resources for the survival of the community (Sorensen 1996: 15).

Marshall's account of citizenship in the modern Europe

In the context of European modernity, national belonging determined the formal dimension of citizenship in the nation-state whereas the substantive content developed together with different phases of capitalism. T.H. Marshall in *Citizenship and Social Class* (1950) gave one of the best-known syntheses of the development of modern citizenship. According to him, citizenship is linked to the development of three sets of rights and is accompanied by the creation of appropriate institutions. Civil rights developed in the eighteenth century and concerned the individual freedoms and justice provided by the courts and judicial system. Political rights were established in the nineteenth century and related to political participation and communal decision-taking procedures. The twentieth century was marked by the emergence of social rights that provide an appropriate level of life linked to education and welfare services. Marshall argued that 'the modern drive towards social equality is the latest phase of an evolution of citizenship which has been in continuous progress for some 250 years' (Marshall 1950: 7).

In Marshall's opinion the establishment of civil rights supported the development of capitalism because individual freedom manifested itself as economic freedom. The satisfaction of social rights, however, was made possible only by increased taxation that worked against the principles of the capitalist market. In a famous phrase Marshall said that: 'in the twentieth century, citizenship and the capitalist system have been at war' (cited in Oliver and Heater 1994: 34). This issue reflects two features of his idea of citizenship: its relationship to the notion of class and its integrative character. As far as the relation to class is concerned, citizenship involves equality of rights and duties, whereas class is a structure of social inequality. Therefore, the growth of citizenship seems to be contradictory to the development of capitalism. The rise of the class system enhanced by the development of capitalism took place in the nineteenth century when political rights were still minimal. The increasing importance of social rights, on the other hand, works against the perpetuation of inequality, although there are limits to 'how far the egalitarian movement may be pushed. In particular, citizenship and the economic system operate with different standards as to what inequalities may be regarded as legitimate' (Hindess 1994: 21).

In his later works Marshall tried to find a compromise between class and citizenship by introducing the model of the 'hyphenated society' of democratic-welfare-capitalism. It was an alternative project of the organisation of social life to the society developed around the single idea of citizenship. As Hindess remarks, the 'hyphenated society can succeed only if it is recognised that both the welfare sector and the mixed economy are contributing to the creation of welfare . . . it is hardly possible to maintain democratic freedom in a society which does not contain a large area of economic freedom' (Hindess 1994: 21).

Discussing the question of the integrative effect of citizenship, Marshall says that it generates 'a direct sense of community membership based on loyalty to a civilisation that is a common possession. It is a loyalty of free men endowed with rights and protected by a common law' (Marshall 1950: 40–41). The concept of civilisation as a common possession denotes the ability of its members to participate in the political and social life of the community to which they belong. Here 'equality of status is more important than equality of income'. The first provides conditions in which other inequalities might be accepted. Marshall argues that 'status differences can receive the stamp of legitimacy in terms of democratic citizenship provided they are not an expression of hereditary privilege' (Marshall 1950: 75–76). Within this concept class inequalities are not legitimated but the idea of citizenship does not exclude other form of inequalities.

Marshall's thoughts (relying upon British experience) may be conceived as a possible answer to solve the problem of the relationship between capitalism and democracy by seeking to reconcile formal equality with the reality of class division. In his opinion, a welfare state providing some social benefits for a citizen would mitigate the negative consequences imposed by the market. The role of social rights guaranteed by social services would be to ensure participation of all citizens in the social and political life of the community. These rights found their full realisation within the framework of the British welfare state. This body of relatively simple ideas appeared to be very influential not only in Britain, but also in American political science.

Origins of European citizenship

For many years the European Community was mainly concerned with market issues, and did not consider the political and civil rights of nationals of member states (Oliver and Heater 1994: 133). It treated individuals as economic actors and in European legislation the term 'workers' was used rather than 'citizens'. The European Assembly, established by the Treaty of Rome, provided the minor political and civil role of individuals, but this body did not have any legislative power. In its most recent incarnation the European Parliament was supposed to express the will of the population of the member states and not the interests of governments themselves.

The first reference to European citizenship was made at the meeting of Heads of States in Paris in December 1974, where it was proposed that a 'working group be instructed to study the conditions and the timing under which the citizens of the nine Member States could be given special rights as Members of the Community' (see Bulletin EC 1974: point 111). At this stage the main concern was with certain civil and political rights, especially the right to vote and to hold public office.

An important step in the process of building 'an ever closer union among the peoples of Europe', as it is expressed in the Treaty of Rome, was the *Tindemans Report* on the European Union presented to the European Council in 1974. First of all, the *Report* called for a democratic commitment to the integration process at the popular level. Tindemans argued that Europe had to listen to 'what the Europeans want and what they expect from Europe'. His ambition was for Europe to move beyond functional economic agreements:

> European Union must be experienced by the citizen in his daily life . . . It must protect the rights of the individual and strengthen democracy through a set of institutions which have legitimacy conferred upon them by the will of our peoples.
>
> (cited in Holland 1993: 61)

Several initiatives by the Commission and the European Parliament were later undertaken to develop these special rights. In 1979 the Commission presented a Directive concerning a right of residence for nationals of member states in the territory of another member state, regardless of economic activity. The precondition of this proposal was awareness that free movement of persons could not be completely realised without a permanent right of residence for all member state nationals. This right was regarded as a first phase in the process of creating European citizenship.

In 1984 the European Council established an *ad hoc* committee chaired by Pietro Adonnino which presented two reports. The first tackled the sensitive issue of border controls and formalities, as well as the right of residence proposed in 1979. The second report drew attention to some special citizenship rights covering the issues of culture, education, communication and symbols of Community identity, such as flags and passports (EC Bulletin Suppl., 85: 18). In 1986 the Commission issued the report *Voting Rights in Local Elections for Community Nationals*. According to this document, free movement denotes that being a citizen in one member state results in possessing the same rights in another member state. So far, member state nationals could not enjoy their political rights in most member states where they were resident as they were not nationals there; at the same time they could not exercise their electoral rights in their state of origin as they were no longer residents there (O'Leary 1996: 36). On the back of these reports the Commission initiated a proposal for a Council Directive on voting rights for Community nationals.

The Single European Act in 1986, amending the Treaty of Rome and aiming at completion of the internal market where 'free movement of persons, goods, capital and services is ensured', provided a minor change in comparison to the earlier Treaty. Within this document, the free movement provisions refer to persons rather than workers. However, the definition of citizens as nationals of all member states was not accepted by national governments that feared the development of 'social tourism' (a term used to refer to an extensive movement of workers from the member states with low social spending to the countries with high welfare standards).

An important step towards a Citizen's Europe was the discussion associated with the Intergovernmental Conference (IGC) preceding the Maastricht Treaty. In the letter to the Irish Presidency in April 1990 Chancellor Kohl and President Mitterrand urged the European Council to initiate preparations for an IGC on Political Union designed to address the need to increase the democratic legitimacy of the Community. A month later Prime Minister González of Spain, in his letter to the European Council, put forward the idea of including in the New Treaty a separate chapter on European Citizenship. According to González, such an initiative would create an integrated space where citizens could enjoy unlimited freedom of movement, residence and access to work together with the right to vote in local elections in member states other than their own. This idea was supported by the Greek delegation who proposed the concept of a 'People's Europe' with a common legal order.

In July 1990 the European Parliament issued a Resolution on the IGC where it called for provisions on European Citizenship, including voting rights for Community citizens in local and European elections in their countries of residence, to be incorporated into the Treaty. It also appealed for provisions against racism, xenophobia and for the protection of fundamental rights and freedoms to be incorporated into the Treaty.

The most engaged position in favour of European Citizenship was taken by the Spanish delegation which, in its note of September 1990, argued that it was necessary to establish a Union citizenship as the 'personal and indivisible status of nationals of the member states whose membership of the Union meant that they had special rights and duties that were specific to the nature of the Union and were exercised and safeguarded within its boundaries . . . and which might also be extended beyond those boundaries' (Laursen and Vanhoonacker 1992: 329). According to Marias (1994: 7), the Spanish Delegation note divided Union citizens' rights into three categories:

1   basic special rights of the European citizen: full freedom of movement and residence; right to participate in municipal elections and the elections to the European Parliament;
2   rights resulting from the dynamic development of the Union especially in the areas of health, education, culture, social relations, consumption and environment;
3   rights exercised by Union citizens beyond its frontiers: diplomatic and consular protection.

Union citizenship in the Maastricht Treaty

The provisions of the second part of the Treaty adopted at the Maastricht Summit in December 1991 developed these values, which, in the preamble to this document, refer to the rule of freedom, democracy, recognition of human rights and basic freedoms, as well as to the rule of law.

The discussion preceding the establishment of the Maastricht Treaty enables us to distinguish several of the objectives behind the idea of European citizenship. First, Union citizenship was designed to improve the status of nationals resident in a member state other than their own behind the position of privileged aliens. In this context, free movement of persons and economically active persons was a precondition of an effective internal market. For this purpose it was necessary to remove all obstacles and introduce new rights (political rights) which would make the free movement more attractive. As is stated in Article B of the Maastricht Treaty, one of the objectives of the European Union is to 'strengthen the protection of the rights and interests of the nationals of the member states through the introduction of a citizenship of the Union'. According to the European Parliament's *Imbeni Report*

> the process of making citizenship of the Union a reality must be understood by citizens of the Member States as a better guarantee that they will effectively enjoy the right to work, a decent standard of living (minimum wages, health care, right to housing etc.) and environmental protection.
>
> (Document A3 1993: 5)

Second, the status of Union citizenship was intended to reduce the 'democratic deficit' that had arisen (1) because of transfers of sovereignty to the Community level where decisions are taken in secret and often by the unaccountable Council; (2) due to the still rather minor role of the European Parliament, the only Community institution directly and democratically elected, but one with comparatively marginal involvement in the EU legislative process; (3) because the executive power of the Community lies exclusively with the Commission and Council (Neunreihter 1994: 300–314).

A third objective was to build a European identity that enhanced the social legitimacy of the European integration programme. The establishment of European citizenship was perceived as a means of achieving public consent and allegiance necessary for the success of the internal market and of economic and monetary union. As O'Leary comments, however, it is not clear 'whether the development of a European identity meant increasing individuals' sense of belonging to the Union or whether it was aimed at making them identify with other citizens of the Union; that is, identifying with fellow citizens to the exclusion of non-citizen residents' (O'Leary 1996: 39).

Fourth, European citizenship was important in identifying the individual dimension of the European Union, in which a series of rights, freedoms and obligations are conferred on its citizens. The key question here, then, refers to the formal aspect of citizenship (mentioned above) which tries to determine *who* is a citizen of the European Union.

In order to realise these objectives the Maastricht Treaty provides the following provisions.

Article F (2) TEU

The Union shall respect fundamental rights, as guaranteed by the European Convention for the Protection of Human Rights and Fundamental Freedoms signed in Rome on 4 November 1950 and as they result from the constitutional traditions common to the Member States, as general principles of Community law.

Article 6 EC

Within the scope of application of this Treaty, and without prejudice to any special provisions contained therein, any discrimination on grounds of nationality shall be prohibited.

Article 8 EC

Citizenship of the Union is hereby established. Every person holding the nationality of a member state shall be a citizen of the Union . . . Citizens of the Union shall enjoy the rights conferred by this Treaty and shall be subject to the duties imposed thereby.

Article 8(a) EC

Every citizen of the Union shall have the right to move and reside freely within the territory of the member states, subject to the limitations and conditions laid down in this Treaty . . . The Council may adopt provisions facilitating the exercise of these rights . . . acting unanimously on a proposal from the Commission and after obtaining the assent of the European Parliament.

Article 8(b) EC

Every citizen of the Union residing in a member state of which he is not a national shall have the right to vote and to stand as a candidate at municipal elections in the member states in which he resides, under the same conditions as nationals of that State . . . Every citizen of the Union residing in a member state of which he is not a national shall have the right to vote and to stand as a candidate in elections to the European Parliament in the member state in which he resides, under the same conditions as nationals of that State. Both rights shall be exercised subject to detailed arrangements adopted by the Council, acting unanimously on a proposal from the Commission and after consulting the European Parliament; these arrangements may provide for derogations where warranted by problems specific to a member state.

Article 8(c) EC

Every citizen of the Union shall, in the territory of a third country in which the member state of which he is a national is not represented, be entitled to protection by the diplomatic or consular authorities of any member state, on the same conditions as the nationals of that state.

Article 8(d) EC

Every citizen of the Union shall have the right to petition the European Parliament in accordance with Article 138 (d) . . . Every citizen of the Union may apply to the Ombudsman established in accordance with Article 138 (e). It is important to emphasise that these two rights are conferred not only on citizens of the Union but also on any natural or legal person residing or having his registered office in a member state.

In the light of the rights enshrined in the Maastricht Treaty and present developments within the European Union, two questions seem to be of vital importance:

1   Does the idea of European citizenship actually realise the objectives assigned to it?
2   Is it a proper concept for the European Union preparing itself and facing the enlargement into central and eastern Europe?

Limitations of Union citizenship

In order to answer the above questions it has to be emphasised that European citizenship is based on the rule of member state nationality, and the procedure within which nationality is conferred and defined by each member state. According to O'Leary:

> the member states thus have ultimate control of access to, enjoyment of, and even forfeiture of, the rights of citizenship of the Union. As a result, no direct link, political or otherwise, has been created between Union citizens and the Union, although this link could be regarded as a fundamental ingredient of citizenship at national level. The use of nationality as a base for Union citizenship also demonstrates that member state sovereignty, rather than promotion of individual rights, remains of ultimate concern to the architects of the Union Treaty.
>
> (O'Leary 1996: III)

Nationality is traditionally based either by birth (*jus soli*) or by descent (*jus sanguinis*). Germany, which exercises a rather restrictive naturalisation process, adopts the *jus sanguinis* as the fundamental principle, while France is known for using the more liberal rule of *jus soli*. Great Britain preserved *jus soli* for some time but, since adopting the 1961 Commonwealth Immigration Act, has become more restrictive and moved towards the *jus sanguinis* as seen in the 1981 British Nationality Act. In 1994 Germany promised limited citizenship rights to third-generation immigrants, provided that their parents had lived in that country for at least ten years and one of them had been born there (Newman 1996: 156). Following the course adopted by other EU countries, France became more restrictive in this matter and in a 1993 law on immigration established the rule of *jus sanguinis* (see Chapter 6 for further details of these developments). However, this law was partially reversed by Jospin's Socialist government, which reverted to the French Jacobin-Republican tradition of *jus soli*.

Union citizenship is therefore fully determined by national citizenship. The member states, not the European Union, decide who might receive the privileges of Union citizenship. According to Evans (1995: 86–110), the reason for this situation is the will to preserve the direct link between member states and their nationals and to exclude any possibility of expansion of Union rights behind the context of this relationship. This practice is contradictory to the rule expressed in a decision of the Court of Justice, which ascribes to the member state the competence to determine who their nationals are, at the same time emphasising the need to realise this competence in accordance with the objectives of European law (notably free movement of persons and the Community's standards in the field of fundamental rights). Several organisations, such as the European Parliament, had wanted European citizenship to be determined on the basis of principles enshrined in the form of a constitutional document incorporating the European Convention of Human Rights. The Maastricht Treaty, however, did not follow this path, as several states (such as the UK) which had not then accepted this Convention within their legal framework did not want to incorporate them via the European Union (Newman 1996: 157). In other words, the member states were not completely prepared to 'denationalise' the issue of 'union citizenship'. Consequently, the use of 'national identity' as a fundamental rule of determination of citizenship led to the creation of a group of second-class citizens and non-citizens of the European Union who became excluded from certain basic rights.

Until the mid-1990s, there was growing evidence that most member states expected migrants to return home after satisfying their needs in the labour markets. The case of Germany is significant here. It used to be extremely difficult for Turkish migrants to obtain the status of citizenship even after living there for two or more generations. There are estimates that in the European Union about ten million people are legal residents without having citizenship status. Since the late 1970s there has been increasing evidence of racism in Europe strengthened additionally by the economic recession (Newman 1996: 161). In several European countries the role of neo-fascist and far-right parties has strengthened. Recent developments, such as the success of the Freedom Party in Austria, are a good example of this phenomenon. It should also be noted that the media play a certain role in the dissemination of negative stereotypes concerning immigrants and linking their presence with increases of crime, terrorism and drug smuggling (Ford Report 1991). In addition, immigration and family reunification policies in Europe, as well as policies on admission and employment, have become more stringent since the 1970s. There is a similar situation with asylum policy as discussed in Chapter 6.

Moreover, with reference to nationals of the member states, the right of residence and movement established according to Article 8(a) is limited by two factors: possession of sufficient resources and possession of sufficient medical insurance. The conditions are not described explicitly in the Treaty, but in the secondary legislation giving effect to the Treaty. This legislation comes from the period preceding the Maastricht Treaty and is contained within three directives (90/366; 90/365; 90/364). The role of the conditions (limitations) envisaged in these directives is to ensure the situation in which member state nationals and their families will not become a burden on the social security policy of the host member state. Although the European Court of Justice has refused to accept the subsistence minimum as a determining factor for free movement and residence, the member states themselves are, in fact, free to determine who benefits from the basic freedoms envisaged in Article 8(a). This article is therefore not a guarantee of the right of free movement and residence because the very realisation of this right depends on the 1990 Directives that are quite restrictive. As a result, this article makes for the emergence of two groups of citizens. The first are beneficiaries of freedom of movement and residence while the second are those excluded from this right (O'Leary 1996: 51). This is especially important in light of the fact that the right of residence and free movement is a crucial factor in the idea of Union citizenship. Realisation of many other rights associated with Union citizenship depends, in fact, on the ability to move freely and reside in another member state.

In addition, the provisions of Article 8(b) concerning electoral rights of Union citizens residing in another member state do not work for the creation of a more direct link between Union and citizens. Important decisions concerning European citizens are not taken at the level of local government and rarely in the European Parliament. All significant matters are decided within the Council or in national parliaments. Moreover, the potential to influence matters directly affecting citizens in their daily lives envisaged in participation in local elections actually depends on competencies exercised by this level of power. This, in turn, depends on the decentralisation of power that varies from country to country.

Taking into account the fact that European citizenship was intended to strengthen a sense of identity with the Union among citizens of the member states, it must be noted that a specific type of identity is being fostered. It excludes long-term legally resident third country immigrants or citizens who do not meet certain economic conditions. According to Herzog's Document: 'the Maastricht Treaty does not create a genuine citizenship of the Union. It simply grants citizens of the Member States rights *vis-à-vis* countries of which they are not nationals. The Union has virtually no obligations towards them' (European Parliament Working Document 1993: 2).

The adoption of nationality as a base for Union citizenship means that the key factor for defining its content was the preservation of national sovereignty rather than the fostering of individual rights and democratic values.

The Amsterdam amendments on Union citizenship

During the pre-Amsterdam debate an IGC was launched at the Corfu European Council at the end of 1994. A Reflection Group was established and tasked with finding how the EU could 'provide a better response to modern demands as regards internal security in the fields of Justice and Home Affairs' (Geddes 2000: 114). The Group also considered the establishment of a 'Union closer to its citizens' and a 'People's Europe' (Reflection Group 1995). Most of the issues developed during the IGC by the Reflection Group referred to migration questions. In March 1996 the official mandate of the IGC was set by the European Council in Turin and its agenda contained three main headings:

1 Union closer to its citizens;
2 More democratic and efficient institutions, especially in the context of future enlargement;
3 Strengthen the Union's capacity for external action and to make more coherent the Union's performance as the European Community (cited in Duff 1997: xxxii).

In comparison to the Maastricht Treaty, Amsterdam is not perceived as a very successful undertaking. Adopted in 1997, the Treaty did not significantly change the existing provisions regarding Union citizenship. It only added to Article 8 that 'citizenship of the Union shall complement and not replace national citizenship' (Duff 1997: 86). This gesture, made explicitly for the Danes after the results of the first Danish referendum on the Treaty of Maastricht, strengthened the sovereignty of the member states with regard to Union citizenship and emphasised a model of the European Community as a union of states (Shaw 2000: 305).

Some changes had been introduced to the Amsterdam Treaty – however, they did not bring about any important consequences. The new Treaty moved the policy on free movement, visa, immigration and asylum from the intergovernmental third pillar to the first pillar of the European Union. In this way it seemed to extend the democratic procedures of the European institutions to legislation in this area as well as to improve the prospect of the principle of free movement of people within the European Community. However, it brought with this shift the intergovernmental procedure of decision-making together with the rule of unanimity.

Another feature of the Amsterdam Treaty concerns the fact that anti-discrimination provisions were written into the Treaty and recognition of human rights was made an explicit criterion for accession to the Union. The Treaty also incorporates into its legal framework the Schengen Agreement (1985) devised by the mainland member states to remove the internal borders of the European Union. However, the flexibility/opt-out protocols added to the Amsterdam Treaty, exempting the UK, Ireland and Denmark from provisions on freedom of movement, weaken the unity of the European Community in this field and limit some rights of citizens (Duff 1997: xxiii–xxxvi). All in all, the Treaty lacks legal uniformity:

> The Amsterdam Treaty will mean the coexistence of dozens of different legal and economic sub-systems over the next ten years, a sort of nightmare resurrection of the Holy Roman Empire.
>
> (quoted after Geddes 2000: 110)

The Charter of Fundamental Rights

At the Nice Summit in December 2000 the member states of the European Union proclaimed the Charter of Fundamental Rights, designed to strengthen the constitutional character of the Treaties and consolidate the basic rights. Moreover, the Charter was to increase protection of individual rights within EU legislation, to create a reference for the European institutions as well as to emphasise the significance of the human rights as a common value for the EU.

In the preamble to the document it is claimed that the Union, taking the inspiration from its moral and spiritual heritage, is built on common and inseparable principles of human dignity, freedom, equality and solidarity. Its foundation consists of the rule of democracy and law. By the establishment of Union citizenship and the area of liberty, security and justice, it puts the individual at the centre of its activities. The Union contributes to preservation and development of shared values with the recognition of a variety of cultures and national traditions of Europe. It also protects free movement of people, goods, capital and services as well as freedom of enterprise.

Furthermore, Chapter I declares that each citizen of the Union is free to find a job, work and to provide services in all member states (ch. I, art. 15). Another important part of the document forbids any form of discrimination with regard to gender, ethnicity, language, religion, or membership of any other minority group. In addition, within the area of application of the TEU any discrimination on the basis of nationality is excluded (ch. III, art. 21).

Despite the very ambitious and moral tone of the Charter it nevertheless remains, so far, only a 'political declaration', which in practice does not have any legal significance. As the host of the Summit, France agreed to its symbolic significance. The Paris position was influenced by objections of the government of the United Kingdom, which regarded the Charter as a first step towards a European constitution and threatened to damage the Nice summit.

Very few member states deem that in future the Charter of Fundamental Rights should become a part of the Union constitution. Such a development would need adjustment of its provisions with the European Convention on the Protection of Human Rights and Basic Freedoms. The European Parliament, a supporter of this development, urged the 2000 IGC to take the necessary measures, a call that was supported by the European Commission. Without the political will of the member states it will not be possible for the EU to sign up to the European Convention on the Protection of Human Rights and Basic Freedoms. Without this development the Charter provisions are not legally binding.

Conclusion

The idea of Union citizenship envisaged in the Maastricht Treaty (and to a certain degree developed in the Amsterdam Treaty) seems not to realise the objectives assigned to it. It does not create any direct relationship between a European citizen and the Union, a condition at the heart of the idea of citizenship. The rights of residence and free movement in other member states are limited by possession of sufficient financial resources and medical insurance. Moreover, electoral rights in the country of residence (that is, the rights to participate in municipal and European Parliament elections) do not increase citizens' influence over the Community since all important decisions concerning Union citizens are taken at the national level and in the European Council. On the other hand, the idea of nationality as a condition for EU citizenship excludes a significant part of society from the benefits of fundamental rights. About ten million legal long-term residents live in the EU without the status of citizenship because they do not have nationality of any of the member states. Immigration and asylum policy within the EU has become more and more stringent as the *jus sanguinis* rule is mainly employed by the member states in their nationalisation procedures. This policy results in a growing number of foreigners and legal residents becoming non-citizens of the European Union. According to Bauböck (1997) the irony of EU citizenship is that, on the one hand, its rights relate primarily to migrants but, on the other hand, determination of the persons to whom these rights apply excludes the great majority of migrants residing in the EU.

It could be argued that these features of Union citizenship are especially important as the EU prepares for enlargement towards central-eastern Europe. The development of Union citizenship clearly suggests that it follows the logic of exclusion. Thus, European citizenship reflects an internal mechanism of European integration that seems to be an extrapolation of the tradition of Western culture based of the principle – as is illustrated in Michel Foucault's work – of exclusion of *the Other*.

Further reading

Antola, E. and Rosas, A. (eds) (1995) *A Citizens' Europe. In Search of a New Legal Order.* London: Sage

Marshall, T.H. (1950) *Citizenship and Social Class and Other Essays.* Cambridge: Cambridge University Press.

O'Leary, S. (1996) *European Union Citizenship. The Options for Reform.* London: IPPR.

Sorensen, J.M. (1996) *The Exclusive European Citizenship: The Case for Refugees and Immigrants in the European Union.* Aldershot: Ashgate.

van Steenbergen, B. (ed.) (1994) *The Condition of Citizenship.* London: Sage.

The nation-state in Europe

Key concepts

- Nation-state
- Territory
- Legitimacy

At the beginning of the twenty-first century there is growing talk that the nation-state – which, for the moment, we will describe as an institution that came into being in Europe at the back end of the eighteenth century – is now in crisis. Indeed, a growing number of writers are arguing that the condition is terminal. For these commentators, those who retain faith in national governments are the flat-earthers of the contemporary era; unable to see beyond the horizon of the nation-state. For those not involved in these discussions, the response may well be: 'So what?' Our answer is that the future of the nation-state is of concern to us all. As the discussion below will show, the rise and transformation of the nation-state has been one of *the* most significant influences on the development of modern Europe. The attempt to build nation-states across Europe has had the most profound effect on those living within the same country, from the development of compulsory schooling through to inter-ethnic relations. As we will show, it has also had important, often dramatic, consequences for international relations.

This chapter explores the rise and development of the nation-state in modern Europe, tracing this process from the late eighteenth century to the contemporary period. We highlight some of the key dimensions of this process, drawing on examples from across Europe. Where possible, we have chosen to demonstrate similarities between the historical and sociological experiences of 'west' and 'east', but it will become apparent that the transformation of the idea of the nation-state has been informed by sometimes-specific regional experiences. Overall, the discussion will show how and why people have come to identify themselves as belonging to a national community. We begin by asking what we mean by a 'nation-state'.

Nations, states, and nation-states

The terms 'nation' and 'state' are often used interchangeably. Politicians, for example, routinely refer to nation when, technically, they are talking about affairs of state. We may nevertheless be aware that there is something slightly different about these two terms. With regard to nation the accent is on cultural matters, such as language, history or religion, while state is more readily associated with politics and policy, such as the welfare state, the military, or government in a broad sense. As we will show in Chapter 4 on nationalism, it is correct to think of nation in this way; a nation is a human population perceived as sharing a common, historic culture. Similarly, state is indeed associated with the formal political sphere, as it refers to the central administration that governs a national territory. If, then, state and nation do not mean the same thing, what is gained by conjoining the two?

For some writers 'nation-state' is a particular type of state. Thus, Horsman and Marshall refer to a 'classic nation-state' that is 'charged with protecting national citizens within secure borders and with the conduct of national economic policies' (1995: xi). Here the modern nation-state is distinguished from earlier European absolutist states, as in the former the state represents the will of the people (the nation) while in the latter the state represents the will of the monarch. If nation-state merely refers to a particular type of political administration it is difficult to see why people in Europe should develop such strong attachments to it. In short, this definition neglects the nation at the expense of the state. Smith (1986b) touches on what is arguably the nub of the issue when he speaks about the 'members of the nation-state'. Building on Smith, we can say that a nation-state is a socio-spatial self-governing *community* – because it has physical limits and because of the social and cultural practices that occur within that finite space – in which it is the task of the state to represent the interests of the national community. Overall, the 'nation-state' is greater than the sum of its parts. It refers not just to the physical space and the institutions that broadly govern it, but also to the wide array of social and cultural practices that foster a popular sense of national identity. We are thus speaking of a political community which, at least in theory, inhabits a common territory and in which all members define themselves as belonging to the same nation.

The development of the idea of the nation-state

From where did the idea of the nation-state develop? There is no single source for the idea of the nation-state. Calleo (1995) argues that the idea draws on the classical Greek tradition of the state, developed, he suggests, by Rousseau in the eighteenth century, and links to the Romantic notion of the cultural nation, expressed by Herder. The French Revolution is often identified as the genesis of modern nationalism, but the French republican tradition does not play heavily on notions of cultural uniformity among 'the people'. Thus, while the French Revolution had an important impact on the development of the idea of the nation-state, in that it identified the nation as the source of political legitimacy, it took the writings of the Romantic philosophers to turn 'the people' into a cultural nation. This group, although especially Herder, is cited by a number of writers as propagating the idea of the nation, in which the community is defined as sharing a common culture that was the product of environment, climate, language and history. It was Herder's belief that an individual belonged to a particular nation, and derived the major part of his individuality from the culture of that nation. From this philosophical basis Herder advocated that territories and government must be organised to reflect Europe's natural division into cultural nations. To do otherwise would be to impose a false order on the diverse humanity of Europe.

Since the late eighteenth century the idea of the nation-state has developed as *the* model for organising political space in Europe. For most, if not all, countries in Europe, however, the realisation of this idea remains an aspiration rather than an achievement. Serious national divisions splinter a number of European countries, such as Belgium, Cyprus, Moldova and the UK. Others, such as Estonia, Latvia and Lithuania, with their sizeable ethnic Russian populations, and Romania (notably the ethnic Hungarians in Transylvania), contain substantial minorities that have frequently been at odds with national government and their fellow citizens. Some countries, such as Greece, the Netherlands, Poland and Portugal, 'have small minorities, but are by now otherwise homogenous' (Smith 1986b: 229). These countries may have comparatively small ethnic or national minorities (where the latter are officially recognised as constituting nationalities), but their existence cannot be ignored.

The situation in the Balkans indicates that the ideal of the nation-state is one which many groups still consider to be worth fighting for. Elsewhere, numerous movements seek independent nation-states, while national governments continue to speak on behalf of 'the nation'. Thus the idea of the nation-state arguably remains as appealing as it was two centuries ago. It is nevertheless becoming more difficult now for states to pursue the ideal of the cultural nation as they once did. In western Europe governments have increasingly promoted a civic version of the nation-state, in which citizens hold multiple identities; identifying, for example, with their ethnic group, their nation and/or with the wider polity of which they are citizens. This version of the nation-state has become a necessity in countries that have experienced considerable immigration, as well as perhaps increased demands for autonomy from ethnic and national minorities. In these cases governments have had to search for new ways of maintaining the unity of the nation-state. As we will see, however, in other countries the state has become firmly aligned with one ethnic group. For us, the important questions are whether we will see a movement away from the ethnic nation-state in Europe, and, if so, how will 'the nation' be defined in this context? Before considering the current and future prospects of the idea of the nation-state, we must understand the routes this idea has taken.

The rise and transformation of the nation-state: 1700s to 1945

Searching for the origins of the nation-state is something of a red herring; since pure nation-states do not exist, as noted above, it is not possible to identify when they came into being. As we have said, however, the *idea* of the nation-state has been enormously powerful in European political history, as governments and political movements have sought to convert the theory into practice. What we need to consider, then, is the nation-state as a process, rather than as an entity. We will therefore focus on three processes: the development of the national territory; the transformation of the state; and the building of popular identification with nation and state.

Dimensions of change

With regard to territory there are two points we should make. The first is that it is broadly acknowledged that the significance of national frontiers has developed gradually, since the 1648 Treaty of Westphalia. This Treaty ended the Thirty Years' Wars that had raged across much of Europe. Among the consequences of the Treaty, arguably the most significant was that it established the principle of sovereignty, thus recognising that sovereigns were the sole source of power within their territory and the representative of that territory in foreign affairs.

The second point is that since this period the state has come to increasingly occupy the entire national territory. Until the late eighteenth century, and more particularly the latter part of the nineteenth century, the state made little impact on the mass of the population throughout the national territory. Navari (1981) argues that until the French Revolution monarchs made little attempt to effect centralisation throughout their realm. Indeed, she suggests, if they had it is very likely that various interested parties would have resisted such moves. Significant changes began to happen from the late eighteenth century onwards. The cumulative effect of change in post-Westphalian Europe was that the state increasingly came to occupy and, indeed, *create* the national space of modern European countries. For example, in 1880 the French Revolution was commemorated for the first time as a national holiday – Bastille Day – to be celebrated across the national territory.

The pivotal change, therefore, is the transformation of the state from its absolutist phase, dominated by the sovereign monarch, to its national phase. From the eighteenth century the state metamorphosed on a number of fronts. In economic and fiscal affairs the state assumed an increasingly mercantilist role in the development of the national economy, and sought new sources of taxation; the British state, for example, introduced a range of new income and property taxes in the late eighteenth and early nineteenth centuries. As in the British case, war was perhaps the primary force behind the drive for new sources of state income. Building these increasingly large forces required vast expenditure; Kennedy (1988) notes that by the late eighteenth century the preparation for war consumed almost 50 per cent of the expenditure of European states, rising to 80 to 90 per cent of a markedly larger expenditure during wartime.

Together, the need for new revenue and the organisation of larger armed services necessitated increased public management of economy and society. The period since the eighteenth century, therefore, saw the expansion of state bureaucratic systems. More generally, by the second half of the nineteenth century the state was assuming growing responsibility for the management of social affairs within the national territory. As Tilly (1992) explains, states developed complex surveillance systems to monitor social conditions, including those that might lead to instability, and to confront problems. The state, too, took responsibility for education, with centralised education systems established within European societies during this period. Education systems became vehicles for promoting cultural uniformity, notably through the use of one 'national' language. The effect of the above changes was that the state increasingly came to have a tangible presence in the lives of ordinary citizens.

To what extent did the state actively seek to cultivate national identity? The state's actions arguably stemmed more from pragmatism than from abstract concerns with a putative 'national' culture. Ideas concerning the latter were undoubtedly influential on individual politicians and for particular nationalist movements – after all, such ideas proved to be powerful legitimising tools – but political authorities clearly utilised the idea of the nation as a means of securing domestic order and advancing their interests. Colley (1992) explains how, during the Napoleonic Wars, the British government employed propaganda to mobilise popular support and volunteers for the war effort. Political authorities were aware that by encouraging such participation on the grounds of patriotism they 'ran an obvious risk of encouraging demands for political change in the future', but, she adds, they 'ran this risk knowingly, because they recognised they had no choice' (1992: 336).

In other instances nationalising programmes were intended to prevent disorder. In the lands that encompass much of modern Estonia, Latvia and Lithuania, incorporated into the Russian empire in the late eighteenth century, local elites enjoyed considerable autonomy until the late nineteenth century when the Russian state promoted the Russification of these lands in order to stem the rising tide of nationalisms. Such contests were also played out elsewhere in Europe. In Hungary a language law was introduced in 1907 which announced that teachers would be sacked if they or their students failed to learn Magyar, the official language. Thus language laws, or provisions concerning language in other laws (such as those concerning education), had the effect of fostering a national language, often at the expense of minority languages. In Spain, first under the dictatorship of Primo de Rivera (1923 to 1930), and then under the Franco regime (1936 to 1975), the use of Catalan as an official language was outlawed, leading to declining numbers of Catalan speakers as generations grew up learning Castilian, the language favoured by the state.

Nationalising programmes were also used to advance the cause of modernisation. Weber's (1978) highly regarded study of the transformation of nationhood in later nineteenth-century France traces how the process of turning 'peasants into Frenchmen' (the title of his book) was orchestrated by the state. For the countries that emerged out of the post-First World War settlement nationalising policies were arguably essential if their populations were to be integrated and their states to function effectively. Crampton comments that inter-war Poland was a 'coat of many colours', which, in addition to a fairly complex ethnic demography, inherited 'three railway systems and economic infrastructures, no less than six currencies, varying educational practices, legal systems which were not completely standardised by 1939, and a multitude of military legacies' (1997: 41). Part of this increasingly interventionist nationalising process involved inculcating national values in order to encourage a commitment to a common national purpose. Andrés and Braster explain how in 1893 the Spanish government declared that the national flag should be flown outside all public schools to symbolise 'love of the fatherland' (1999: 83). Often these strategies were intended to address what the political authorities viewed as the adoption of the wrong values. Thus in Prussia in 1911 the Ministry of Culture issued a decree on 'Youth Cultivation', in response to the perceived drift of Prussian youth towards socialism and official concerns about the declining standards of physical health among young males and the consequences for the Prussian military.

By the twentieth century, then, the state had gone from being a relatively distant force in the lives of ordinary people to one that increasingly regulated everyday life. What impact did these policies have on the broad mass of the population?

Where records of public opinion are available they do not lead to any conclusive opinion. Colley notes that during the Napoleonic Wars state propaganda in Britain cultivated a fear of French invasion, and historical records show that 'nightmares of a violent French invasion' were widely shared at the time (1992: 324). Other historians argue that fear of invasion does not necessarily lead to identification with the national state. Gemie (1998) shows that in the Val d'Aran in the Pyrenees, which was annexed by France in 1812, locals were not swayed by fears about political unrest in Spain or by the efforts of Napoleon to encourage identification with France.

Developments throughout the nineteenth century arguably strengthened the sense of loyalty to nation and state. We certainly know that, by 1914, millions of men were willing to fight 'for their country'. When war broke out, and the propaganda machines got to work, nationalist feelings ran high. Stories that came back from the battlefield quickly evolved into legends. Segel (1999) comments that tales of the efforts of General Piłsudski, the liberator of Poland by the end of the war, encouraged large numbers of young Poles to join his legions. Therefore, in the period up to the end of the First World War conflict, international rivalry and xenophobia may have contributed a great deal to the success of the idea of the nation.

Nationalist propaganda and the First World War

World War I, and the effect of the propaganda that accompanied it, illustrated how effective state-sponsored nationalism and xenophobia were in mobilising popular opinion. Poster art, for example, became an effective medium in communicating images of the enemy (especially of 'the Hun' in British WWI posters) and in encouraging the public to buy war bonds. Ferro points out that in France the writer René Benjamin alone sold 150,000 copies of his pro-war publications, while adding that during the War pacifist groups in France 'were not able to make themselves heard at all' (1999: 301). Meanwhile, in those territories that would emerge as independent countries after 1918, such as Poland, propaganda was utilised by elites to engender national consciousness. The effects of war propaganda nevertheless produced a backlash. In poems such as *Blighters* by Siegfried Sassoon, and *Dulce et Decorum est* by Wilfred Owen, both of whom served in the War (Owen was killed a week before Armistice Day), writers did not disguise their vitriol at the manner in which they saw the public so taken in by war propaganda. In Germany the celebratory tenor of music-hall performances was lowered as, by 1915, awareness of the scale of German losses was becoming clearer to the German public.

The direct impact of the other activities of the state, such as the centralised education systems established in the latter part of the nineteenth century, is less certain, however. We do know that the centralised education systems had the impact of reducing the numbers of those able to speak minority languages, and especially those who could speak only these languages. In the UK the decline in the numbers of Welsh speakers begins from the establishment of the first centralised primary system of education, as English, and not Welsh, became the language of modernisation. The impact of such policies, while having some immediate impact, was nevertheless felt only generations later.

Social conflict, involving first the European peasantry and then, in the early twentieth century, the industrial working classes, demonstrated that, despite the progress of European societies, the supposed unity of the nation was an illusion. A number of countries – among them Denmark (1849), Greece (1864), France (1875) and Norway (1898) – had seen the extension of universal male suffrage in the nineteenth century, but these changes did not prevent further, serious outbreaks of social conflict. Stone (1999) notes that in Germany over half a million people went on strike in 1905, while in Italy there were 1255 strikes involving 327,000 workers in 1911. While the governments and rulers of Europe had done much to promote a sense of mass national identity in their countries at the time, they nevertheless were forced to confront separatist nationalists, frustrated workers, socialists, and – as the growth of a nascent fascism in Italy showed – nationalists who wanted the state to represent a particular vision of the nation.

The rise of fascism

Fascism is an ideology that, arguably above all else, holds that the state should have total control of all aspects of society, and that the individual must be subject to the authority of the state. The term derives from the Latin, *fasces*, a cylindrical bundle of wooden rods bound together around an axe, and which is broadly regarded as symbolising power and unity. The development of fascism in Europe took different forms, but as a generic ideology it advocates the need for radical changes to purportedly corrupt political systems and the establishment of a new regime, and insists that the integrity of the nation is being threatened by, among other factors, liberalism, individualism, and by the actions of other ethnic groups or 'races'. As a political movement fascism has its origins in the movement started by Benito Mussolini in Italy in the period following the First World War, and which came to power in Italy during the 1920s after a period of civil unrest (to which the fascists made a significant contribution). It was, however, the rise to power of the Nazis in the 1930s that inspired fascist movements elsewhere in Europe, such as in Hungary, Romania, and, with markedly less success, in Britain.

If the war fanned national identities that acted as bridges over the chasm created by social class, the effect was temporary. The political systems, especially those of the states that had been recently established by the Treaty of Versailles, began to creak, and then, in some cases, to break, in the face of growing ethnic tensions and political chaos. In Poland, for example, by 1925 there were some ninety-two registered political parties, thirty-two of which had seats in Parliament, while between 1919 and 1934 Estonia experienced twenty-one different governments! Poor economic conditions, deep social divisions and a weak civic culture – features that applied to many European countries, east and west – proved to be fertile conditions for the right.

While the parties of the right took many forms, their general popularity derived from their promises to engender stability and national strength. The rhetoric of the right, from the *Estado Novo* ('New State') of Salazar's dictatorship in Portugal to Mussolini's 'New Italy', played heavily on national regeneration. As the nation became an increasingly exclusive community, Jews were commonly identified as a group against which it was defined, though they were not the only minority group viewed in this way. Some of the newly independent countries began with honourable intentions; in Estonia a liberal constitution gave considerable cultural autonomy to cultural minorities. During the 1920s, however, divisions between ethnic Germans and ethnic Estonians developed into more troubled relations. In other parts of Europe, the right assumed a far more terrible form than in the Baltic (not that this region was free of fascist movements), most notably in Nazi Germany. In Romania, too, the fascist Iron Guard movement, established in 1930, gathered mass backing, as did the Arrow Cross movement in Hungary. The 1930s Depression compounded problems caused by existing social and political divisions.

Between the latter half of the nineteenth century and the beginning of the post-Second World War era, the state played an increasingly significant role in transforming popular identities. When added to an environment in which national rivalries loomed large, this strategy undoubtedly succeeded in fostering a mass sense of national identity. Returning to one of the issues with which we began this section – the extent to which the people living in the national territory identified with the nation – it is evident that few countries, if any, could claim to have achieved a stable settlement. In a growing number of cases, especially during the inter-war years, the solution to the problem of overlap between state and nation was resolved by a range of policies, from repression of minorities to forced migration.

An east–west divide?

One issue that features recurrently in discussions of the development of the nation-state, and nationalism, in Europe is the matter of an east–west divide with regard to the operation of the idea of the nation-state. How much support is there for this argument?

The first of these issues concerns the manner in which individual states were established within the two regions. Smith (1991) identified two routes to nationhood – bureaucratic incorporation and vernacular mobilisation – that correspond to two different types of nationalism: territorial and ethnic. In the first pairing – bureaucratic/territorial – the state develops over a lengthy period around an 'ethnic core', which incorporates peripheral elites into the dominant ethnic group via the new state bureaucratic structure. Thus, territorial nationalism seeks the integration of the population of the territory by developing a civic culture that would overlay, or even replace, an individual's ethnic or regional identity. In contrast, in the process of vernacular mobilisation the nation is identified as one ethnic group, and ethnic nationalism seeks an independent nation-state for that group. In short, the former process begins with a state and leads to a nation, while the latter starts from the nation and ends with a state. Using a similar model Schöpflin (1995) identifies the development of nationhood in a number of western countries as fitting the former categories, such as France, the Netherlands and Sweden, while states in eastern Europe tend to fall into the latter. Péteri (2000) prefers to view the division as being between those states in the West that developed into civic nation-states, with a public culture that seeks to embrace all those living in the national territory, and those states of central and east Europe that emerged out of the imperial states.

On a general level, there are good grounds for supporting this argument. It is nevertheless important to note Péteri's (2000) point. The relatively lengthy history of the existence of the countries of western Europe, even allowing for some border movements, has enabled the gradual transformation of the state. Even where new countries emerged during the nineteenth century, such as Belgium and Italy, the process has involved building the state around a broad civic culture. Belgium is a difficult case to fit into this model because, since independence in 1830, the new state faced opposition from Flemish speakers over the use of French as the official language of Belgium (Flemish became an official language in Belgium in 1898) and before the end of the century a Walloon nationalist movement, comprising French speakers, had emerged to counter the influence of Flemish nationalists. Thus one could ask whether, with such disputes, Belgium could be rightly regarded as broadly characteristic of an aspirant civic nation-state. The answer is that the 'civic' quality is to be found in the intentions of the state, rather than in whether or not all citizens of the country identify with nation and state. Belgium, therefore, may be regarded as being of a broadly civic form.

The difference is evident in comparison with many of the countries of central-east Europe that emerged out of the imperial states, and wherein nationalist movements had been campaigning for independence for a number of decades. All of these movements were directed towards securing the independence of a particular ethnic group, whether Estonians, Hungarians or Poles. If it had been possible to create a perfect fit between all those who identified themselves as Hungarians, for example, and their new national territory, then there might be few problems. As we have explained, however, territory never fits with ethnicity in this way. All the new states created by the Treaty of Versailles contained substantial minority populations. In 1921 newly independent Poland contained a Ukrainian minority that accounted for 14 per cent of the total population, while non-ethnic Poles comprised over 30 per cent of the population (Romania at the same time had a similar sized ethnic minority population). When many of the new countries were established, then, there was a profound clash between the aspirations of the dominant political elite, and their supporters, and the actual ethno-social conditions in the territories. In Yugoslavia, perhaps the country with the most complex political arrangements in central-east Europe at that time, the state formally spoke on behalf of all Yugoslavs, but from the start bore the imprint of Serbia; Serbs dominated both government and army during the inter-war years. Of the new states, only Czechoslovakia survived with a functioning parliamentary democracy during the inter-war years, but even here there were significant disputes between German and Slovak separatists and the state over perceived Czech dominance.

There is, then, a case for arguing that in the countries of central-east Europe which emerged out of the imperial states the state assumed an ethnic as opposed to a civic form. Some of the new states began with different intentions. We have already noted the cases of the Baltic states. The first republic of Czechoslovakia, too, was founded on a liberal constitution that gave considerable cultural autonomy and political freedom to its constituent ethnic groups (although denying them regional political autonomy). In all of the states in the region, however, the new institutions reflected the interests of the dominant ethnic groups. In all cases the elites who dominated the new states believed they had a right to do so, because, for example, of their efforts during the war (as in the case of Serbia). It is also the case that in some countries the new elites had little intention of sharing power with the country's minorities and that they would use power to weaken old enemies (thus land reforms were often used to remove power from ethnic groups that had previously dominated the rural economy in certain regions).

As we will see, the rise and dominance of communism in the region for much of the second half of the century served to throw a fire blanket over ethnic divisions within the countries (although, as we will also show, they were far from eliminated).

Post-war Europe

Discussion of the transformation of the nation-state in the post-Second World War era has tended to focus heavily on the process of European integration, and, more recently, on the impact of globalisation. Other chapters in this book treat these themes more fully, and consequently they will not be covered in much detail here. It would nevertheless be impossible to talk about the evolution of the idea of the nation-state without some reference to European integration. There is, however, a danger that the EU becomes synonymous with 'Europe', when clearly it is not. We will nevertheless point to some common experiences across Europe. The following discussion continues to explore the three processes – the development of the national territory, the transformation of the state, and the forging of popular identification with nation and state – which informed the preceding section. In doing so, we will briefly address three key areas: communism; European integration; and political culture and restructuring.

Communism

The communist regimes that assumed power in central-east Europe in the three or four years after the end of the Second World War sought to suppress expressions of 'bourgeois nationalism', such as the influence of religion (so important for national identities in the region). In addition, it was planned that industrialisation would bring workers together from different countries, and thus serve to break down attachments to national identities. More particularly, the 'purges' of the 1940s and 1950s by the communist regimes sought to directly eliminate perceived nationalists from the party ranks. When thirteen senior members of the Communist Party of Czechoslovakia, including the country's deputy prime minister, were put on trial in 1952 (eleven were subsequently executed) one of the charges levelled at them was that they were 'nationalist traitors'. Some of the most brutal purges against nationalists occurred within the Soviet Union itself during the 1930s. In Ukraine, the largest of the Soviet republics after Russia, its political leaders were killed, as were many other opponents of Stalin's Russification strategy, and all elements of Ukrainian culture were either banned or Russified.

The communist regimes were not averse to harnessing the power of nationalism, however. In Romania, Ceaucescu, leader of the Romanian Communist Party and the country's president from 1974 to 1989, was among the most openly nationalist of the communist dictators. Under his regime, the decreased emphasis on the teaching of Russian contrasted with the promotion of Romanian identity. Undoubtedly the leading proponent of the efforts to give socialism a national, rather than international form was Tito's Yugoslavia. Yugoslavia had been expelled from the Cominform (Communist Information Bureau) in 1948, a body established by the main European communist parties in 1947, while Tito himself was locked in conflict with Moscow and other communist regimes in central-east Europe. Tito's brand of socialism was inseparable from the Yugloslav identity, which he developed in an effort to reconcile the various national and ethnic factions within the country.

Thus, while communism and nationalism appear to be mutually opposing ideologies, a number of communist leaders throughout the post-war period mixed the two. The Soviet Union had initially sought to get around the problem of its multi-ethnic and multinational composition by allowing the republics considerable autonomy. The republics were nevertheless constructed around 'nations'. Although under Stalin's (1926 to 1953) and Brezhnev's (1964 to 1982) regimes the republics experienced a diminution in their powers, these changes failed to diminish the challenge of separatist nationalism.

The experiences of central-east Europe today provide abundant evidence that communism failed to eradicate the significance of ethnic and national identities and indeed underline that the institutional structures and ideological innovations employed during the post-war era *contributed* to ongoing awareness of national identity. These sentiments were not, then, suddenly rediscovered after the demise of Soviet influence. Rather, ethnic and national identities and tensions were present throughout the Soviet era, albeit not expressed as openly or as powerfully as today. Studies of the breakup of the former Yugoslavia, for example, often point to the resurgence of nationalism after the death of Marshal Tito, the President of Yugoslavia from 1948 to 1980, but nationalist tensions between the constituent republics and the federal government had been going on for a decade before. Significant expressions of nationalist dissatisfaction with the federal arrangements date back to the 1960s, while the new constitution of 1974, which considerably increased the power of the republics, was an attempt by Tito to curb the competing nationalist tensions within Yugoslavia. Similar tensions were evident in various parts of the Soviet bloc, including the USSR itself. Batt (1998) comments that the influx of workers from Ukraine and Russia to the Baltic republics to meet the demand for industrial labour succeeded in increasing national animosities. Indeed, as with the former Yugoslavia, the USSR inter-republic rivalry and tension was a constant feature of the country's history. In this environment, nationalism became an effective tool for opposing Moscow's influence and policy, and as the Soviet system attempted to reform in the 1980s, the challenges from disaffected nationalist elites increased. In the end, many elites preferred to go it alone as independent nation-states rather than to continue within the framework of the USSR. As we will see below, the 1980s and early 1990s also witnessed the beginning of a period of political restructuring in the Soviet bloc countries of central-east Europe.

European integration

If, in central-east Europe, the post-war era saw the rise and demise of one possible contender to life beyond the nation-state – international socialism – in western Europe, the process of European integration has continued to strengthen during the same period. The EU does not yet offer a vision of life after the nation-state, nor are there any real signals that it is likely to do so. Integration has nevertheless sponsored considerable debate about what the process entails for those countries that become members of the EU. After all, as we show elsewhere in this book, membership carries serious implications for the relative autonomy of the state. The original architects of integration – people like Jean Monnet and Robert Schuman – believed, too, that the process was needed to combat nationalism and international rivalry. So, then, what has integration meant for the European nation-state?

Integration has not had a great deal of impact on people's identification with their country relative to identification with 'Europe'. European citizens – that is, those people who, by virtue of their citizenship of a member state, are simultaneously citizens of the EU – participate in lower numbers for European elections than for national elections, and their turnout in the former has decreased since the first elections to the European Parliament in 1979. It would seem, therefore, that the EU does not rank as highly as the nation-state in the minds of EU citizens. People in central-east Europe are more likely to feel European than their counterparts in the EU, however; a study in the late-1990s shows that 60 per cent of Poles and just over 40 per cent of Czechs believed their European identity to be as strong as their national identity (Leonard 1998). Yet this same study argues that while people may identify with 'Europe', in most cases this does not translate into identification with the EU. Protests against the EU – such as the Danish decision not to join the EMU and the protests of British and French farmers against EU policy – nevertheless suggest that people believe the EU *is* affecting the ability of their national governments to do things they were once able to do. These frustrations may manifest themselves in disaffection with formal politics, but there is not a great deal of evidence that these changes are diminishing the appeal of nationalism or persuading most of the people that national government is no longer relevant. Identification with their nation-state still appears to be the highest form of political loyalty in Europe.

This is perhaps not surprising, as all European governments continue to play heavily on national rhetoric no matter how overtly pro-integrationist they are. Indeed, in his acclaimed study *The European Rescue of the Nation-State*, Milward (1992) argues that the governments who signed up to the European Coal and Steel Community, the first institutional landmark in the integration process, did so to advance domestic interests that, without the framework of the ECSC, would not have been realised. Milward holds that a bundle of economic, political and social interests concerned post-war European governments, chief among them being the need to rebuild their economies, to foster a more inclusive social consensus that would generate the support of the agrarian and industrial working classes, and, especially on the part of the French government, to contain Germany. European integration, Milward argues, allowed the first wave of participants in the process (Belgium, France, the Federal Republic of Germany, Italy, the Netherlands and Luxembourg) to do exactly these things. For example, when the Belgian coal industry, hitherto one of the country's main employers, began to experience problems in the late 1950s, the ECSC initiated a restructuring plan involving large subsidies for retraining and aiding the restructuring and modernisation of the industry.

Without this support unemployment would have risen and prosperity decreased, weakening the legitimacy of the state. Thus, integration has enabled the state to portray itself as representing the interests of 'the nation'. Governments have certainly been keen to portray integration as assisting with the interests of the nation-state, and there is a good deal of reason behind these arguments. For example, the decision of two British governments to seek, unsuccessfully, membership of the European Economic Community (established by the 1957 Treaty of Rome) in the 1960s came after a realisation that the UK could not survive on its trading links with the Commonwealth and the European Free Trade Association. For Spain, membership of the EEC in 1986 was broadly perceived to be necessary for the 'full recovery of national self-esteem' (Jáuregui 1999: 273–274). Equally, in Poland in 1997, like Spain in the mid-1980s a country emerging from a period of being in Europe, but not part of Europe, the government's National Strategy for Integration spoke of how 'Poles perceive the idea of including their country in the integration of Europe as part and parcel of political and economic transformation' (Committee for European Integration 1997).

At what cost, however, has come this dependency of the nation-state on integration? The first twenty years may be portrayed as strengthening the European nation-state, but the period since then has exacted a higher toll on governments. With the transfer of further powers, notably over economic policy, and as opposition parties and movements have become increasingly vocal about the dangers of further integration, so governments of current and prospective member states have increasingly had to point to what would happen if they did *not* surrender the powers they have surrendered. Even if integration does bring benefits, will national citizens be able to accept further transfers of powers and still view their national governments as more significant than the EU? The Danish rejection of EMU in 2000 (in opposition to the pro-EMU stance of the government) and the Irish rejection of the Treaty of Nice in 2001 suggest that national electorates are finding further integration difficult to accept. The next decade will be crucial, as the progress of the euro unfolds and as the next wave of entrants joins the EU. It is highly unlikely, however, that the EU will rapidly become a focus for the loyalties of national citizens. It is rather more likely that deeper integration will bring a further crisis of the national state, although the *idea* of the nation-state will retain its allure.

Political culture and restructuring

Both of the above developments highlight the international dimension to political restructuring – by which we mean actual changes to the political and constitutional architecture – in Europe in the post-1945 era. Both of these changes held, and in the case of the EU continue to hold, considerable implications for the idea of the nation-state, especially how 'the nation' is defined, but they do not alone explain the changing fortunes of the idea of the nation-state. In central-east Europe, although the influence of Moscow penetrated many aspects of the foreign and domestic policies of the Soviet bloc countries, and of the internal affairs of the Soviet republics, local disputes between neighbouring countries as well as tensions between ethnic groups and nationalities within countries were significant in shaping the vision of the socialist nation. In north-west and Mediterranean Europe, too, these problems are critical influences on how the nation is envisaged by competing political camps. To what extent did these forces compel political restructuring?

In the case of each of the countries of north-west and Mediterranean Europe the post-war period saw a gradual redefinition of the dominant idea of the nation. We have already noted that membership of the EU always involves a process whereby the nation and its interests are portrayed as being compatible with European integration. For some of the countries of western Europe the demise of their empires provoked much debate about the country's changing place in the world, and what this meant for the country's identity. In the post-war era the Belgian, British, Dutch and French empires experienced demands for independence, sometimes accompanied by armed conflict or war, which caused terminal damage. Elsewhere, the return of democratic regimes after periods of dictatorship, as in the cases of Greece, Portugal and Spain in the mid-1970s, similarly led to fundamental changes in the political architecture and, more gradually, changes to the political culture. Whether it was the end of empires or dictatorships (or both), these changes initiated a process of redefining the dominant idea of the nation. In Spain, for example, where 'autonomous communities' were established in the Basque Country, Catalonia and Galicia in the late 1970s and early 1980s (there are now seventeen such regional units), Article 2 of the 1978 constitution enshrined the 'indissoluble unity of the Spanish nation, the common and indivisible motherland of all Spaniards'.

Demands for autonomy from 'stateless nations' (McCrone 1992), as in the case of Spain, have led to political restructuring in a number of west European countries. Besides Spain, in the post-war period Belgium, France and the United Kingdom have changed their political structures to accommodate such demands. Belgium has undoubtedly seen the most radical efforts to address demands for increased autonomy and independence. Here the devolution of considerable powers to regional governments has led to discussion about the function of the Belgian state relative to the regional units. In this instance, then, the very existence of the nation-state has been questioned. France, in contrast, has devolved little power as a result of regionalist and nationalist demands. The exception is the island of Corsica, which has seen a violent struggle for independence, and which has been awarded more powers than any other region of France. In general, however, French governments, whether left or right, seem unwilling to abandon the idea of the unity of the republic.

In France, as in many other western European countries, there are nevertheless moves to broaden the idea of who belongs to the national community. Thus the French football team, which won the World Cup in France in 1998, and which included numerous members of France's ethnic minority populations, was widely hailed as reflecting the cultural diversity of the modern French nation. The need to redefine the nation in a more inclusive manner is among the greatest political pressures facing western European states. In Germany, the period after unification in 1990 has seen efforts to find a new way of speaking about the German nation, including, most recently, the position of Germany's resident non-citizens: the so-called 'guest workers', mostly hailing from Turkey. In the UK a report produced by an independent body entitled *The Future of Multi-ethnic Britain* (Parekh 2000) sparked considerable controversy when it was published. Among the main messages of the report was the suggestion that the 'national story' needed to be retold to better reflect the contribution that Britain's ethnic minority populations have made to 'Britain'. By the late 1990s other countries, such as Denmark and Sweden, were experiencing similar debates. At their heart lies the matter of how it is possible to accommodate ethnic diversity while maintaining common values. Up to the 1960s many states would have pursued an assimilationist approach to minorities. This was a policy that was first applied to erode regional attachments in the late nineteenth and early twentieth centuries, as we have already noted, and which was then used to ensure that immigrants embraced their adopted national culture. Today, most mainstream political parties in western Europe officially view such policies as unacceptable, while broader cultural changes among the wider population have made it less likely that such policies would be supported. In addressing this task, as the governments of west Europe will have to do, it will be necessary to consider a radical evaluation of what 'nation-state' means, and *can* mean, today.

This task will not be limited to west Europe. Over the next decade *all* European states will have to confront this matter. In central-east Europe some countries, such as the former Czechoslovakia and Yugoslavia, saw very fundamental changes in order to address separatist demands. Others are beginning to feel the winds of change. The communist era meant, however, that states were unable to go through the nationalising phase to the same extent as west European states had done in the late nineteenth and early twentieth centuries. In central-east Europe nationalism was one of the main factors in the decline of Soviet hegemony over its satellite states; indeed, a noted commentator on the region describes 1989 – the year that saw the beginning of the region's revolutions – as the 'finest hour of East European nationalism' (Glenny, 1993: 204). It is perhaps not surprising, therefore, that since the demise of the Soviet empire central-east Europe has seen widespread efforts to 'nationalise' the state (see Brubaker (1996) for an interesting discussion of this development).

In some cases the transition has been made easier by virtue of the existence of a relatively homogenous population, as in the case of Poland, although whether the country's minorities would see things this way is debatable. Other countries in the region have found it more difficult to engage in nationalising programmes without causing concern to, and in some cases discriminating against, minority populations. Leaving aside for a moment especially difficult cases such as Croatia, Serbia and Macedonia, the experiences of other countries in the region illustrate the difficulties of seeking to implement the principle of the nation-state in countries with substantial ethnic minority populations. In Latvia, for example, the campaign for independence was broadly multi-ethnic, and there were plenty of well-intentioned discussions about the position of ethnic minorities, especially Russians, within the new Latvia. When Latvia gained independence, however, the new government disenfranchised one-third of the population by declaring that only those who had been Latvian citizens prior to 1940 (when the country was annexed by the USSR) and their descendants could hold citizenship. Related laws meant that only citizens could own property, bear arms and be employed in the civil service. Latvia, therefore, metamorphosed into an ethnic nation-state, rather than the civic nation-state that had been discussed prior to independence. The upshot of this development was that the political culture moved towards the right, while ethnic minorities became, understandably, increasingly frustrated by their non-citizen status. New legislation in 1998 has led to a substantial increase in the number of naturalised citizens (that is, non-ethnic Latvians acquiring Latvian citizenship), although almost 25 per cent of the population still did not hold Latvian citizenship.

Latvia is far from unique in this respect. Its neighbour, Estonia, introduced similarly restrictive citizenship legislation when it gained independence from the USSR. New legislation in 1995 made it easier to acquire citizenship, but the 1998 language law, making Estonian the official language of business, once again provoked criticism from the EU and Russia about the ethnic character of the state. Slovakia, too, has witnessed inter-ethnic difficulties, notably between ethnic Slovaks and ethnic Hungarians, the latter of which comprises more than one-tenth of the country's population. While ethnic minorities hold citizenship, the post-communist period has seen a rise in Slovak nationalism, especially during the administrations of Vladimir Mečiar.

There are nevertheless signs that the countries of central-east Europe are taking significant steps towards creating or fostering civic states. Situations in many countries may still be far from ideal for many ethnic minority groups, but there are signs that governments are intent on making the state more inclusive. In contrast to a number of other newly independent countries, Slovenia introduced a relatively liberal constitution on seceding from Yugoslavia in 1991, which gave citizenship to immigrants who had permanent residence and employment in the country for six months prior to independence. Hungary established elected councils for its large Roma population in 1998. There is much that remains to be done, however. Countries such as Bosnia-Hercegovina, Croatia, and the rump Yugoslav Federation, especially Serbia, have experienced terrible conflict since the beginning of the 1990s. The death of Franjo Tudjman in Croatia in 1999 and the end of Milošević's reign in Yugoslavia, the two figures who exacerbated the rise of Croatian and Serbian nationalism in the 1980s, have broken symbolic links with the past; it remains to be seen whether the new regimes will be able to forge strong civic societies.

At present, it appears that central-east Europe comprises three types of countries: those that are making relatively comfortable progress to a broadly civic political culture (such as Hungary, the Czech Republic, Lithuania, Poland and Slovenia); those that are experiencing some difficulties in their transition, but which are nevertheless showing signs of progress (such as Bulgaria, Estonia, Latvia and Slovakia); and finally, those where the state still bears an especially strong ethnic imprint (such as in Croatia and Serbia). Given the short history of genuine *de facto* independence for all of these countries, time will tell whether the civic nation-state, instead of its ethnic cousin, becomes the future for central-east Europe.

Conclusion: where next for the nation-state?

Crystal ball gazing is fraught with difficulties, so before we make any statements about the future let us outline some fairly uncontroversial observations.

- Perhaps the most significant observation we can make is that nation-states are not permanent features of European history. This chapter has shown that there are particular reasons why people come to imagine themselves as belonging to nation-states, and why this idea has come to be *the* mode of organising political space in Europe. We nevertheless know that it was not always this way. Indeed, most of the states of the former USSR had not previously existed as nation-states prior to the 1990s, while many other states in Europe did not exist as fully democratic nation-states – wherein people held full citizenship rights – until the late twentieth century. So, even when we speak of the universality of the nation-state, we should remember that this is a fairly recent phenomenon. The first observation we would like to make, therefore, is that there is no inherent reason why people should always wish to identify themselves as belonging to nation-states.

- A second observation is that patterns of change make it increasingly difficult to speak of a single, national culture anywhere. In reality there never *was* such a thing, but politicians and others chose to speak as if 'our' culture was a timeless entity, handed down from one generation to the next. National politicians and some of the primary national institutions display an awareness that the nation is not an unchanging entity. In 1999, for example, the British Broadcasting Corporation issued a new set of guidelines to journalists informing them that it is no longer acceptable to use terms such as 'nation' and 'British' where it is possible that national groups may have different experiences. The movement of people, ideas, images and commodities brings new cultural experiences that, in turn, mean that is less likely that the nation is imagined by the mass of the population in the way it once was. It is difficult to measure the impact of these cultural changes on a people's sense of national identity, but given what we know about how national consciousness was generated it seems fair to argue that as the key cultural and political processes change, so will our attachment to the nation.

- A final observation is that people have less trust and faith in political institutions than in previous generations. Studies have shown, for example, that trust in Parliament varies from 18 per cent in Ukraine and 32 per cent in Italy through to 57 per cent in Lithuania and 59 per cent in Norway; even at the highest end, these are not impressive figures (see Budge *et al.* (1997) for a discussion of this research). Diminished trust in Parliament does not necessarily lead to a diminished sense of national identity; indeed, in some cases it may actually lead people to back radical nationalist parties which promise to 'reform' the state and Parliament. Political institutions have nevertheless been crucial to the development of national consciousness over the past 200 years. If public faith in these institutions diminishes, does this mean that the sense of nationhood will weaken?

- This is unlikely to happen. If nationhood is to substantially weaken, where are its rivals? Despite the chatter about 'region-states' (Ohmae 1996), there is little indication that regions are capable of rivalling the emotive power of the nation. It also seems highly improbable that the challenger will be bigger than the nation-state, at least not for some considerable time to come. If people are disaffected with the national state because it seems distant from their concerns, then they are unlikely to switch their loyalties to a supranational body; Leonard (1998) reports that 98 per cent of EU citizens had no connection with the EU. The possibility of global government, meanwhile, remains the stuff of science fiction! Across Europe people may be frustrated with the state, but they remain keenly attached to the idea of the nation-state. Where the state faces domestic challenges, it is more often than not from movements seeking to establish their *own* nation-states.

- The future, then, remains national, albeit adapting to changing times. Laws, government and society need to be underpinned by some broad values that enable people to engage, for most of the time, in relatively harmonious relations. Up to now, political elites defined these values as reflecting the culture of a particular group. As we have argued, in multi-ethnic and multinational societies – which is what *all* European countries are – such prescriptive notions of the nation are outmoded. The future of the idea of the nation-state, therefore, is to find ways of developing inclusive values capable of holding together culturally diverse political communities. From east to west, there are signs that reflections on this task are beginning; the future will be to make them work.

Further reading

Brubaker, R. (1996) *Nationalism Reframed*. Cambridge: Cambridge University Press.

Crampton, R. J. (1997) *Eastern Europe in the Twentieth Century – and after*. London: Routledge (2nd edn).

Milward, A. (1992) *The European Rescue of the Nation-State*. London: Routledge.

Pierson, C. (1996) *The Modern State*. London: Routledge.

Nationalism in Europe

Key concepts

- Nation
- National identity
- Nationalism
- Secession

In the opening sentences of his book *Nationalism* (1960), Kedourie remarks that nationalism 'is a doctrine invented in Europe at the beginning of the nineteenth century', concluding that it is one without which we might well have been better off. Whether or not one agrees with Kedourie's negative assessment, there is no doubt that nationalism has had a significant impact on the development of Europe since the late eighteenth century. Although not entirely on its own, nationalism has nevertheless kept generations of cartographers busy, as the borderlines of European countries have been redrawn time and time again. Nationalism has played a pivotal role in modern European political history, producing events of far-reaching consequences, but it has also, rather more mundanely, pervaded our everyday culture. Thinking of ourselves as belonging to a nation, or as having a national identity, are among the most commonplace ways of positioning ourselves in relation to others. In short, nationalism, nations and national identities have become part of the fabric of modern European life.

Today, the European love affair with the nation shows little substantial sign of abating. What sustains this popular attachment to nations and national identity? Why does nationalism remain such an integral element of European political culture? The primary concern of this chapter is to explore why nationalism emerged, and why it has continued to be capable of mobilising people in each of the countries of Europe. We begin this analysis by considering how 'nation' and 'nationalism' might be defined.

Nations and nationalism in a European context

In the dramatis personae of the history of modern Europe, the nation would be among the leading players. Since the late eighteenth century the idea of the nation has developed as arguably *the* principal source of political legitimacy for European states. During this period, too, nationalism, as an ideology and a movement, has been among the chief political forces reshaping the political map of Europe. The changing fortunes of empires and states, and the lives of those inhabiting these territories, have in large part unfolded in the shadow cast by these phenomena. Nations and nationalism have therefore been implicated in some of the most profound political changes of the past two centuries.

So, then, how are we to understand these powerful forces? What are 'nations' and 'nationalism'? To take the nation first, ironically, for a phenomenon that generates so much emotion, researchers have sometimes been puzzled by this question. Seton-Watson (1977), in a widely respected study of nationalism, comments that he is 'driven to the conclusion that no scientific definition of the nation can yet be devised; yet the phenomenon has existed and exists' (1977: 5). Other writers have reached similar conclusions, and they, like Seton-Watson, have sought recourse in the idea that nations exist if people feel they belong to one.

Nations do not just exist in people's imaginations, however. The nation, or, more accurately, a vision of the nation, is embodied in many social institutions, from education systems to government, as well as across the spectrum of high and popular culture.

Representing the nation: high and popular culture

Since the nineteenth century themes of national identity and nationhood have informed all manner of cultural practices, including art, architecture, classical music, film, literature and theatre. In the case of classical music the list of composers who, especially at the turn of the nineteenth and twentieth centuries, embraced nationalism, and sought to find some expression of the nation and their sense of attachment to it through their music is considerable, including Sibelius (Finland), Grieg (Norway) and Chopin (Poland). Some pieces of classical music were adopted by nationalist movements or have come to be associated with nationalistic occasions, such as Verdi's *Chorus of the Hebrew Slaves* (which became an anthem of Italian nationalism in the mid-nineteenth century) and Edward Elgar's *Pomp and Circumstance March No. 1*, perhaps better known as *Land of Hope and Glory* (which first became popular in the UK during the First World War). In addition, a number of composers during this period drew on folk-songs as inspiration for their compositions, such as the Russian composers Rimsky-Korsakoff and Tchaikovsky. In the twentieth century film has been a key arena in which ideas of nation and nationhood have been played out to European audiences. The importance of film is that it has the capacity to reach an audience beyond the scope of many other cultural practices and because it has the power to *make* history, rather than simply recording it. Thus a movie such as *Braveheart*, the 1995 film starring Mel Gibson as William Wallace, who had waged war against the English King Edward I in the late thirteenth and early fourteenth centuries, has arguably created an awareness of Scotland as a nation distinct from Britain. Films that do not attain the international commercial success of *Braveheart* can still generate awareness of issues of nationhood among domestic audiences; Jerzy Hoffman's 1999 historical epic, *Ogniem i mieczem* ('With Fire and Sword'), for example, which portrays civil warfare in the Polish-Lithuanian Commonwealth in the seventeenth century, met with critical and popular success in his native Poland.

In addition, people generally speak of belonging to a nation if they can locate themselves within a group distinguished from others by putatively objective criteria, such as language or religion. Some academic commentators hold that groups share common cultural markers, especially where that group resides within a recognised national territory. Thus A. D. Smith, the most prolific and perhaps the most influential writer on nationalism, defines a nation as a group of people 'possessing common and distinctive elements of culture, a unified economic system, citizenship rights for all members, a sentiment of solidarity arising out of common experiences, and occupying a common territory' (1998: 188).

Some writers, including ourselves, nevertheless find the idea of a common national culture highly problematic, because any notion of a 'common culture', even at the most abstract level, is always open to dispute. Even Poland, commonly cited as an example of a largely ethnically homogenous country, has citizens who are ethnic Belorussians, Ukrainians and Germans. In practice, it is not possible to speak of a common national culture. Instead, writers such as Brubaker (1996) maintain that rather than asking what a nation *is* we should look at how particular visions of that nation are articulated. Thus, in observing the development of post-independence politics in former-Soviet republics such as Belarus, Estonia and Kazakhstan, Brubaker holds that one of the key issues for analysts is to explore how the nation is defined by the new ruling elites.

In spite of these differences of opinion, there is broad opposition to the idea of the 'immemorial' nation. If Mazzini, one of the chief architects of Italian unification during the mid-nineteenth century, believed that the Italians were a 'people . . . known from time immemorial by the same name, as the people of Italy' (quoted in Cowie and Wolfson 1985: 277), most scholars accept that before the 1500s people in Europe had little conception of belonging to a nation as that term is understood by writers such as Smith. Llobera (1994), for example, argues that by the late medieval period it is possible to discern nascent expressions of national consciousness, yet points out that such sentiments were held only by small groups of people in these territories and argues that what 'France' meant in the fourteenth and fifteenth centuries for these people cannot be equated with modern expressions of French identity.

Indeed, a number of writers argue that the significance of ethnic markers, such as language or religion, dates to the late nineteenth century, until when the nation was largely conceived in a political manner as a 'people' of a largely unspecified ethnicity. Hroch (2000) makes a convincing case for the position that between the 1820s and the 1840s emerging patriotic societies were vehicles for the promotion of ideas of nationhood centred on interpretations of national culture and utilising the vernacular languages. Hroch nevertheless argues that in the case of these nationalisms, it was only in the second half of the century that they received anything approaching popular support. In Ireland, too, the latter part of the nineteenth century saw the formation of Gaelic societies, such as the Gaelic League in 1893, for the promotion of the Irish language and other cultural activities, and to advance an idea of Irish national identity and nationhood.

Why the idea of the nation has been able to generate such support across social strata will be tackled in the next section of this chapter, but it is evident that this development would not have been possible without the contribution of nationalist movements across Europe promoting the ideology of nationalism. Contrary to a belief that nationalism grows out of an innate sense of national identity, to paraphrase Gellner (1983) it is nationalism that gives rise to the nation and not the other way round. As an ideology and movement nationalism dates largely to the nineteenth century, although we can trace its origins back to the eighteenth century to the French Revolution and to the views of prominent intellectuals such as the philosopher Herder. Smith provides one of the most widely accepted definitions of nationalism, stating that it is 'an ideological movement for the attainment and maintenance of self-government and independence on behalf of a group, some of whose members conceive it to constitute an actual or potential "nation"' (1998: 188). As an ideology, nationalism offers a world-view that represents people as divided into culturally discrete nations and which naturalises our attachments to our nation.

Categorising nationalism

Nationalism is not a singular phenomenon, however, and events across Europe highlight the diversity of nationalism. Some nationalist organisations, for example, are openly hostile to foreigners, such as the Front National in France and the Freedom Party in Austria, while others, especially most national governments in Europe, officially favour a multicultural nationalism. It is, moreover, difficult to speak of nationalism in the singular when referring to particular countries. 'French Nationalism', as expressed through the country's political parties, may take the form of the nationalisms of the Front National or the Mouvement National Républicain on the far-right, or the Gaullist Rassemblement pour la République and the Rassemblement pour la France on the centre-right. There are even marked differences between avowedly nationalist parties within a country. Thus the Volksunie and the Vlaams Blok in Belgium both advocate independence for the region of Flanders, but the Vlaams Blok, which has radical anti-immigrant and anti-Francophone policies, is to the right of the Volksunie.

Given this diversity, it is not surprising that central to the study of nationalism have been classificatory systems that tend to distinguish nationalisms either chronologically (see Snyder 1954) or by location (see Breuilly 1993). To what extent can typologies help us understand the diversity of nationalisms in Europe? One device, found variously in the work of Kohn (1967), Smith (1986a) and Schöpflin (1995), categorises nationalisms in Europe along 'territorial' and 'ethnic' lines. For Schöpflin (1995) nationhood and state nationalism in west Europe, as in Britain, France, the Netherlands and Sweden, have been underpinned by processes of state formation that fostered a relatively strong civic culture capable of holding together different ethnic groups within a common territory. In contrast, in most of the new countries of central-east Europe emerging from the late nineteenth century onwards the state was unambiguously the representative of a dominant ethnic group. Schöpflin cites the case of inter-war Romania, in which the state was aligned with the interests of ethnic Romanians at the expense of some 30 per cent of the population comprising ethnic Hungarians, Germans, Roma and Russians, among others.

The east/west dichotomy is nevertheless far from satisfactory. Such typologies can be hostage to the normative judgements of scholars. Moreover, even the scholars who utilise this methodological device add qualifications. Smith (1995) comments that 'civic nationalism', commonly viewed as more tolerant of ethnic difference and as being more typical of the national state nationalism in west Europe, 'delegitimizes and devalues the ethnic cultures of resident minorities and immigrants alike, and does so consciously and deliberately' (1995: 102). In this way, Weber (1978) illustrates how the French state promoted a standardised history through a public education system created by a series of laws in the 1880s, and promoted the primacy of standard French over regional vernaculars (up to the late nineteenth century only a quarter of those living in France spoke standard French). In contemporary Europe, the government of Estonia introduced a range of policies designed to promote a multi-ethnic society in the late 1990s, but its State Integration Programme is directed towards ensuring that minorities, especially the large Russian minority, are able to speak the Estonian language and participate in Estonian culture.

Some scholars have developed other bases of classification. Breuilly (1993) develops one of the more interesting alternative typologies, distinguishing between three types of nationalism: unification nationalisms; reformist nationalisms; and separatist nationalisms. Since the nineteenth century, Europe has witnessed a number of high-profile unification nationalisms. Italy and Germany, founded in 1870 and 1871 respectively, were the product of unification nationalisms, as these movements brought together populations that had never before lived within one national territory. More recently, unification nationalisms have achieved some notoriety, principally because of the conflicts in the Balkans where Bosnia-Herzegovina fragmented along ethnic lines as Croat and Serb nationalists sought to 'reunite' elements of this republic with their respective republics and where ethnic Albanians in the Balkans have pursued a vision of a 'Greater Albania' that would join the territories of Kosovo in Yugoslavia and the western region of Macedonia with Albania.

As the case of the Balkans illustrates, many unification nationalisms are also separatist since they will involve secession from another country. Of the two, however, separatist nationalisms have been the most common in Europe. In the nineteenth and early twentieth centuries separatist nationalisms played important roles in breaking the grip of imperial rule across Europe from the Russian Empire in the east to the British in the west. An indication of the impact of separatist nationalisms is the emergence of a considerable number of new countries in the closing and opening decades of the nineteenth and twentieth centuries, among them Romania (1878), Norway (1905), Bulgaria (1908) and Albania (1912). The late twentieth century witnessed a strengthening of separatist tendencies across Europe. Central-east Europe has seen the most dramatic changes, with Croatia, Serbia, Slovenia and Macedonia seceding from Yugoslavia in 1991, the breakup of the Soviet Union in the same year, and the fragmentation of Czechoslovakia in 1993. Western Europe continues to experience a strengthening of separatist nationalism. Northern Ireland and the Basque Country have been the focus of media and academic attention because of the armed conflicts in those regions, but in recent years the prospect of the secession of Scotland from the United Kingdom and the fragmentation of Belgium, while still some way off, should nonetheless be considered seriously.

Breuilly's third type of nationalism – reform nationalism – refers to an opposition movement that seeks to move the state and society in a radical nationalist direction. In Europe, Breuilly is primarily interested in the fascist movements in Germany, Italy and Romania that developed in the 1920s and 1930s. In examining these cases Breuilly explores why these types of movements were successful in these instances, and why, comparatively, fascist movements in Britain and Spain did not achieve the same success (perhaps the main factor is an underlying political crisis, and the inability of other movements to position themselves as the national opposition).

Breuilly's typology nevertheless deliberately excludes a range of other nationalist movements in Europe, because he is concerned with 'significant' nationalist movements that pose a 'serious challenge to the state' (1993: 8–9). Thus he is not interested in movements such as those of Bretons in France, ethnic Germans in Poland or ethnic Hungarians in Romania. Billig in his excellent *Banal Nationalism* nevertheless cautions against discriminating against some forms of nationalism because they do not have the high profile of others. As he comments, 'if sociological nets are for catching slices of social life, then the net, which sociologists have marked "nationalism", is a remarkably small one: and it seems to be used primarily for catching exotic, rare and often violent specimens' (Billig 1995: 43). If we follow Billig, then these smaller movements and, at a more sublime level, the everyday reminders of the nation, just as much as those in Catalonia, Flanders or Croatia, reveal the enduring appeal of the idea of the nation.

The rise and transformation of nationalism in Europe

So far we have said little about why nationalism emerges in Europe and what factors contribute to its development. Both of these issues are nevertheless central to our understanding of nationalism. As we will show, there are two ways of exploring these issues. The first deals with the long-term rise of nationalism, and focuses on the forces that led to its early development in the eighteenth century and its subsequent transformation. We are therefore interested in the impact of concomitant social changes, such as the rise of industrialisation, the development of the modern state, or other such significant social transformations. In contrast the second approach is what Brubaker (1996) terms an 'eventful' analysis of nationalism, in which the accent is on nationalism activated in particular conditions.

Before we turn to these issues, let us make two opening points about the rise and transformation of nationalism in Europe. First, nationalisms and national identities have been constant features of European societies since the second half of the nineteenth century. This is not to say that the form and content of nationalisms in European societies have remained the same, for they have not. Equally, it is important that we do not view nationalism as something that disappeared off the radar after the end of the Second World War only to reappear at the close of the twentieth century, when it played such a pivotal role in the fragmentation of the former Yugoslavia, Czechoslovakia and the Soviet Union. Too often commentators, whose myopia may be partly attributed to wishful thinking, have been surprised by 'resurgences' of nationalism. Cobban (1969) observes that opinion among British and American writers during the Second World War was that the principle of nationhood should not be allowed to form the basis of a post-war political order. As he remarks in memorable terms, for these writers nationalism was a 'survival of a dead age, the ghosts of Garibaldi, Mazzini, Byron, Bolívar, come back . . . to haunt an age in which all they stood for no longer has any right to exist' (1969: 13). Later, Smith (1979), responding to the growth in support for nationalist movements and political parties in regions in which modernisation was supposed to have eroded the appeal of separatist nationalisms, such as Brittany, Catalonia, Flanders, Scotland and Wales, comments that 'the so-called "demise of nationalism" in mid-century Europe has been more apparent than real' (1979: 152). Moreover, we can lose sight of the significance of nationalism across Europe if we view it as something that happens only in seemingly pathological situations, such as Northern Ireland, the Basque Country, Bosnia, Kosovo and Moldova, or in contexts where emotions have been stretched to breaking-point, as in the rivalries between Croatia and Serbia, or, sometimes, between western governments such as between those of France and the UK. If we follow

Billig's (1995) advice, then, by broadening our definition of nationalism to include all the habits and practices by which the nation is reproduced, it becomes apparent just how embedded nationalism is in all European societies. So, then, we should not be surprised at the recent high profile of nationalism across Europe.

The second opening point is more specifically concerned with three key dates in the transformation of nationalism in order to clarify what we know about this process. One date, the fifteenth century, is a baseline, in that there is widespread agreement that nationalism does not date to before this period. Political rhetoric can sometimes result in the wholly incorrect view that nationalism dates back a thousand years or more, but even J. A. Armstrong (1982, 1995), who, perhaps more than any other writer, has argued for the need to recognise the deep historical roots of nationalism, argues that nationalism as the 'conscious demand for political expression of the nation' (1995: 35) does not pre-date this point. Prior to this period a number of factors limit the development of a popular sense of nationhood (for further details on this issue, see our discussion of the development of the nation-state). This has not, however, prevented disputes between rival national groups or countries in which figures or events are claimed as part of the history of their respective nation.

Disputed histories: the case of Greece and Macedonia

The Republic of Macedonia, often known as the former Yugoslav Republic of Macedonia (FYROM), has been in dispute with neighbouring Greece since the former became independent in 1991, over its right to use the title 'Macedonia' and over the appropriation of certain symbols. For the Greek government the problem is that 'Macedonia' is the name of its northern province, and thus it views FYROM's claim to this name as an irredentist aspiration. The Macedonian government, however, believes its claim to the name to be an historic right. For both sides, evidence to support their respective cases rest with interpretations of the region's ancient history which sees figures such as Alexander the Great as an early Macedonian or Greek national figure. This dispute was only partially addressed by a special Accord, signed by the governments of both countries in 1995, in which, among other issues, it was agreed that if one country believed that any symbols 'constituting part of its historic or cultural patrimony' was being used by the other then the accused country would have to change or justify why they would not alter their practice. Greece nevertheless continues to refuse to recognise the right of its neighbour to utilise the name of 'Macedonia'.

Another seminal date is the back end of the eighteenth century, specifically the French Revolution. This event is broadly recognised as marking the genesis of modern nationalism, as it founded the new political order on the principle that the people constituted a nation and that the nation, in turn, was the sole source of political legitimacy. The wider significance of the French Revolution was that it provided a model for similar movements seeking to overthrow what they viewed as despotic regimes, such as the 1794 Polish rebellion against the Habsburg, Prussian and Russian empires which occupied sections of land formerly belonging to the Polish crown, and the 1798 United Irishmen's rebellion against the British crown. The legacy of the French Revolution was political, and as a model for later nationalisms it was largely devoid of ethnic content. This is why the third key date – the latter half of the nineteenth century – is so important, as it is a period in which ethnic factors come to play an increasingly important role in nationalisms. Thus, historians such as Hobsbawm (1990) and Breuilly (1993) convincingly argue that the unification campaigns in what were to become Germany and Italy were underpinned by political concerns, and that it was only after these new states were established that ethnic notions of the nation gained a wider currency.

Why nationalist movements should gather the popular support that they did is an important question. What is it about this ideology that it has been able to sustain an appeal unmatched globally by any other single ideology? It is difficult to say with any certainty why the idea of the nation developed in the first instance. We know that the idea of popular sovereignty (that is, rule by 'the people') had been in circulation since the seventeenth century, and given form by Cromwell in England and Wales. We also know that this concept gained in importance throughout the eighteenth century, culminating in the French Revolution. The growing interest in popular sovereignty can be traced to the broader intellectual culture that was part of the Enlightenment, in which the ideas that humans were equal in nature and that government should reflect this state were the subject of much discussion. Intellectual enquiry may also have kindled interest in national culture across Europe, albeit among a small, educated elite. Throughout the eighteenth century there had been growing interest in archiving history in museums, and these institutions became dedicated to organising the history of the nation and region. During the eighteenth century national museums were established in Naples (1738), Paris (1750), London (1753) and Madrid (1771), while royal collections were opened to the public in Vienna (1700), Dresden (1746) and St Petersburg (1765). Hroch (2000) tells us that the pioneers of nationalism, those scholars who took an active interest in historical and cultural affairs without being necessarily committed politically to nationalist ideals, were inspired by a 'patriotism of the Enlightenment type, namely an active affection for the region in which they lived' (2000: 23).

What about the broad mass of the population, however? Records of the opinions of the views of ordinary Europeans are not extensive during this period, so we know little about why people actually found the idea of nation appealing. The best that we can say is that a combination of factors has been responsible for the initial appeal of the idea of nation. National consciousness was undoubtedly fired by national rivalries and warfare, especially since the increasing scale of warfare from the 1500s meant that it touched the lives of growing numbers of ordinary Europeans. Colley (1992), for example, gives us some indication, through study of personal letters, auto-biographies and local registers, of how important opposition to Napoleon and the French was in popularising British national consciousness in the late eighteenth and early nineteenth centuries. Shafer (1972) argues that similar sentiments were aroused as Napoleon's grip extended over Prussia, Spain, and the northern regions of what was to become Italy. Once established, it took little time before other regions experienced the principles of popular sovereignty and national self-determination in action. Greece had seceded, after a war, from the Ottoman Empire by 1829 and Belgium separated from its union with the Netherlands, with which it had been joined since 1815, in 1839. Therefore, when mixed with feelings of hostility and resentment, the idea that a 'nation' should have the right to self-government evidently held considerable popular appeal.

This principle is one of a number of factors that help to explain the long-term appeal of nationalism in Europe. Just as the French Revolution inspired national revolutionaries elsewhere in Europe, so too the ideal of national independence produced its own momentum; even the memories of failed insurrections made impressions on later generations. For populations that resented being tied to others by virtue of sharing the same territory, nationalism became – and remains – a potent ideology. Smith (1996) notes that in the Baltic republics of Estonia, Latvia and Lithuania, for example, the launch of the popular fronts (the nationalist opposition to the Soviet system) in the late 1980s was marked by declarations of the illegality of the incorporation of these territories into the USSR in 1940. Arguments about democracy are often tied to such declarations, in that the annexing state is usually held to be unrepresentative of the 'will of the people'. Thus, Sinn Fein, a party campaigning for the unification of Ireland (and the secession of Northern Ireland from the UK), takes part in the electoral process in Northern Ireland but refuses to send its elected representatives to the British Parliament. It is not just separatist movements, however, that have utilised the idea of the 'will of the people'. In recent years writers such as Miller (1995) have used this idea to develop what has been termed 'liberal nationalism', after the work of another writer, Tamir (1993).

There is nevertheless a step that necessarily precedes people's support for nationalist movements: people must perceive themselves as belonging to nations. As this attachment is not natural, people need to *learn* to think of themselves as being part of a nation. To use a sociological term, people need to be 'socialised' into thinking of the world as being naturally divided into nations. How does this happen? First, people need to be convinced that 'their' nations exist as real entities, so that they can identify with them. Second, these people need to be encouraged to identify with 'their' nation. On the first issue there are a number of factors that help to persuade people of the existence of their nation. We have already noted that intellectuals interested in folk history were among what Hroch (2000) terms the 'pioneers' of nationalism. By the late nineteenth century writers busily creating national histories had superseded these pioneers. Moretti (1999), for example, analysing historiography in Italy shortly after unification in 1870, points to the growing number of professional historians dedicated to demonstrating the ancient origins of a unified Italy. Indeed, he quotes one historian as arguing that his research was not 'merely of scientific need, but also a patriotic duty' (1999: 114). The period from the mid-nineteenth century onwards saw a remarkable growth in nationalist propaganda that helped to spread the idea that people belonged to cultural communities, and that this difference was sufficient to warrant a separate national state and government. Such studies also lend a sense of objectivity to nationalist claims, and thus further reinforce the existence of the nation. For many people their nation has come to be synonymous with the country in which they live (although the existence of separatist nationalisms illustrates that not all people feel this way), largely as a consequence of the actions of the state, which we will consider below (and which are examined in more detail in Chapter 1). Calhoun (1997) argues that maps, depicting the world as divided into national societies, have been enormously important in reinforcing a belief in the existence of nations. National emblems, icons and figures, too, act as visible declarations that nations exist in the real world, rather than simply in our own imaginations.

Many of these phenomena also encourage identification with the nation. Nationalist historiography will always involve a narrative that helpfully identifies 'our' glories, while simultaneously pointing to the deeds of enemies. National icons and emblems, while part of the tapestry of Billig's (1995) 'banal nationalism', are nevertheless also part of the mass rituals and celebrations in which 'the people' come together as a nation. If these phenomena foster attachments to 'our' culture and history, others forge identification with 'homelands'. National anthems, many of which do not date beyond the mid-nineteenth century, often make direct reference to the relationship between land and identity. The first line of the Lithuanian national anthem, for example, refers to 'my homeland, land of heroes', that of Finland opens with 'our land, our land, our fatherland', while the national anthem of Wales combines an attachment to land and history, *Mae Hen Wlad Fy Nhadau* ('Land of My Fathers'). Indeed, as Bryson and McCartney (1994) observe, homeland is one of the three most common references in national anthems (the other two being history and conflict/struggle). National memorials are also interesting in this respect, as, by virtue of being located throughout the national territory, they make links between the local and the national and nationalise public spaces. Hobsbawm (1990) notes, for example, that in the immediate decades following the unification of Germany in 1871 there was an energetic phase of building national monuments. Elsewhere, Gaffney (1998) points out that throughout Britain there are estimated to be 50 to 60,000 war memorials.

Icons of the nation: flags

For centuries flags have been used as markers of identity, especially in battle, and of territory. States increasingly began to use flags in the medieval period, although the flag of Denmark, the *Dannebrog* ('Danish Cloth'), is the oldest national flag in continuous usage, dating to the thirteenth century. Today, national flags are present at all public national ceremonies, such as sporting events and national holidays, although they also fly permanently from many public buildings across Europe. They are, in short, part of the performance of nationalism. Although there is a fair degree of originality with regard to the colours and the visual designs on flags, there are some common patterns (such as the 'Scandinavian cross' found on the flags of Finland, Norway and Sweden, and the tricolour, the earliest example of which is the French flag) and some commonality with regard to what various colours symbolise (black usually symbolises the wealth of the soil, while yellow or gold will often represent the wealth of the country). Given the nationalist preoccupation with territory it is perhaps surprising that only the flag of Cyprus carries an image of its territory. The esteem in which the national flag is held is evident in the fact that numerous countries have laws relating to the design and use of the flag. In Finland, for example, a law dating from 1978 stipulates that anyone using or selling a flag that does not meet the specifications as laid down elsewhere in the Act will be fined for 'disobeying regulations about the Finnish flag', while adding elsewhere that when the Finnish flag is publicly flown alongside other flags it must be 'placed in the most valuable position'. Similar attention is often given to the process of creating new flags. The design of the 'Union Jack' flag of the UK dates back to the seventeenth century, when it was created by King James VI to symbolically bring together the Kingdom of Great Britain. It has remained largely unchanged (apart from changes to the proportions of the constituent elements of the design) since the early nineteenth century, when it was altered to include the emblem of St Patrick after Ireland became part of the United Kingdom of Great Britain and Ireland in 1801. Similar efforts to ensure that national symbols are inclusive of different factions in the national community were evident when Bosnia and Herzegovina in the late 1990s, in negotiation with the United Nations, had to establish a flag that would symbolise the aspirant unity of the country and which would satisfy national groups that had been engaged in a civil war during the early 1990s.

Since the nineteenth century, then, the nation has become woven into the ideological fabric of European society. We nevertheless have to ask whether there is something, or a combination of forces, which, at a deeper level, underpins the appeal of the idea of the nation. Some writers have, for example, linked the rise of nationalism in Europe with the development of industrialism and capitalism. For Gellner (1983) nationalism is a by-product of the rise of the industrial society. Gellner suggests that a mobile labour force was necessary to develop a successful industrial economy, and that this, in turn, required a basic level of education provided by the state to overcome linguistic barriers within the country and to create a geographically mobile labour force. For Gellner, it is this public education system that generates a mass sense of national identity; people come to identify with the new culture. Conflict occurs partly because the modernisation process is uneven, and that cultural and class divisions develop between those who have been socialised into the new culture and those who, while living in the same country, speak a markedly different dialect or language. Fault lines also emerge between the new dominant culture and those who adhere to cultural practices that have withstood the tidal wave of modernisation, such as religious groups. Where these divisions emerge counter-nationalisms develop. Other writers, such as Hobsbawm (1990) and Anderson (1991), have attributed the development of nationalism to capitalism, rather than industrialisation. For Hobsbawm, nationalism aids the creation of large-scale national economies, necessary for the effective expansion of capitalist enterprise, by consolidating a unified national territory. Anderson's argument focuses instead on 'print-capitalism', claiming that the decision by publishers to turn away from Latin to vernacular languages in search of new markets for their commodities essentially created new cultural-linguistic communities. By standardising certain vernaculars – below the level of Latin, but above the many spoken vernaculars – print-capitalism enabled relatively large populations to share the same printed information, whether in the form of newspapers or literature. In short, this development enabled people to imagine themselves as belonging to a larger cultural community. Moreover, the new printed languages also enable the spread of the ideology of nationalism itself.

Other commentators, however, are less convinced of the role of industrialism and capitalism. For Smith (1998), the above approaches leave him asking why the masses should find the ideas 'invented' by elite social groups so appealing, or, addressing Anderson, why people should want to imagine themselves as belonging to nations just because print-capitalism makes it possible for them to do so. Moreover, Smith maintains that because writers such as Gellner and Hobsbawm claim that nationalism does not have roots outside modernity, they have difficulties in explaining why nationalisms emerge in some places and not in others. Anderson does nevertheless suggest that part of the appeal of nationalism is its spiritual nature, comparing it to the world religious imagined communities that preceded the era of the nation. Gellner, too, has provided us with an account which explains that people identify with their nation because of the public culture into which they are assimilated, but, again, Smith is not satisfied with the strength of this argument.

Instead, Smith (1986a, 1998) suggests that we need to understand the pre-modern origins of nationalism to see how and why certain nationalisms flourish in the modern era. Smith's argument is that national cultures cannot just be invented; rather, modern nationalist movements draw on elements of pre-existing ethnic cultures and it is the use of these cultures that ensures the idea of the nation has a popular resonance. Smith holds that there have been two main routes to nationhood in Europe: bureaucratic incorporation and vernacular mobilisation. The former is characterised by those countries, such as England, France and Spain, where the state has developed over a number of centuries, during which the mass of the population is gradually assimilated into the culture of the dominant ethnic group. The latter process – for Smith, characteristic of central-east Europe – is marked by the transition that occurs when an ethnic group is mobilised by elite groups from within its own culture and drawing on myths and traditions appropriated from the pre-existing ethnic culture. The particular advantage of Smith's approach is that it also combines some of the elements present in the work of Gellner and Hobsbawm, notably the role of the state.

These approaches, then, offer us a 'deep' explanation for the rise and spread of nationalism in Europe, even if there is considerable disagreement between individual writers. Overall, we might say that there is no one single factor that explains why in the nineteenth century nationalism should hold such an enormous appeal for so many ordinary Europeans. For each of the writers mentioned above the primary mover is the intelligentsia, a relatively elite social group, and they offer good reasons why this group should find nationalism appealing (such as their career paths being blocked because of their ethnic identity). We can nevertheless speculate that, in general, a combination of factors generated and have sustained popular national consciousness in Europe since the nineteenth century, from war and international animosity to the impact of national public cultures and, more recently, nationalising popular cultures.

These general explanations nevertheless need to be supplemented by factors that can cause support for nationalist movements to surge in certain instances. Some factors may contribute to unrest and hostility towards the state, without being the main cause of the growth of nationalism. Thus, for example, an economic downturn in the former Yugoslavia in the late 1980s undoubtedly contributed to social unrest, but economic circumstances were not the main cause of what unfolded in the country a couple of years later. We are looking instead for changes that push the category of nation to the fore of public policy, political rhetoric and popular feeling: this is nationalism as a 'contingent event', to use Brubaker's (1996) phrase. Brubaker himself looks at some of the structural changes that occurred in central-east Europe and the former USSR, tracing their influence as catalysts in promoting mass national consciousness. Brubaker considers the consequence in the USSR of institutionalising nationhood, by, for example, marking an ethnic nationality (such as Georgian, Russian or Ukrainian) on internal passports.

Similarly, we might argue that the acceleration of European integration in the 1990s illustrates how 'nationness' can unfold as an 'event', when people find themselves suddenly utilising the category of nation. A more specific example is the case of the UK, where, after elected national assemblies were established in Northern Ireland, Scotland and Wales, national identity quickly became an issue of considerable public debate and concern, albeit for a relatively short period of time.

Nationalism, then, may not simply be the product of deep structural forces, such as industrialism or capitalism. The significance of Brubaker's analysis is that it alerts us to how nationalism and national identity can quite suddenly move to centre stage, rather than slowly emerge as experiences passed down through generations. Overall, however, we need to combine perspectives in order to understand the rise and development of nationalism. For example, events in the former Yugoslavia in the late 1980s and early 1990s may have compelled large sections of the population to identify with their ethnic nationality in ways which they had hitherto not done so, but these circumstances did not create the categories of 'Croat' or 'Serb'; rather, these identities had been shaped over generations. It may not be essential to understand today what caused the emergence of nationalism two hundred years or so ago, but it does help us to appreciate that while similar conditions exist, nationalism is likely to remain a potent force. Moreover, as we will show below, perceptions of historical divisions, as much as contingent events, are both important factors in explaining why hostilities develop between national groups.

Nationalism: conflict and conflict resolution

No account of nationalism in Europe would be complete without some consideration of how we may address the serious tensions that may develop between national groups. After all, Europe has seen many wars over the past two centuries in which nationhood has been a major issue for combatants. What, then, are the lessons of this history? What are the ways in which we can resolve major nationalist disputes?

The first strategy is intervention by the international community. Tensions over nationalism have, on occasion, necessitated responses from the international community. In the late nineteenth century, nationalist revolts against the imperial powers, especially within the territories belonging to the Ottoman and Russian empires in central and eastern Europe, caused shocks across Europe. Thus, revolts in the provinces of Bosnia and Herzegovina, followed by uprisings in Serbia and Bulgaria against Ottoman power, and a subsequent massacre of 12,000 people in Bulgaria by the Ottomans, managed to envelop all the European Great Powers because of the strategic importance of south-east Europe. The 1878 Treaty of San

Stefano, which marked a temporary cessation of conflict in the region, led to the subsequent establishment of Romania and Serbia as independent states, for example. Perhaps the most significant example of a response by the international community, however, is the 1919 Treaty of Versailles, in which the principle of national self-determination was applied to reorder the territories of the defeated powers at the end of the First World War. Borders were redrawn on the grounds that peace in Europe was best preserved if borders reflected putatively national divisions across Europe, although this logic was not extended to the territories of the victorious powers. Thus, the Versailles agreements saw the emergence of a number of new states – Czechoslovakia and the Kingdom of Serbs, Croats and Slovenes (changed to the Kingdom of Yugoslavia in 1929) – and the establishment of others – Austria, Poland, Hungary – which had existed in earlier forms, albeit with different borders.

In modern times the Balkans has, again, seen interventions by European states in response to nationalisms. As civil war was unfolding in Yugoslavia in 1991 the European Community established the Badinter Commission to arbitrate between the various parties. The ensuing negotiations and divisions within the EC never-theless compounded the problems in Yugoslavia, as Germany unilaterally recognised Slovenian and Croatian independence in December 1991 and January 1992, respec-tively. This move ran contrary to the EC requirement for unanimous agreement among its members and flew in the face of warnings that this policy could well exacerbate problems. The EC collectively followed this move with official recognition in January 1992, but the negotiations over recognition of these states and the other republics of Yugoslavia seeking recognition, such as Macedonia, revealed that the principle of national self-determination by the international community was not applied uniformly. Thus, recognition of Croatia progressed in spite of evidence that it did not meet the standards of human rights and protection of national minorities, as set out by the Badinter Commission. Recognition, then, did not address a problem that had been central to the civil wars: the treatment of national minorities residing within the republics. The problems of intervention in the Balkans illustrate that outside intervention is no guarantee of lasting stability. This should not be a great surprise, since intervening governments, while desiring peace, have no wish to remain committed in the long term. The primary desire is to bring a halt to conflict and, sometimes, to establish consociational political structures.

The case of Yugoslavia illustrates a second potential outcome of addressing nationalist tensions within a national territory: secession. As was noted earlier, secessionist nationalisms are to be found in most European countries, and some countries, such as France, the United Kingdom and Spain, face challenges from a number of such movements. Only in a few instances over the twentieth century, however, have secessionist movements been successful in securing independence for the nation which they claim to represent. Movements in Ireland had been campaigning, and sometimes fighting, against British rule over the island since the late eighteenth century. In 1920 partial success was achieved with the establishment of the Irish Free State (which became the Republic of Ireland in 1949 when the territory seceded from the British Commonwealth). A section of the island, which became Northern Ireland in 1920, remained under British rule, although different types of Irish nationalist movements campaign for the unification of this territory with the Republic of Ireland. In the final decade of the twentieth century secessionist nationalist movements played key roles in the demise of the USSR and the former Yugoslavia. Although in Yugoslavia, and in some of the republics of the USSR, such as Ukraine and Moldova, the campaign for independence was either marked or followed by armed conflict, this is not always the case with secession. The breakup of the USSR, especially given the size of the territory, was achieved relatively peacefully, and the creation of the Republic of Slovakia and the Czech Republic out of Czechoslovakia in 1991 was secured without any fighting.

The failure of any secessionist movement in western Europe – with the exception of Ireland in 1920 – to secure its objective demonstrates that governments are reluctant to concede to separatist pressures, even where, as in the case of the Basque Country, Corsica and Northern Ireland, significant armed conflicts have developed. Political and social systems have therefore been largely successful in ensuring that national pride, where it differs to attachments to the national state, does not spill over into mass support for extreme secessionist movements. Even where voters have supported movements committed to secession via democratic pressure, as in Flanders or Scotland, support has not yet reached levels that would force national governments to concede sovereignty over a territory. In the case of those states in central and east Europe, as well as across the former USSR, that did fragment, the weight of evidence illustrates that the system was no longer viewed as legitimate by the mass of the population. In Czechoslovakia, for example, tension between Czechs and Slovaks was present throughout the history of the country, and had increased in the post-war era. In the case of the former Yugoslavia, one commentator (Lendvai 1991) argues that the roots of secession pre-date the Second World War because of perceived Serb monopolisation of power.

The decision to allow part of a national territory to secede or to move towards a peaceful fragmentation, as in Czechoslovakia in 1991, may be necessary, especially if relations between national groups are disintegrating or have already done so. On the surface, secession will often bring an end to large-scale manifestations of hostilities, as in the Republic of Ireland, Slovenia, many of the former Soviet republics, and the Czech and Slovak republics. There is, however, plenty of evidence that post-secession states will go through a nationalising process, in which the culture of the dominant ethnic group is embedded at the expense of minorities. Post-independence, the Irish Free State (later, the Republic of Ireland) was virtually dominated by Fianna Fail, a party that entrenched the doctrine of the Catholic Church in state institutions and in the new constitution adopted after secession from the British Commonwealth. In a more extreme situation, post-independence Croatia, under the leadership of Franjo Tudjman, underwent a process of Croatianisation, a development that made life more difficult for ethnic Serbs. It is far from inevitable that post-independence states will experience this kind of politics, but the efforts to establish a new identity, combined with hostility to the previous regime, does mean that cultural pluralism is unlikely to accompany democratic pluralism. The Baltic states of Estonia and Latvia have had troubled relations post-independence with their large ethnic Russian minorities. Latvia, for example, denied citizenship to many ethnic Russians and Russophones from 1994 to 1998.

Some states, in an effort to stem threats to the existence of the country, will seek to change the internal balance of power in order to accommodate difference. In Czechoslovakia there had been some attempt to accommodate tensions in the early

1970s, when a federal structure replaced, at least in theory, the centralised state governed from Prague. This measure was, of course, ultimately unsuccessful in maintaining the integrity of the state. It nevertheless highlights how governments are willing to restructure political arrangements within a country in order to accommodate demands for increased autonomy on the part of groups claiming to represent the interests of what Guibernau (1996) calls 'stateless nations' within the national territory. As Chapter 5 on regionalism illustrates, there are varying political arrangements across Europe. Federal systems exist in a number of European countries, such as Austria and Germany, which have existed since the post-war reorganisation, whereas Belgium has moved to a federal structure because of the increasing demands made by Flemish and Walloonian separatists. Without yet venturing down the federalist route, in other European countries political restructuring has given varying levels of autonomy to sub-state territorial units. In Spain, after the death of General Franco, the 1978 constitution established a number of 'autonomous communities' in a move designed to reconcile the unity of the Spanish state with the demands of sub-state nationalist movements. Thus Catalonia, nationalist movements in which date back to the nineteenth century, became an autonomous community, and it seems unlikely that it will demand independence from Spain. In the UK in referendums in Scotland and Wales a majority of those who participated (in Wales only 50.1 per cent of the electorate voted) voted in favour of the government's plans to establish devolved governments in these territories. Popular support for the Scottish National Party and Plaid Cymru in Wales has fluctuated since the 1960s, when both parties secured their first elected representatives to the British House of Commons, but pressure for devolution grew throughout the 1980s and 1990s. The constitutional changes in the UK since 1997 have been an attempt to address the problems experienced by the British state.

A third strategy for addressing nationalist pressures within a state, then, is to restructure political arrangements in order to enable greater self-government for sub-state territorial units. Decentralisation may sometimes occur because of a reorganisation of relations between different tiers of government, rather than as a direct response to internal schisms. Such changes can nevertheless enable central government to address territories where separatist pressures are particularly strong. France began a process of decentralisation in the early 1980s, in the course of which it granted supplementary powers to the island of Corsica. This move was designed to address the challenge presented by support for separatist parties and, in particular, as a response to the escalation of guerrilla attacks by armed Corsican separatists.

Such changes to constitutional arrangements are nevertheless measures that states will only consider if the threat to the legitimacy of the national state is considerable, and if other avenues have been exhausted. Before this stage is reached it is likely that the state will have sought to appease nationalist movements and political parties by enacting special legislation that will enable members of the group which they represent to have an aspect of their cultural identity officially recognised. Often this may take the form of giving official recognition to a minority language.

In the late nineteenth century the Austrian part of the Habsburg Empire was riven by language disputes, and because of the intermixing of nationalities within the kingdoms and territories hostilities were not easily resolved. The imperial government in Vienna nevertheless allowed Czech to be given equal status with German in the Bohemian civil service in order to appease Czech nationalism (Stone 1999). Many countries in contemporary Europe allow minority languages to be used in public institutions, such as schools, local government, civil service and courts. At one end of the spectrum is Belgium, whose federal structure divides the population into the Flemish and French cultural communities. Other countries have introduced laws that address the demands of certain ethno-national groups. In the UK, for example, a number of laws since the late 1960s have gradually increased the status of the Welsh language, which now has parity with the English language in all areas of the public sector in Wales. In the states of central and eastern Europe applying to join the EU, the issue of the rights of minority groups – notably sizeable ones such as the Hungarian minority in Slovakia, the Roma in the Czech Republic, Slovakia, Hungary and Romania, and the Russian minorities in Estonia and Latvia – are of increasing significance as the EU monitors political change. In its 1999 report on the progress made by candidate countries, the European Commission claimed that some 'continue to face difficulties in finding the right balance between legitimate strengthening of the state language and the protection of minority language rights', highlighting the situations in Latvia and, in particular, Estonia.

Recognition strategies can be important in promoting a healthy civic culture and social integration within a country. Refusal to introduce such strategies may contribute to a strengthening of nationalist cleavages within a society, as in the case of the divide between ethnic Latvians and Russians in Latvia. Recognition strategies, especially where combined with some measure of political restructuring, may be sufficient to stem popular support for secessionist parties. In Catalonia and Wales, for example, parties that formerly espoused separatist policies are now committed to working within the existing territorial arrangements. In other cases, however, recognition strategies have not prevented a growth in support for secession. Thus in Spain, while the 1978 constitution gave Basques (along with other national groups) a measure of political autonomy, this has not halted Basque secessionism.

Faced by internal challenges some states have chosen to pursue a contrasting approach: nationalising strategies. Such strategies are typical of post-independence states, as has happened in some of the Baltic states. These strategies are nevertheless not limited to post-independence states. Since the late nineteenth century, when nationalisms began to challenge states and empires across Europe, one response has been to crack down on tolerance of domestic minority nationalities and promote the culture of the dominant national group. Cobban (1969) remarks that while in 1870 Polish regiments in the Prussian Army marched into battle playing Polish tunes, a few years later this would not have been tolerated by a German government determined to Germanise ethnic Poles living in Germany. In Spain, under Franco, Basque and Catalan languages and cultures were viewed as threats to the Spanish nation, and were consequently repressed. In Northern Ireland, where the settlement of the 'Irish Question' had created a small self-governing province dominated by Protestants loyal to the British state, the Unionist Party used its domination of the devolved Parliament to repress the minority Catholic population and anything construed as non-British culture.

Nationalising strategies may succeed in halting critical threats from sub-state nationalisms, but they are not necessarily long-term solutions. In some territories where such strategies have been employed, challenges to the state have reappeared. Therefore, despite the repression by Franco, Basque and Catalan nationalisms survived and became key elements of democratic Spain. Similarly, despite the strategies of the Unionist Party in Northern Ireland, Irish national consciousness continues to exist and the challenge of Irish nationalism to the existence of Northern Ireland's place in the UK has not gone away. It should nevertheless be noted that in western Europe serious challenges to the existing nation-state are the exception rather than the rule.

Overall, then, there are a number of strategies for tackling problems arising from nationalist tensions within a national territory. The strategy chosen, and its impact, will depend on the nature of the regime within the country. As we have shown, in western Europe threats to the state have been limited, and recognition strategies and, in some instances, a degree of political restructuring have been sufficient to contain or neutralise them. In a number of the countries of central and east Europe divisions between national groups remain real challenges for governments if they are to maintain, or, in some cases, promote social cohesion.

Conclusion: nations, nationalism and European integration

If the reader takes away one idea from this chapter it should be an understanding that nations are not natural forms of human organisation. Studies have shown that there was a time when people did not think of themselves as belonging to nations. Indeed, we have suggested that it is only since the late nineteenth century that national identity has become a mass phenomenon. We have outlined some of the reasons why the idea of the nation was, and remains, appealing to so many people across Europe, but equally we know that circumstances have conspired to encourage this identification with the nation.

So, if nations did not always exist in the past, can we assume that they will not always exist in the future? An answer to this question takes us into the realm of speculation, because the end of the age of nationalism is still not in sight. The nation will almost certainly experience a serious demise in fortunes in the future, but what – or what *different* forms of society – will take its place is far from clear. It appears that nations and nationalism will remain with us for the rest of this century at least. To conclude, there are three reasons why we believe this to be so.

- First, life in Europe remains organised around national societies, despite the flows of ideas, commodities and people that all European countries have experienced in the post-war period (because of the restrictions imposed by the communist regimes, central and east European states have experienced this change relatively recently, but they are experiencing it nonetheless).

Education, media, and the spheres of government closest to Europeans are still organised on national bases, despite the advance of integration. While these sectors, which were so crucial in forging attachments to nations in the nineteenth and twentieth centuries, remain primarily national it is difficult to understand how Europeans will genuinely imagine themselves as living outside of national territorial units.

- Second, what interest would Europeans have in abandoning national societies, and organising themselves along different, possibly transnational, lines?

European integration may have brought benefits to Europeans – and many of those living in the applicant states evidently believe that such benefits will be extended to them – but research shows that most Europeans feel that the EU is not in touch with their concerns (see Chapter 8 on European identity for further discussion of this point). Similar attitudes may be expressed towards national governments in Europe, and some citizens may be unhappy with the state of the economy and society some of the time, but these are not reasons to abandon national societies. Indeed, while integration brings some costs in terms of policy decisions in some areas no longer taken solely by national government, as Milward (1992) argues, integration has allowed national governments to advance 'national societies'. In short, then, it is difficult to imagine a challenger emerging that would even remotely encroach on the place of the nation.

- Finally, far from diminishing, over the past decade or so we have been reminded of the continuing appeal of the nation, and the still prominent role of nationalism.

The desire for independence on the part of movements across Europe, and the recent successes of some in central and eastern regions in achieving it, demonstrates that the idea of the nation has lost none of its popular appeal. In the EU nationalism has been fanned by integration, especially over the contentious issue of who best represents the 'national interest'. During the past ten years, for example, the UK has seen the emergence of the Referendum Party and the UK Independence Party, both of which are committed to the UK's withdrawal from the EU. In contrast, many minority nationalist parties are pro-EU precisely because they believe the policy of subsidiarity will enable them to advance their interests by enabling them to participate in policy-making in the EU. In the applicant countries similar arguments are made in favour of membership; national governments play on national sentiments to argue that membership advances the national interests of the country.

Nations and nationalism, then, look set to remain key players in European society for some time to come. That we know that there was a time when neither existed does not make it easier to imagine a time when, again, they will no longer have an impact on the European stage. To be sure, many European societies – from east to west – are contemplating what national identity means today, a development that has been prompted by considerations of immigration as well as the position of minorities, but many Europeans would find it difficult to contemplate life without nations.

Further reading

Brubaker, R. (1996) *Nationalism Reframed*. Cambridge: Cambridge University Press.

Caplan, R. and Feffer, J. (eds) (1996) *Europe's New Nationalism*. Oxford: Oxford University Press.

Lynch, P. (1996) *Minority Nationalism and European Integration*. Cardiff: University of Wales Press.

Schulze, H. (1996) *States, Nations and Nationalism*. Oxford: Blackwell

Smith, A.D. (1995) *Nations and Nationalism in a Global Era*. Cambridge: Polity Press.

Chapter 5

Regions in Europe and 'a Europe of the Regions'

Key concepts

- Regions
- Regionalism
- Regionalisation
- Committee of the Regions
- Structural Funds

Across Europe, in the closing decade of the twentieth century, the 'region' is stepping out of the shadow of the nation-state. While formal systems of regional government are not novel, over the past decade the region, regionalisation and regionalism have moved squarely on to the policy agenda across European countries, as well as at the level of the European Union. It is not just national policy-makers, however, who are exercising their judgements on this matter. Within European countries, pressure has come from politicians elected to regional assemblies, from assorted political parties and organisations representing regional business interests, and from sections of the population living in these regions.

Region, regionalisation and regionalism

Region.   As used in this chapter 'region' refers to territorial units that exist between the levels of local and national government. These are, then, administratively defined territorial units, as in the case of the German *Länder*, the Spanish autonomous communities, or, in the case of the United Kingdom, the territories governed by the devolved administrations in Northern Ireland, Scotland and Wales.

Regionalism.   Refers to the manner in which certain political parties and other organisations have promoted the distinctiveness of the region. Regionalism, therefore, is both a political ideology and strategy, utilised for the purpose of securing advantages for the region.

Regionalisation.   This term refers to the process of devolving, or transferring, powers from central government down to regional administrations. Regionalisation may occur when central government seeks to improve the management of regional affairs by, for example, administrative reorganisation and enhancing regional economic development. Regionalisation may also occur as a consequence of the devolution of political powers whereby central government meets the demands of a given population for a greater degree of political autonomy.

In this chapter we will address two principal issues. First, we will examine some of the varying forms of regional government in operation across Europe. Second, we will explore the region within the context of EU policy.

Regions in Europe in the post-war period

When employed to analyse empirical conditions at the sub-national level across Europe the concept of 'region' has a chameleon-like quality. There are, for example, considerable differences between the Austrian and German *Länder* on the one hand, and the nominal regional entities that are the focus of regional development bodies in Greece or the Republic of Ireland on the other. Indeed, the fact that some regional polities, such as North Rhine-Westphalia in Germany, manage budgets larger than the national state budget of Denmark or Greece underscores the considerable disparities between regions across Europe. Even without drawing attention to such extremes of difference, the most cursory evaluation of conditions across Europe

Table 5.1 Examples of different forms of regional administration in Europe

Federal states	Regionalised unitary states	Devolving unitary states	Classic unitary states
Austria	Italy	France	Bulgaria
Belgium	Spain	Netherlands	Estonia
Germany	United Kingdom	Portugal	Finland
Yugoslavia		Czech Republic	Greece
Switzerland			Hungary
Russian Federation			Romania
			Poland
			Sweden
			Republic of Ireland

reveals that there exist varying levels of administrative, economic and political decentralisation between countries, as well as, in a number of cases, within them. How, then, can we categorise the differing empirical conditions found across Europe in order to develop a more general comparative framework? The four-dimensional approach utilised by Bullman (1996) to categorise differences between regional entities in the EU provides a useful starting point, although the original typology has been adapted to take into account political changes in Europe.

Federal states

Austria, Belgium, Germany, the Russian Federation, Switzerland and the Yugoslav Federation possess federal structures. In addition, prior to political changes in the 1990s Czechoslovakia, the former Yugoslavia and the USSR were organised on a federal structure. Federal systems of government are characterised by a division of powers between the federal government and regional governments in which each tier of government has designated executive and legislative competencies in certain fields. Thus federal governments may, for example, retain control over defence matters or relations with other countries, while regional governments may have control over education or social policy. Disputes do, however, arise between federal government and regional government over which tier has responsibility for a particular area of policy.

There are nevertheless marked differences in the way in which federalism is practised in each of these countries, although there is a greater degree of commonality between the systems operating in Austria and Germany. Austria's federal system is divided between the *Nationalrat*, to which members are directly elected and the *Bundesrat*, the latter comprising members appointed by the nine directly elected federal assemblies (*Landtage*). The principle that the political balance should be in favour of the *Landtage*, enshrined in the Austrian constitution, does not bear closer scrutiny. The areas over which the *Landtage* have sole legislative authority are comparatively limited (to topics such as pre-school education, planning regulations and nature preservation) when viewed in relation to the wide array of areas over which the federal government enjoys a legislative monopoly (see Gruber 1997; Honauer 1999). In Germany, while there remain areas of mutual legislative exclusivity for the governments of the sixteen *Länder* and the federal government, there has nevertheless been a movement towards increased cooperation between the two structures across a wide range of policy areas. A major factor behind this 'co-operative federalism' (Gerstenlauer 1995; Benz 1998) has been the impact of EU policy on legislative areas for which the *Länder* governments are responsible, and the desire of the *Länder* to ensure that they can exert an influence over the direction of federal policy in relation to the EU.

If the German and, to a lesser degree, the Austrian systems of federalism allow for appropriate modes of contact between the regional and federal levels of government, in Belgium the federal system that was created in 1988, and which was reformed more radically in 1993, tips the balance in favour of the six sub-national units: the three cultural 'communities' (the Flemish, French and German-speaking communities) and the three territorial 'regions' (the Brussels Capital Region, the Flemish Region and the Walloon Region). Since the 1988 reforms these sub-national units have expanded their legislative portfolio, and since 1993, in particular, they have been able to undertake international agreements with other states. Moreover, as a result of the 1993 reforms the communities and sub-national entities are entitled to participate directly in discussions within the EU Council of Ministers in areas where authority is shared with the federal government or where the issues under discussion are exclusively subject to the control of the sub-national units. Thus, as Kerremans and Beyers (1996) argue, the 1993 reforms allowed the regions and communities to legally operate at the 'Second Level', rather than the 'Third Level' at which regional bodies conventionally function.

Federal systems can be useful in helping to maintain the overall territorial unity of a country by giving a level of self-government to regional minorities. Belgium, for example, has moved to a federal system to accommodate the growing demands for autonomy from its constituent groups. The Russian Federation, home to twenty-one republics, has seen a war against nationalists in Chechnya, but elsewhere has managed to hold together. There has also been some discussion that Moldova will move to a federal system in order to accommodate some of the demands of separatists in the Gagauzia (largely populated by ethnic Turks) and Transdniestria (largely populated by ethnic Russians and Ukrainians). As we noted earlier, federalism does not prevent further political fragmentation. In the cases of Czechoslovakia, the USSR and the former Yugoslavia the federal system could not cope with competing nationalisms. Federal systems, then, do not always satisfy the demands of nationalist opposition movements.

Regionalised unitary states

The political situations in the above countries, most notably in Belgium, are far from the norm across the rest of Europe. Regional political bodies nevertheless exercise varying degrees of legislative and executive competence in other European countries. In the typology outlined by Bullman (1996) Italy is characterised as a 'regionalised unitary state'. Spain and the United Kingdom may also be characterised as regionalised states, though technically they are 'union', rather than 'unitary' states, as they are multinational polities.

Devolution in the United Kingdom

Following referenda held in Scotland and Wales in 1997, and in Northern Ireland in 1998, devolved administrations were established in three of the territories of the United Kingdom. Each of these institutions has emerged in response to different kinds of political circumstances. In the case of the Northern Ireland Assembly this is evident from the manner in which legislation and voting is conducted to ensure that there is sufficient cross-community co-operation. In addition, there are some significant differences between each of the devolved administrations with regard to their respective powers. Of the three institutions, the Scottish Parliament holds the most extensive range of powers. This 129-member body possesses primary legislative competence (i.e. legislation that does not have its origins in the UK Parliament in London) over a range of policy areas, such as health, education, housing, and most areas of criminal and civil law. The Scottish Parliament also holds tax-varying powers. The 108-member Northern Ireland Assembly holds full legislative and executive authority over the fields of economic development, education, agriculture, the environment, finance and personnel, health and social services. The sixty-member National Assembly of Wales possesses secondary legislative powers, meaning that it has, within legal limits, the right to apply the provisions of laws made by the UK legislature in such a way as to suit the specific conditions in Wales. A Joint-Ministerial Committee has also been established to co-ordinate relations between the British Prime Minister and the heads of each of the devolved administrations.

Of these three countries, Spain has experienced the most comprehensive regionalisation process. In the 1978 constitution provisions were made for regions to form elected regional governments with varying degrees of legislative and executive authority, although, as is routinely observed, the constitution proclaims the continued 'indissoluble unity of the Spanish nation' (Morata 1995; Luelmo and Williams 1999). The constitutional changes of 1978 nevertheless accorded a greater degree of autonomy to the regions of Catalonia, the Basque Country, Galicia and Andalusia in recognition of the cultural distinctiveness of the inhabitants of these territories. Since 1989, however, all seventeen devolved regions enjoy 'full autonomy', although the extent of the powers of individual devolved governments varies considerably.

Similarly, in Italy, where the 1948 constitution provided for the establishment of fifteen directly elected 'ordinary' councils and five directly elected 'special' councils, there are differences between the constitutional status of particular regions (including, between the 'special' and 'ordinary' councils, different financial arrangements with central government). Where there exist differing levels of autonomy within regionalised unitary states the process of decentralisation is complex, and different constitutional arrangements for particular units lead, almost inevitably, to growing pressures on central government to address the conflicts that arise as a consequence. Thus central government in Madrid has had to address claims that Catalonia and the Basque Country, for example, are privileged to the disadvantage of other regions. In a similar manner, Plaid Cymru in Wales maintains that the National Assembly for Wales should possess the same legislative powers as the Scottish Parliament.

In the case of each of these countries, however, central government continues to act as the primary locus of political power, and can claim a constitutional entitlement to oppose legislation passed by regional governments where the latter conflict with the legislation passed by the former. In Italy, for example, the councils do not possess primary legislative powers and therefore must work within the legislative framework established by central government. Morata (1995) has noted that similar conflicts exist in Spain, where, in the first decade of the existence of the autonomous communities, more than 800 legal cases had arisen from incidences where central government had blocked decisions taken by the regional governments. This situation does nevertheless highlight how regionalisation alters the relations between central government and the regions, particularly where devolved governments have been established. Under these changed conditions central government faces greater pressure to establish structures for resolving disputes between regions and the centre, not least because of the need to maintain support for the governing political party among the electorate in the regions.

Devolving unitary states

The situation in 'devolving unitary states', Bullman's (1996) third category of regional government, generally involves greater restrictions on the autonomy of regional bodies, as well as differences in the form of these bodies. As with the other categories of regional government, however, there are considerable differences between countries. Portugal, as established in the 1976 constitution, is divided into three forms of regions: the 'autonomous regions'; the 'administrative regions'; and, since 1991, the 'metropolitan areas'. Of these categories, only the first has any political significance, where the autonomous regions of the islands of the Azores and Madeira have established formal devolved governments that exercise executive control over regional issues and possess some legislative functions. In contrast, the administrative regions are rather more nebulous entities. Reforms in 1991 advanced the development of regionalisation, creating the new metropolitan regions, but, as Pereira (1995: 272) comments, the administrative regions remain an 'intermediate level of government at a not-yet-attained decentralisation goal'. France represents another example of a devolving unitary state, where directly elected regional assemblies have existed since state reforms in 1982. Moreover, the reforms of 1982 also established a regional assembly in Corsica, with a more extensive range of powers than those held by other French regions. The powers of the twenty-two regions are tightly circumscribed, being limited to the areas of planning, regional economic development, and post-16 education and training. The evolution of the role of the regions in French political life represents part of a broader strategy of redefining the relations between central government and the various levels of sub-national government, from the regions down to the communes (the level closest to the French citizen). If, as a number of commentators argue, the potential of the French region remains unfulfilled, due in large part to the existence of significant alternative modes of sub-national government, the role of regions in the Netherlands is even weaker. The Netherlands is divided into twelve 'provinces', each of which is overseen by a directly elected council. As with the French regions, the Dutch provinces are mainly entitled to be involved in provincial planning issues, but their powers are even more limited than their French counterparts.

Some countries in central-east Europe have engaged in far-reaching reorganisation of sub-national government, including establishing directly elected regional governments. In the case of the Czech Republic, for example, its 1993 constitution makes provisions for the establishment of regional self-government. Although it was not until 1997 that a law was passed establishing this new tier, and not until November 2000 that the first elections to the new regional governments took place, there are now fourteen regional governments within the Czech Republic.

Classic unitary states

The relative degrees of autonomy enjoyed by French regions and Dutch provinces are nevertheless in advance of the powers held by regional units in 'classic unitary states'. This mode of government characterises all the Nordic states (although Finland's Åland islands enjoy a directly elected regional assembly), Greece, the Republic of Ireland and most central-east European states. In some unitary states a regional tier of government does not exist at all, although there will be various levels of local government. In other 'classic unitary states' there is a regional tier of government, although these are usually for largely administrative purposes and do not have legislative authority.

As with the place of regions within the above categories, the situation in 'classic unitary states' is nevertheless not static, and in each of these countries there have been recent moves towards developing the role of regional bodies. In Greece, for example, one of the most resolutely centralised countries in the EU since the mid-1980s, there have been growing internal demands for state reform. To date this had led to elections to the country's fifty-two prefectures (or local government) although the thirteen regional councils are still directly appointed by central government. In Finland and Sweden, too, the past decade has seen growing discussion about the place of regions within the wider polity.

Perhaps the most fundamental changes have occurred in central-east Europe. All the countries in the region have initiated reform of domestic political structures. In large part this has involved coming to terms with the legacy of the communist era, during which sub-national governments served the interests of the state. A major task, then, has been to rebuild confidence in sub-national government. In the first instance, much of the energy was directed towards revitalising local government, with attention turning more recently to the regional tier. Poland, for example, began this process in 1990, when the local government elections were the first to be held for fifty years. New constitutions in the early 1990s also provided the framework for governmental reform at all levels. In 1999 further changes led to the creation of sixteen self-governing regions to replace the former system of forty-nine centrally administered regions. There is little doubt that the region is becoming a more significant unit within the changing political culture of central-east Europe. Since the beginning of the 1990s nearly all the countries in the region have developed regional development plans (see Bachtler and Downes 2000). There are, as yet, few signs that other countries in central-east Europe will move in the direction of directly elected regional government, as the Czech Republic has done.

As these latter examples illustrate, even within the most centralised of unitary states there are pressures for momentum in the direction of enhanced regional involvement in legislative and executive processes. Indeed, the changes in the UK that have occurred since 1997 highlight how the political relations between the national and regional levels of government can change dramatically in a relatively short space of time. Movements in this direction can arise for a number of reasons. First, regionalisation may occur as a consequence of a top-down rationalisation of sub-national tiers of government. This is a factor that has gained increasing significance because of developments unfolding at the level of the EU, as is the case in the reforms in the different cases of the Netherlands and Greece, for example. In addition, the countries of central-east Europe are currently witnessing moves to restructure or create a regional level of government after the demise of communist centralised planning. In each of these countries there had existed differing forms of sub-national spatial organisation, but, as Horváth (1995) suggests, the generic three-tier module applied in each of these countries was based on the Soviet model and was used to implement central government strategies. As a consequence, the reorganisation of regional government in central and eastern Europe involves coming to terms with the manner in which these units operated under the communist regimes in the past and recognising the necessity for a new role for regional units with a degree of self-governing authority. Second, regionalisation is implemented to address disparities in economic circumstances. In France deteriorating economic circumstances in a number of regions, along with demographic changes in others, provided a great deal of the impetus for the state reforms of the early 1980s, and serve to partly explain why the regions have come to be responsible for measures concerning regional economic development and training. Third, regionalisation may arise as a response to regionalism. This is most evident in the privileged position of the Basque Country, Catalonia, Andalucia and Galicia in the 1978 Spanish constitution, in the special statute relating to Corsica in the French reforms of 1982, as well as in the precarious settlement in Belgium. A final factor, and one that has gained increasing importance since the 1980s, is the political change at the level of the EU. The fostering of the concept of a 'Europe of the Regions', the impact of the structural funds and the institutionalisation of a regional dimension to the policy-making process at the level of the EU have, together, served to simultaneously generate pressures for regionalisation within existing member states, as well as among those states applying to join the EU, and to create a more fertile environment for the promotion of regionalist objectives. EU policy has had a particularly significant impact on the countries of central-east Europe, where the regional strategies and the moves towards regionalisation have been heavily influenced by preparations for accession to the EU. It is to the impact of EU policy that this discussion now turns.

European regions and EU policy

Throughout the 1990s, for policy-makers across the EU the place of the region prompts a range of questions. What are the most effective measures for reducing regional social and economic disparities across the EU? How can regional politicians best contribute to policy-making at the level of the EU? What form should the dialogue take between regional and national government with respect to national positions on EU business? What is the potential impact of the widening membership of the EU for regions, especially those with more serious economic and social difficulties, within existing member states? These are policy matters about which there is a great deal of dispute and which, due in part to the specificity of national arrangements over regional government, it is impossible to speak of uniform regional or national responses (see Keating 1998). What is clear, however, is that the trajectory of European integration over the past two decades has pushed issues relating to the role of regions in this larger process and, in turn, its impact on regions, increasingly on to the political agenda. In drawing attention to some of the key dimensions of this changing climate we settle on three issues: first, the evolution of an EU regional policy since the late-1980s; second, the implications of the Structural Funds; and finally, the role of regional politicians and organisations within the policy-making processes at the level of the EU.

The evolution of EU regional policy

Taking the first of these dimensions, there is some debate as to the origins of an EU regional policy. Armstrong (1995), for example, traces the genesis of EU regional policy to the establishment of the European Regional Development Fund (ERDF) in 1975. Hall and van der Wee (1995), however, argue that the 1988 reforms of the Structural Funds (see below) mark the start of a 'genuine regional policy since interventions in this field prior to then were essentially actions by the Community in support of nationally-determined regional policy' (1995: 9). There is nevertheless a common ground between these two positions. It *is* the case that the creation of the ERDF, to assist social and economic disadvantaged regions, marks the origins of an EU regional policy, but it is also evident that the member states exerted a great deal of control over the dispersal of the funds and largely opposed the transfer of regional development powers to the level of the EU. Since 1975, subsequent reforms to the ERDF, and the Structural Funds more broadly – in 1979, 1988, 1993 and 1998 – have, however, involved a shift in the balance of the relationship between the member states on the one hand, and the EU (and, in particular, the European Commission) on the other. The key point in this shift was the reforms that were introduced in 1988, which saw the creation of a new set of objectives for tackling social and economic problems across the EU.

Evidence of the new balance in this relationship is apparent in that after 1989 it was the EC that defined the areas which would be eligible for assistance. Whereas previously it was the member states who drew up the maps defining eligible areas, this change was indicative of the growing authority of the EU in the field of regional policy. Aside from the changing political currents, there is also a qualitative change in the form of EU regional policy that distinguishes the objectives up to the mid-1980s from those of the subsequent period. From the creation of the ERDF, EU regional policy has involved assisting socially and economically disadvantaged regions, but in the period after the mid-1980s there has been a growing emphasis on economic and social cohesion across the EU. Crucial to this redirection of regional policy objectives was the new momentum given to the completion of the Single European Market (SEM), enshrined within the 1986 Single European Act, especially the necessity of ensuring the gradual elimination of impediments to the functioning of the SEM. To realise this larger objective, since 1988 the goal of working towards economic and social cohesion has been channelled through three broad regional objectives: to assist those regions where GDP is less than 75 per cent of the EU average; to aid the restructuring of declining industrial regions; and to address the conditions in particularly problematic rural regions. Following the 1992 Treaty on the European Union (TEU), in the negotiations on which there was a broad acknowledgement among member states about the desirability of further promoting economic and social cohesion, the funding for this goal was increased by 40 per cent between 1993 and 1999, from 21 billion ecu to 30 billion ecu. The most recent radical changes to EU regional policy have been implemented in accordance with the planned expansion of the membership of the EU to include some of the states of central and eastern Europe.

The EU Structural Funds

Central to the plans for widening the membership of the EU to some of the states of central and eastern Europe are the Structural Funds. As we have already noted, for the EU the Structural Funds represent a key device in the efforts to bring about an ameliorative change in the economic and social conditions across the member states. Together, the Structural Funds constitute the collective title for four funds: the European Regional Development Fund (ERDF); the European Social Fund (ESF); the European Agricultural Guidance and Guarantee Fund (EAGGF); and, since 1993, the Financial Instrument for Fisheries (FIFG). The reforms of 1988 led to a reorganisation of the way in which these funds would be dispersed by creating a common set of seven objectives for their utilisation, three of which were specifically marked for particular kinds of regions: Objective 1, dedicated to the structural adjustment of the poorest regions in the EU; Objective 2, for declining industrial regions; and Objective 5b, for enabling the development of rural areas. In 1993 the Structural Funds were again subject to reform, principally due to the increased emphasis on economic and social cohesion, and regional policy more especially, within the TEU. Among the changes to the Structural Funds were: the establishment of the FIFG; the addition of an Objective 6 programme for the development of extremely under-populated regions; the broadening of Objective 3, previously for addressing the problem of long-term unemployment, to include actions designed to tackle youth unemployment; and the creation of a new Objective 4 now targeting the adaptation of workers to industrial change.

From 1999 onwards, the Structural Funds will have been reformed even more radically, with the reorganisation of the previous seven objectives into three broad objectives (for a discussion of the evolution of the Structural Funds up to 1999, see Michie and Fitzgerald 1997; see Morgan and Price (1998) for a discussion of the post-1999 reforms to the Structural Funds). This most recent shake-up in the role and dispersal of the Structural Funds is largely concerned with improving their efficiency and altering the relations involved in the management of the Structural Funds. Thus, with regard to the former, the proportion of the EU population covered by the Structural Funds will be reduced from 51 per cent to between 35 and 40 per cent in order to maximise the impact in especially disadvantaged regions, and, with respect to the latter, in future there will be a greater involvement of regional governments and local authorities in the dispersal and management of funding. Another substantial development in the recent reforms is the increase in the level of funding available under the three redefined objectives. The amount available for the phase to run 2000 to 2006 will be increased by 38 per cent from the funding for the previous phase, 1993 to 1999. Built into the 2000 to 2006 budget will be a separate allowance for the planned new entrants, such as the Czech Republic, Hungary, Poland and Slovenia, amounting to approximately one-sixth (€45 billion) of the total €275 billion.

The decision to reduce the percentage of the EU population covered by the Structural Funds has been driven by a recognition that funds which are too widely distributed will not have a sufficient impact on the most seriously disadvantaged regions and by the attendant costs of enlargement. Questions of funding – from how it should be raised to how it should be dispersed – are politically sensitive issues, with disputes revolving around further increases in the financial contributions to the Structural Funds to the efforts of some member states to exert increased national control over regional policy, as well as over the general effectiveness of the Structural Funds in realising their intended objectives (Bachtler 1998). Referring to the case of Wales, for example, Thomas argues that the significance of the Structural Funds with regard to economic conditions in Wales must be 'qualified with respect to both its scale and nature' (1996: 213). In particular, Thomas points out that much of the funding in Wales has gone to 'hard infrastructure' projects (such as roads), while not enough has gone to projects designed to foster indigenous economic development (such as business support and training initiatives). Other commentators have been generally more positive about the impact of the Structural Funds in reducing regional disparities across the EU, but argue that if further substantial increases in the levels of funding available do not transpire this will inevitably have a negative impact on the success of regional policy (Armstrong and de Kervenoael 1997; Bachtler 1998). This question becomes all the more pressing when the matter of enlargement of the EU is taken into consideration. In spite of the statements from the European Commission about the political and economic imperatives for ensuring cohesion within future member states, the subject of enlargement is often reduced by some regional and national players to the issue of cost. The specific implications of the impact of enlargement for EU regional policy are difficult to project, but there is little doubt that this development will ensure that spending on regions within existing member states will have to be more focused than at present, even with an increase in the budget of the Structural Funds. In this changed political environment compromises will be necessary to ensure that the most disadvantaged regions in existing member states continue to benefit from targeted funding, while also contributing to the development of the new member states. As enlargement progresses and as increasing amounts of the Structural Funds move eastwards, the likelihood of discontent will increase within regions that have been major beneficiaries of the Structural Funds, such as in Greece, the Republic of Ireland, Portugal and Spain. The form of the solution to this dilemma reached by the member states and the European Commission will impact on much more than EU regional policy: due to the considerable significance of this policy to the broader objective of enlargement, it will have a bearing on the relations within an expanded EU.

Regional involvement in the EU

The 1998 reforms to the Structural Funds, in particular the changes to the management of their deployment, highlights the issue of the role of regional and local authorities in the planning and implementation of EU regional policy. As we have already noted, across Europe the specific arrangements between the national and sub-national levels of government vary from one national context to another, but it is nevertheless possible to speak of an increased regional participation in structures of governance in many European countries throughout the 1990s. In the context of the EU, the regional level has been given an added boost with the establishment of the Committee of the Regions.

The Committee of the Regions

The Committee of the Regions began life in March 1994, as provided in the Maastricht Treaty on European Union. The Committee comprises 222 members (and 222 alternates who can attend in place of temporarily absent members), and the membership is roughly divided between representatives of regional and local government. Members are appointed for four years by the Council of Ministers, following selection by national governments. The largest national delegations come from France, Germany and the UK, who each have twenty-four representatives on the Committee, and the smallest, with six representatives, comes from Luxembourg. The respective domestic role of these tiers can have a quite considerable impact on the nomination of members; in the case of some member states (such as Germany and Spain) the overwhelming majority of representatives are drawn from regional government, while in other member states (such as the Republic of Ireland) the representatives are taken from local government. Building on the growing regional dimension of EU social and economic policy, and more particularly on the success of other 'informal' regional groupings within the EU (such as the Assembly of European Regions), the creation of the COR was designed to give representatives of sub-national political institutions some input into decision-making in the EU. This role has, however, been formally restricted to a consultative one through which the COR may be requested by either the Council of Ministers or the European Commission to deliver an opinion on legislation and policy initiatives in those specific areas of competence defined within the TEU. Originally the Committee had to be consulted in five areas (economic and social cohesion, trans-European infrastructure networks, health, education, and culture), but since the Treaty of Amsterdam came into force in May 1999 a further five areas have been added (employment policy, environment, social policy, transport and vocational training). The COR may, in addition, deliver judgements on issues outside of its specific remit, and although neither of the main EU institutions is obliged to pay any attention to these pronouncements, the Parliament has used some of the recommendations of the COR in these 'extra-curricular' areas in formulating its own amendments to EU legislation (Warleigh 1997).

Indeed, the nature of its membership is a reflection of the differing national arrangements for regional government that was the subject of our discussion in the previous section. Created by the 1992 TEU, the Committee of the Regions acts as an advisory body to the main EU institutions on regional policy matters. The impact of the Committee of the Regions on policy formation has been the subject of considerable dispute, especially given that the main institutions are not formally obliged to accept the former's recommendations (Kennedy 1997; Warleigh 1997). The Committee of the Regions lacks political clout in its own right, but it is evident that both the European Parliament and, more particularly, the European Commission have made good use of its work. Notably, the European Commission, in its relations with the Committee of the Regions, has often accorded it a *de facto* status that exceeds its *de jure* remit.

Clearly the Committee of the Regions provides a channel through which regional or local government politicians can directly take part in the policy-making process in the EU. Some of its members are nevertheless already entitled to take part in the business of the Council of Ministers by virtue of the specific arrangements made between national and regional government in some member states. Thus elected representatives of regional government in Belgium and Germany can, in certain policy fields, be involved in negotiations in the Council of Ministers. These are, however, the exceptions to the general practice across the EU. In Spain and Italy plans to move towards more formal institutional processes for involving the regions in the drawing up of national responses to EU policy matters have not yet borne significant fruit (Mazey 1995). In the UK, the importance of the Joint Ministerial Council, which will bring together the heads of the devolved governments and the British prime minister, will be judged in time.

If formal institutional arrangements for a regional input to national policy responses are absent in most EU member states at present, regional players nevertheless pursue their objectives through informal lobbying. Differences in levels of organisation are again present with respect to lobbying. A growing number of regional and local authorities are establishing their own offices in Brussels in order to be better placed to monitor developments and lobby relevant EU politicians. The Scottish Office, for example, although part of the domestic infrastructure of the British government, established an office in Brussels in 1999. In addition, regional interests are lobbied via commercial offices based in Brussels. As successful as some of these ventures are, they are nevertheless not an alternative to formal structures for a regional input to the formulation of national policy. As numerous commentators maintain, the increasing regional dimension to EU policy has not led to a uniform improvement in the standing of regional players in relation to national planning, although some regions have prospered rather better than others (Martin 1997; Smith 1998).

Future trajectories

The plans for improving communication and collaboration between national, regional and local government under the 1998 reforms to the Structural Funds are intended to facilitate greater participation from sub-national actors in directing EU regional policy. The extent to which this will be successful will become clearer this century, as the midway point of the next phase of the Structural Funds will require holders of funding to account for how objectives are being met. By way of a conclusion, we shall briefly identify two matters that will be crucial to the future of regions across Europe.

First, the progression of regionalisation programmes across the EU member states and other European countries. There has been a general move in this direction, but there exist considerable disparities in the levels of regional political autonomy. The process of European integration has acted as a powerful pressure on national governments to reform state structures, and the moves towards greater regional and local government involvement in the management of EU funding programmes post-1999 should continue the momentum in this direction. Significant reforms to political structures within European countries are rather more difficult to predict, as the case of the changes in the United Kingdom illustrates. It is, however, likely that further reforms to local and regional government, although not necessarily the establishment of devolved regional assemblies, will occur within countries such as Estonia, Poland and Hungary as they continue to prepare for entry into the EU.

Following on from the above point, a second matter is that it will be necessary to enhance our understanding of the conditions within given regions across Europe. Research highlights that, while prevailing economic conditions are pivotal for the successful development of a region, the ability of regional bodies to create an environment conducive to inward investment and local economic development is also a key factor, as the cases of Baden-Württemberg, Germany, and Emilia-Romagna, Italy, illustrate (Cooke *et al.* 1995; Garmise 1995). Other commentators, however, are not so convinced of the transferability of lessons from one region to another. Lovering (1999), for example, criticises the application of generic models of regional development, arguing that it is necessary to develop a better under-standing of the local conditions and problems in a region in order to establish models for development and policies that take account of regional differences. Increased regional self-government may serve to produce an improvement in the economic and social conditions in regions across Europe, as, indeed, might an emphasis on technological innovation. It may, however, be argued that further ameliorative change in regions across the expanding EU will require changes in the way in which EU policies address the diversity of regional conditions across the territory as well as to how representatives of regional government participate in the policy-making process both in member states and at the level of the EU. There are signs that the EU is moving in this direction. In the 2001 White Paper on *European Governance* the

European Commission states that it wishes to see greater involvement of local and regional government within EU policy processes, through increased participation in developing the member states' position on EU policy and by becoming directly involved in implementing EU policies in certain fields at the regional level. The Commission also recognises the need to pay more attention to local and regional conditions in drawing up and implementing EU policy in future.

Conclusion

As a combined consequence of political reforms that have taken place in a number of European countries, demands from sub-national organisations and political parties and EU policy, the region has become an increasingly significant aspect of European politics over the past decade.

- There are nevertheless significant variations between the different modes of regional administration across Europe. We can, however, distinguish between four principal modes: federal systems of government; regionalised unitary states; devolving unitary states; classic unitary states.
- Pressures for strengthening regional involvement in legislative and executive processes can occur for a number of reasons. These include: central government-led political reforms; to address regional disparities in economic and social development; as a consequence of demands from sub-national organisations and political parties; and as a result of EU policy initiatives.
- European integration has had a considerable impact on regions, both directly and indirectly. Directly, EU policy initiatives, especially the Structural Funds, have directed attention towards regional disparities across the EU and have served to galvanise regional mobilisation on the part of political parties and business interests, among other groups. Indirectly, the growing discussions about the most appropriate levels of decision-making for the implementation of EU policy, as well as about the need to take such decision-making closer to EU citizens, have raised questions about the necessity of a 'third level' of governance below the transnational and national levels, respectively.

Further reading

Bache, I. (1998) *The Politics of European Union Regional Policy*. Sheffield: Sheffield University Press.

Le Gales, P. and Lequesne, C. (eds) (1998) *Regions in Europe*. London: Routledge.

Loughlin, J. *et al.* (1999) *Regional and Local Democracy in the European Union*. Luxembourg: Office for Official Publications of the European Communities.

Wagstaff, P. (ed.) (1999) *Regionalism in the European Union*. Exeter: Intellect.

Migration and asylum-seeking in Europe

Key concepts

- Immigration policies
- Asylum and asylum-seekers
- Race and racism
- Anti-discrimination policies

Background

Migration to Europe is generally perceived as a post-1945 phenomenon hastened by labour shortages in the more highly industrialised countries such as the former West Germany, France and the UK. In fact, as shown in Chapter 3, many European countries had for centuries been involved in exploration, colonisation and imperialism. Such activities led to the development of notions of racial superiority and inferiority as well as legislation in many countries that today would be regarded as blatantly racist. 'Race' and 'nation' became synonymous in the nineteenth century – an idea that still prevails among many right-wing ideologies (Banton 1999).

Colonial populations associated with European powers were systematically marginalised and excluded during the nineteenth century. Even in the case of France, where the policy was to provide the potential for the colonised population to obtain French citizenship, this rarely happened in practice. Similarly, the *assimilação* policy of the Portuguese had little impact. This exclusion again reinforced stereotypes and further generated racist attitudes towards minorities whether they were actually 'foreign' or merely non-Christian.

The early decades of the twentieth century provide evidence of racism becoming more formalised. In Britain, for example, the Aliens Act of 1919 led to the deportation of over 30,000 'enemy aliens', many of whom were Jews and originally from countries such as Russia, Hungary, Turkey, Austria and Germany. In the same year the race riots at many British ports led to the repatriation of 600 black men. By the 1930s in Britain a virtually total 'colour bar' was operating. In practice this meant that black people were denied accommodation, service in cafes and restaurants, and entry to places of entertainment. The idea that black people and Jews were somehow inferior became deeply rooted at this time even in communities where a black population had been well established. In Cardiff, for example, in 1935 there were about 3000 non-European seamen, and yet the local police made the assumption that all of them were aliens even if proof could be shown of British citizenship. In France immigration had been encouraged after the First World War in the face of labour shortages, but by the 1930s during the period of economic slump, repatriation and deportation became commonplace. In Germany a similar policy was adopted to the extent that the numbers of foreign workers were reduced by at least three-quarters of a million between 1907 and 1932, many of whom were Poles. By 1935 it became illegal for Jews, gypsies and black people to marry Germans and a certificate of 'marriage fitness' had to be produced.

Although it may be thought that the ultimate racism displayed by the Nazi regime would act as a warning, racism remained rife in the years following the Second World War. Anti-Semitism became a feature of British cultural life; and yet citizens of the British Empire (from Pakistan, India and the Caribbean, for example), following the 1948 British Nationality Act, were allowed to move to Britain relatively freely – a situation that prevailed until the first of the immigration acts in 1962. A similar pattern existed in the Netherlands where Indonesians and Surinamese were initially welcomed. In many European countries migrants were perceived and defined simply as guest workers (Fenton 1999); more often than not this arose because of the absence of colonies from where labour could be recruited. Nowhere was this more prevalent than in the former West Germany. The periods of labour shortages in the

1950s and early 1960s strongly encouraged the import of labour whether from (former) colonies or elsewhere.

Even though the period from the early 1970s to the present day has been characterised by a labour surplus in most European countries, there has nevertheless been a huge amount of in-migration from the West Indies, Western and Southern Asia, the Mahgreb, parts of Latin America, Western and Eastern Africa and, more recently, from eastern Europe and the Balkans. As immigration expanded and economic buoyancy declined, so individual European nations introduced restrictions on immigration and continue so to do to the present. This was the case regardless of how liberal or otherwise the nation. Immigration was unrestricted to Sweden until the late 1960s; Italy had no restrictions until the 1970s. West Germany officially had a 'no-immigration' policy prior to 1978 as applied by the 1965 Aliens Law. The demise of the Soviet Union and the reunification of Germany generated a vast influx of East Germans into West Germany, and of ethnic Germans from east-central Europe and the former Soviet Union into the united German state. The revised Foreigner Law of 1990 made for more open immigration, although the Kohl administration did subsequently reimpose some controls.

The actual nature of immigration and of immigrants themselves varies considerably across the EU and a discussion of the situation prevailing in a sample of EU countries makes this clearer.

France

The case of France is an interesting one since its former colonial interests led to large-scale immigration of people who technically were French subjects from South-East Asia, the West Indies, West Africa and, of course, the Mahgreb. The combination of the economic difficulties of the 1970s and changing political attitudes had the effect on immigration experienced in many other European countries. The election of the Socialists under Mitterand in 1981 certainly generated a more tolerant attitude and in 1984 migrants were, by law, allowed rights of permanent residence. Immigrants were also mobilised to seek further political and human rights (see, for example, the work of *Fédération des associations de solidarité aux travailleurs immigrés* or the *Conseil des associations immigrées en France*). The pressure groups more than the political parties fought for greater rights for immigrants. During Mitterrand's re-election campaign in 1988 he was remarkably quiet on the issue of immigration, although the harsh residence card regime was effectively abandoned in 1989.

By the 1990s the immigration 'problem' had become publicly identified as one relating to the non-integration of Islamic groups, coupled with the increasing political militancy of a number of immigrant groups. Muslim identity and militancy came to the fore, especially in relation to Algerians and other Mahgrebian groups and most particularly among second-generation individuals within such groups. Muslims were, in a sense, forced into a minority ethnic identity situation by the legal expectations obtaining at the time.

In France, then, there appears not to have been too much consistency in policies relating to immigrants, but even where public policy has prevailed, both institutional and individual racism remain common in France. France has long advocated the need for a strong relationship between nationality and citizenship, even though at times the rhetoric has perhaps been stronger than the reality. This is an issue to which we return later in the chapter when the broader European position is discussed since – in principle – the Treaties of Maastricht and Amsterdam brought together a range of social, civil and political rights.

United Kingdom

As indicated above, immigration to the UK has a long history with some seaports (e.g. Cardiff, Liverpool and Glasgow) having been home to black people for well over a century. In the post-1945 period the first significant piece of legislation was in 1948 when Commonwealth citizenship was granted to all those from Commonwealth countries. The following year the political rights of Irish immigrants were guaranteed (Ireland had recently withdrawn from the Commonwealth). During the 1950s immigration was encouraged in order to make up the shortfall in the labour market, particularly in unskilled, male and menial occupations. By 1962 limits had been placed on immigration by the Conservative government and the 1964 election was characterised by overtly anti-racist speeches. Such anti-racism in the public arena continued into the early 1970s as witnessed by the outpourings about 'rivers of blood' from Enoch Powell and the apparent support he received from members of his own (Conservative) Party.

During the 1970s a different form of racism became apparent that emphasised cultural rather than biological differences. In this way debates about citizenship and national identity have incorporated race and racism. Cultural differences have included religion, language, customs and ethnicity and as such have had a deep influence on social institutions in the legal, educational and political spheres. A series of immigration laws placed progressively greater restrictions on the right to migrate to the UK. The 1981 and 1988 Acts very significantly reduced the rights of Common-wealth citizens to settle in the UK and more recent legislation has made the position even more difficult for aspirant migrants from any country.

Given the relatively long history of immigration to the UK it is perhaps surprising how the generic term 'immigrant' is still applied to second- or third- or even fourth-generation individuals given their full British citizenship and their identi-fication with things 'British'. Indeed, the very term 'British' has been the subject of some debate. Well over three million British inhabitants belong to 'ethnic minorities'.

Germany

Germany presents a unique case largely because of having been a divided nation and the impact previously of *Heimatvertriebenen, die Mauer* and latterly *Ossis* and *Wessis*. But, arguably, the key issue since the 1950s in the Federal Republic of Germany (FRG) was the plight of the 'guest workers' (*Gastarbeiter*). These were individuals, largely from South-Eastern Europe and North Africa, whose status had always been insecure and highly precarious. These workers, often in the FRG for decades, had little entitlement either to German citizenship or to enfranchisement. During periods of labour shortage, as seen above, guest workers were welcome, but by the recessions of the early 1970s onwards their position became even more marginal with public opinion urging a forcible return to the countries of origin.

> East Germany was host to thousands of migrant or 'contract' workers (some estimates go as high as 200,000) from around sixty different countries by 1989 (for example, an estimated 60,000 Vietnamese, 52,000 Poles and 8000 Cubans) who were almost completely segregated from the indigenous population except at work. For the majority, accommodation comprised separate hostels, thus ghettoising these workers. With reunification, overt nationalistic hostility towards these migrant groups quickly surfaced.

In West Germany the position was different since the Basic Law suggested an ethnic definition of citizenship, so making it hard, if not impossible in practice, for immigrants to gain such citizenship. In spite of this, following reunification, Germany became a haven for political refugees. About a million refugees seeking political asylum have fled to Germany since 1989, a large proportion of whom were from Eastern Europe or from the disintegration of the former Yugoslavia, Bosnia, Herzegovinia and from northern (Kurdish) Turkey.

Racist incidents towards migrants, particularly in the eastern part of Germany, have been widely reported in recent years with arson attacks on hostels for asylum-seekers, defenestrations of Africans from trains and physical attacks on Polish commuters near the border. Although those directly responsible appear to come from extreme right-wing allegiances, opinion polls show middle class support for such actions.

Sweden

Swedish neutrality during the Second World War and, indeed, its very strong economy before the war meant that in the immediate post-war period Sweden was able to capitalise on its position through several big export-led industries such as Volvo, Ericsson, ASEA and SKF. What was required was not capital as in many post-war economies but labour, and during the 1950s cheap labour from Italy and Yugoslavia in particular was imported in abundance. The Swedish welfare model that developed at that time attempted to be completely inclusive, overtly protecting the interests of the disadvantaged and the weak in society. Coupled with the welfare state were the social democratic industrial relations policies that defused the potential for industrial strife and, relatively, promoted wealth for all. The 'common good, the 'state' and the 'public interest' prevailed over and above the 'individual'.

By the 1960s the wave of industrial migrants from Mediterranean areas was followed by large numbers of African and Asian refugees who tended not to stay for long periods. By the late 1960s and 1970s political refugees from Spain, the Middle East, eastern Europe and Latin America were arriving in significant numbers. The relative lack of restrictions on immigrants and refugees led, in the 1980s, to an influx of migrants from all over the world and this continued through to the early 1990s when, for example, 60,000 Bosnian refugees were granted asylum.

By the 1990s, however, the Swedish economic bubble had begun to burst with large-scale unemployment and macro-financial difficulties. For the first time, Sweden imposed limits on immigration and even repatriated long-term resident immigrants.

The question is raised of the extent to which immigrants have actually been integrated into Swedish society in spite of the long period of a relatively open-door policy, certainly compared to other European countries. The metropolitan areas, perhaps inevitably, have the largest concentration of immigrant groups, and distinct districts for different groups are to be found within such areas. Possibly the most famous (infamous?) of these is Hammarkullen in Gothenberg with its dominant ethnic groups from Turkey, Iran and East Africa. Hammarkullen became a police no-go area, and was frequently the scene of street fighting where the local authority seemed unable to find a solution to the often conflicting interests and demands of its multi-ethnic population. This has not been a unique situation. In many Swedish urban communities there has been a growing consciousness and awareness among immigrant groups – a consciousness and awareness that racism and discrimination are rife in Swedish society and that the Social Democratic Party had perhaps lost its way in terms of encouraging a multicultural society. There is also evidence that a growing identification with black culture (with its potential for exclusion and discrimination) among some immigrant groups is contributing to greater segregation. This is evident in areas such as Uddevalla (north of Gothenberg) where violence and counter-culture elements have come to the fore. Equally, in many of Gothenberg's suburbs all the classic indicators of an underclass have emerged among young people of Turkish, Vietnamese, Lebanese and Latin American origin and, indeed, even among some elements of Swedish youth.

The very liberal policy relating to immigration to Sweden and for acquiring citizenship (originally simply a residence qualification of seven years and often less) has now been adjusted following the huge numbers of refugees arriving from Bosnia, Kosova and Somalia. The model to which many European countries might have aspired has moved to one which is remarkably similar to that prevailing in these other countries.

Southern Europe

Countries of southern Europe such as Italy, Greece and Spain have traditionally been places of out-migration with many of their nationals being the guest workers of Germany, Switzerland, France and Belgium within Europe or settled migrants in countries such as the USA, Australia and Canada. However, as Anthias and Lazaridis (1999: 3) suggest,

> In recent years a major reversal of historical patterns has developed, with the Southern European countries becoming receivers of migrants (both poor migrants and highly qualified experts) and of refugees, from non-European countries . . . Southern European countries may function today as the 'entrance

hall' to the EU and often serve as a 'waiting room' for many migrants who have as a destination the Northern EU countries.

The scale of this 'major reversal' is significant. King (1997: 10), for example, estimates the numbers in the mid-1990s to be around 3.5 million of whom only under a half were legal migrants (King and Konjhodzie 1995: 47). These immigrants come from a wide range of countries including those of east and central Europe, North Africa and Mediterranean non-EU countries such as Turkey. Included also are a growing number of 'retirement' migrants especially from northern Europe and the USA who pose particular problems of their own for the host country.

How can all this be explained? The economies of many southern European countries attract migrant, albeit temporary and sometimes seasonal, workers in industries such as agriculture, tourism, construction and domestic service. Jobs in such industries are often casualised and flexible. They may be attractive to migrant workers even though they are low paid, temporary and insecure – precisely the characteristics that make them unappealing to the indigenous population. Nevertheless, such jobs are often part of the 'informal' or hidden economy. Entry to many of these southern European countries is relatively easy since they are all bounded on at least one side by extensive coastlines, borders in mountain areas or by extensive island networks. Such physical characteristics compare starkly with the border situations of many north European countries.

As many of the southern European countries moved from being countries of emigration to ones of immigration so their policies changed – in most cases moving to situations prevailing in northern European countries. This has been the case in Portugal where illegal immigration has become a criminal offence and where the naturalisation process has been extended from six to ten years, in Spain where the rights of asylum-seekers have been curtailed and both Italy and Greece where the residency requirement for naturalisation has also been extended to ten years.

Lessons from Europe

The above brief review of the position in a range of European countries demonstrates that there is no uniform approach to handling matters of immigration and race. On the contrary, each country more or less pursues its own policies and these policies appear to derive *inter alia* from history, pragmatism and political ideology. Although it might be argued that some convergence has occurred between European countries, harmonisation of policies has certainly not (Crouch 1999). EU policies themselves, as indicated below, have led to some convergence but immigration and citizenship are two of the most crucial areas where it is clear that national interests and national identity seem to be stronger motivators than international governance.

As far as labour immigration is concerned, the influence of macro-economic factors cannot be over-emphasised. In each of the north European countries examined the immediate post-1945 period was one of labour shortage and, as a consequence, the flow of immigrants into these countries was welcomed. What actually happened to immigrants upon arrival and during their sojourn differed significantly. In France, for example, the idea was that immigrants should be given the right to permanent residence; it should be recalled that a large proportion of immigrants came from countries previously under French colonial rule and could be easily assimilated culturally into French society. West Germany, as seen in the blatant use of the word *Gastarbeiter*, clearly saw labour immigrants as temporary residents who were 'guests' who could overstay their welcome, even though they had been positively invited and recruited in the first place. Implicit also was the idea that guest workers would rotate in the sense that after some period of working abroad guest workers would return to their country of origin and be replaced by others. In the UK the first waves of post-Second World War immigrants were fairly easily assimilated, coming, as with immigrants to France, from actual or former colonies of the host country. Furthermore, the demand for labour and the decline in the fertility of the indigenous population ensured the need for labour immigration. Again in Sweden the buoyant economy in the immediate post-war period and the emphasis on exporting industries created the demand for immigrant labour for a sparsely populated country.

In each case, the change in fortunes of national and international economies from the early 1970s onwards produced changes in the demand for labour and, in turn, changes in public and political attitudes towards immigrants. Nevertheless, the actual numbers of immigrants continued to rise but the nature of the immigration differed. Instead of being driven by the prospect of immediate work, for many the motivation was the desire to join extended family members or – increasingly – escape from political oppression (Rex 1998). During this decade, for each of the countries analysed and for most other west European countries immigration became a problem. Some have seen this rather more dramatically in referring to a 'global migration crisis' generated by the forces of globalisation on the developing world. The problem was not only a major social one for immigrants themselves but also for governments as conflict arose and as, in some eyes, the social and cultural fabric of a particular nation appeared to be undergoing fundamental change.

However, as seen above, different countries have addressed 'the problem' in different ways. The underlying French policy of assimilation continued, the German policy of separation was, if anything, strengthened following reunification and the UK policy of subordination through pluralism each showed different solutions to the same fundamental 'problem'.

Asylum-seekers

In more recent years most EU countries have had to cope with the issue of asylum-seekers, whose reasons for seeking residence are obviously different from those of labour migrants and who do not necessarily derive from source countries displaying similar cultural features to their 'hosts' or, indeed, necessarily to each other. The problem remains, however, that the terms 'immigration' and 'asylum' are often used synonymously, with no real distinction being made between the economic migrant and the political refugee.

All EU member states have bound themselves to certain obligations under the 1951 Geneva Convention (amended by the 1967 New York Protocol) and the Universal Declaration of Human Rights (UDHR). Of particular relevance here is the fact that the Convention bestows on those with a well-founded fear of persecution (based on race, religion, political opinion, nationality, etc.) the right of protection in the country to which they have fled. In both cases the obligations were made and accepted before movements of refugees reached current levels. Three factors in particular have significantly increased the numbers of those seeking asylum in EU member countries – the demise of the Soviet Union, the violent disintegration of former Yugoslavia and what Joppke (1997: 262) calls 'jet-age asylum-seeking'. Geddes (2000: 26) makes the point that between 1950 and 1980 the numbers of asylum-seekers were small but that the situation had begun to change by the 1980s with numbers peaking in July 1992 when 80,000 applications were made in that month alone across member states. Such huge numbers raised suspicions in some quarters that many asylum-seekers might not be genuine but might essentially be economic migrants using the Convention as a shield. Certainly the number of asylum applications to Germany rose to a staggering 438,000 in 1992 (65 per cent of the EU total); the respective figures in the Netherlands were 13,000 in 1987 to 52,000 in 1994 and in the UK from 6,000 in 1987 to 73,000 in 1991. Since then numbers have remained high following the conflicts in Bosnia and Kosova and the movement from Romania and the Czech Republic, in particular, of large numbers of the Roma population.

Some EU countries (Germany, Austria, the Netherlands and Sweden in particular, and more recently the UK) appeared to be more popular choices of destination for asylum-seekers and such countries were somewhat overwhelmed by the sheer numbers. Furthermore, asylum-seekers have been accused of 'shopping around', since the reception they are likely to receive in different countries differs. In 2000 within the fifteen EU countries almost 400,000 asylum-seekers lodged asylum applications.[1] The largest groups originated in Yugoslavia, Iraq, Afghanistan and Iran. However, the actual granting of asylum status remains low – in the EU as a whole only about a quarter of asylum-seekers were successful in their applications in 1999. This, of course, varies considerably by country. In the UK, for example, in 2000 more asylum applications (97,860) were received than in any other EU country; yet the proportion recognised as genuine between 1998 and 1999 was 72.5 per cent, even though only 12.1 per cent were actually granted refugee status. Although Germany bore the brunt of asylum-seekers in the 1990s, the number of asylum-seekers has more than halved in recent years so that by 2000 the number stood at 78,760. In 1999 a mere 13.5 per cent were recognised as genuine cases although 11.3 per cent were granted refugee status. A further comparison is with Belgium where per 1000 inhabitants in 2000 to 2001 there were more asylum-seekers than in any other EU country (4.4 compared to the UK with 1.5, Germany with 0.9 or Spain with 0.2). Clearly, the pattern of asylum-seeking across EU countries is variable as indeed are the countries of origin.

The European Commission had tried to introduce a policy document on the integration of third state nationals but a ruling by the European Court made clear that this went beyond the Community's jurisdiction. The Maastricht Treaty introduced intergovermental decision-making and within that context the Commission has sought to produce EU-wide proposals. Thus, member states have tried to develop common policies and done so in the absence of European legislation.

The 1985 Schengen Agreement on asylum and visas involving the EEC founder members minus Italy was subsequently ratified by all member states with the exception of the UK, Ireland and Denmark with a view to implementation in 1994. The aim was to harmonise among the signatories matters relating to frontier controls and procedures for use with asylum-seekers and to abolish internal border controls. However, as Geddes (2000: 27) succinctly puts it,

> The connection between free movement within the single market and its impact on immigration and asylum policy means that 'fortress Europe' is linked with single market liberalisation. *Freedom of movement for some begets tighter control over movement by others* [our italics].

In the event, the 1990 Dublin Convention was agreed by all member states and it sought to overcome the problem of an asylum-seeker simultaneously seeking refugee status in more than one EU country. This has been seen as a significant European development since the decision of one member state became binding on all others, thereby raising again the question of national sovereignty. The 'one chance' rule has been criticised by the UNHCR which claims that the Dublin Convention fails to adhere to the Geneva Convention nor, indeed, to the European Convention on Human Rights.

The Treaty of Amsterdam did introduce a new Article 13 to the EC Treaty:

> Without prejudice to the other provisions of this Treaty and within the limits of the powers conferred by it upon the Community, the Council . . . may take appropriate action to combat discrimination based on sex, racial or ethnic origin, religion or belief, disability, age or sexual orientation.

Furthermore, the Treaty of Amsterdam moved matters relating to visa, asylum and immigration policies to the intergovernmental first 'pillar' from the third, meaning in effect that these matters became the concerns of the EU institutions and, in particular, the European Court of Justice. However, the UK and Ireland remained outside the protocol for integrating the Schengen Agreement and Denmark reserved the right to choose whether or not to adopt EU legislation on these matters.

Nevertheless, EU policy on asylum remains incoherent because those policies that do exist have been made intergovernmentally and are largely designed on the basis of national considerations. However, the position is slowly changing. Following the call for action made at the European Council meeting in Cardiff (June 1998), a 'High Level Working Group on Asylum and Immigration' was established by the EU in January 1999 charged with producing an integrated strategy. Moving very swiftly, the Working Group produced five action plans for specific countries (Afghanistan, Iraq, Morocco, Somalia and Sri Lanka) of asylum and immigrant origin and these plans were endorsed by the Council in October 1999. Furthermore, the European Parliament addressed the general issues in April 1999 but appeared not to move too far from the traditional 'fortress Europe' position in that a very clear distinction was made between asylum as a basic right and migration as an economic issue. In other words, the emphasis remains on trying to contain or reduce the numbers of asylum applicants and on formalising 'returning' procedures.

Although EC funds have recently been made available for help with the reception and voluntary repatriation of asylum-seekers and refugees (€26 million in

2000), it has not proved possible for member states to agree on a wider system of burden-sharing. However, in 1999 the Tampere European Council recognised a need for harmonisation in the areas of admission criteria and the conditions for residence. Related to this has been the Commission's proposal for a directive on the right to family reunification as a step towards improving integration of third-country nationals. This proposal could go some way to harmonising policy across member states in an area where there currently exist considerable differences. At present, though, there is no single asylum policy derived from the harmonisation of national policies, and attempts by countries such as Germany to move towards such a policy have foundered in recent years. Asylum policies are still perceived by many member states as examples of where national sovereignty should override any European-wide policy. The Treaty of Amsterdam has gone some way towards indicating the need for such a policy and some tentative first steps have followed, but much still needs to be done before a realistic European policy can be said to exist. Apart from Amsterdam, if a policy can be said to be emerging, it has been achieved largely through stealth and intergovernmental policy networks. The Treaty might suggest that intergovernmentalism has become less dominant with the growth of supra-nationalism.

Racism and anti-discrimination policy

For many years the position on anti-discrimination policy was similar to that on asylum-seekers in the sense that the EU was a 'policy laggard' (Geyer 2000: 164). Indeed, it is debatable whether any distinctive European-wide policy could be distinguished insofar as racism rarely appeared on any agenda. Racial discrimination is not mentioned in the original treaties (unlike gender and nationality) largely because these were dominantly economic treaties but also because race had not become a political issue in the 1950s. By the late 1960s and early 1970s it most certainly had in many European countries and, as seen above, was driven by economic factors and economic downturn in particular. This led to various actions in most Community countries such as the French anti-racist laws in 1972, the 1976 Race Relations Act in the UK, or the anti-racism law in Belgium in 1981. This legislation was, however, made at the level of the nation-state and was neither influenced by nor actually influenced European (lack of) policy. It took the EC twenty-seven years to arrive at its Joint Declaration that supported the 1950 European Convention of Human Rights and Fundamental Freedoms.

The 1984 European elections generated some success for extreme right-wing political parties espousing racist doctrines, even though overall the Parliament had a left-wing majority. The former were clearly a matter of concern to the latter and a committee of enquiry was established (reporting in 1985) with the aim of examining the rise in Europe of both racism and fascism. The committee's report caused sufficient concern for the EC to issue its Joint Declaration against Racism and Xenophobia, but, as with the rhetoric associated with asylum-seekers, the Declaration was little more than a piece of rhetoric given that no major policy initiatives followed nor, importantly, were any financial resources committed to eradicating racism. A similar position ensued with the 1989 Social Charter.

Prior to 1990, therefore, no specific European policies for curbing discrimination on the grounds of race existed in spite of the fact that many member states were witnessing a growth in racist activities. Even the 1990 Resolution on the Fight against Racism and Xenophobia went no further than being exactly that – a resolution. The Dublin Council meeting in 1990 referred to its concern at recent racist outbursts, and similar concern was expressed at the 1991 Maastricht Council meetings although the actual Treaty is far from explicit about the formulation of policy to combat racism and xenophobia other than the commitment to comply with the 1950 European Convention. Another committee was established and its report (the Ford Report) in 1991 made disturbing reading with its seventy-seven recommendations. This report, coupled with various proposals made during the process of ratifying the Maastricht Treaty, led to the formation (and, importantly, the funding) of the EC Migrants Forum concerned, among many other things, with the inclusion of rights of migrants many of whom were non-white. The most important recommendations of the Ford Report were adopted by the Parliament in 1993 (although by 1999 only three had actually been implemented) and in the same year the Green Paper on social policy had clear anti-discrimination strategies spelled out. The ensuing White Paper in 1994 appeared to be more positive in terms of providing funding for anti-racist projects, developing an employment code of practice and in establishing monitoring mechanisms.

By the mid-1990s the earlier rhetoric was slowly turning into action. The Social Action Programme (1995 to 1997) designated 1997 as the European Year against Racism and Xenophobia, developed a code of conduct to combat racial discrimination and created an action plan. At the same time the Parliament resolved three times to develop anti-discrimination policy. The formation of the European Observatory of Racism and Xenophobia was agreed at the December 1996 Council meeting. Although in 1997 (the designated year against racism) only €5 million had been allocated for projects to combat racism, funding increased considerably after that.

As noted above, the Treaty of Amsterdam in 1997 did introduce a new article (13) that enabled a clearer and stronger policy to develop and to enshrine this in EU law. This has yet to happen. However, it is clear that the pace of policy development has quickened in the past decade in spite of the reluctance of the Council to implement Article 13 so far. Although international law exists there is a glaring absence of specific European law on the issue of racism.

Discussion

Issues relating to race and immigration provide an interesting example of the continued strength of national policies rather than EU policy. This chapter has clearly shown that the position of ethnic minorities and immigration and anti-discrimination policies have been held to be the concern of the individual nation-state. The examples discussed show the various ways in which different countries have addressed these matters. Each country, in the post-Second World War period, passed its own legislation and dealt with issues such as border controls in their own way. However, things are changing as the matter of European integration has come more to the fore in EU thinking and strategy.

As common European law has been enacted and as European political institutions have become stronger, so the power of the individual nation-state to impose its own policy on immigration has been reduced. Coupled with this has been the strengthening of human rights and within them of citizenship rights. Part of the reason for this move towards a European position rather than a collection of individual national positions has been the changing nature of (would-be) immigrants themselves. From the end of the Second World War through to the 1970s immigrants to the various countries were broadly, but not exclusively, from former colonies or were guest workers. The political changes in central and eastern Europe from 1989 onwards and the protracted unrest in the Balkans produced new types of potential and actual immigrants. As seen above there has been a dramatic increase in the numbers of political refugees who, in turn, have claimed political asylum status. Similarly, the increased opportunities for would-be immigrants to travel more easily have increased their numbers and from parts of the world previously not sourced.

The EU itself has, of course, found itself in a confused position here. On the one hand, the numbers and types of immigrants seeking to settle in EU countries has changed and, on the other, EU policies, as part of the move towards greater integration and common identity, have almost deliberately provoked the diminution of cultural and national barriers and differences. In an attempt to overcome this confusion the EU has adopted a series of policy measures that are strictly 'European' in nature and go beyond anything that the nation-states themselves have generated (Layton-Henry 2001).

The position of those non-EU migrants who have gained admission to Europe but who do not yet have citizenship in their country of residence raises some interesting questions as a result of Schengen. These so-called 'third country nationals' are, under existing conventions, inferiors compared to EU nationals since they do not appear to have the right of free movement throughout the EU. It also raises the vexed question of how citizenship may be harmonised within the EU.

This chapter has shown how different EU states, through legislation, have dealt with immigration matters with each country arriving at different positions as a result of history, economics, culture or political persuasion. Until the EU has common laws relating to anti-discrimination, nationality and immigration, the overarching aim of improving human rights and protecting minority status is unlikely to be achieved.

The Treaty of Amsterdam in 1997 certainly went some way towards addressing such issues, especially clarifying immigration and asylum matters within the 'third pillar', but to argue that there now exists a clear policy of immigration within the European Union would be an exaggeration. Overall, though, race and immigration are unresolved questions in spite of the extensive rhetoric and posturing on the part of the Commission and the IGC. Symbolic acts such as pronouncing 1997 as the European Year Against Racism and Xenophobia remain just that – symbolic. Until there is a clear and forceful legislative position taken by the EU on these matters, national policies and prejudices will prevail – often to the cost of immigrants and ethnic minorities themselves. But increasingly, 'the response must be European because these are now European issues' (Geddes 2000: 175).

Further reading

Carr, F. and Massey, A. (1999) *Public Policy in the New Europe*. Cheltenham: Edward Elgar.

Geddes, A. (2000) *Immigration and European Integration. Towards Fortress Europe?* Manchester: Manchester University Press.

Gundara, J. and Jacobs, S. (eds) (2000) *Intercultural Europe*. Aldershot: Ashgate.

Joppke, C. (1999) *Immigration and the Nation-State*. Oxford: Oxford University Press.

Konstadinidis, S. (1999) *A People's Europe: Turning a Concept into Content*. Aldershot: Ashgate.

Human rights – the European experience

Key concepts

- Human rights
- Universal Declaration of Human Rights and Fundamental Freedoms
- The European Convention for the Protection of Human Rights and Fundamental Freedoms
- The European Court of Human Rights
- The European Charter of Fundamental Rights

Fifty years ago, when Allied soldiers walked into Auschwitz and Belsen and the camera showed people around the world the horror of what had gone on inside, the world vowed that it would never happen again. The horror of Bosnia is that, fifty years on, not only war but ethnic cleansing as a direct object of war, is once again scarring the lives of people in Europe.

(Ashdown 1995: 9)

Introduction

Human rights are those rights we are entitled to by virtue of our humanity. One of the most basic and fundamental rights is the right to life. The above quote highlights that even though we have witnessed the development of a wide range of human rights initiatives even this one basic right is not always upheld. This chapter concerns itself with the patchwork of human rights initiatives within Europe. It argues that human rights have traditionally been bound up with national sovereignty and consequently have largely been hampered by a lack of commitment and implementation both at European and nation-state level. Traditionally, human rights have held 'no sacrosanct quality' but rather are 'proclaimed or ignored in accord with the interests' of individual nation-states (Mansell 1999: 71). Following this line of argument, the chapter will outline the development of human rights documents and initiatives in a European context, suggesting that rather than adding to the array of documentation already in place it is now time to ensure that existing treaties are put into practice in a more consistent way.

Rights were once seen as primarily the concern of the nation-state. Before the Second World War a generally accepted principle within international affairs was that of 'sovereign determination' – how a state treats its own citizens is an internal matter and not the legitimate concern of 'outsiders'. Although this principle is to a large extent still adhered to today, the post-Second World War Tribunals at Nuremberg and Tokyo decreed that international rules protecting human rights take precedence over state laws. While we may now be used to this idea, this was the first time in history that this notion had been espoused legally. The trials rejected the defence of obedience to superior authorities in matters of responsibility for war crimes (Held 1995a: 102). The principles established at Nuremberg have however proven difficult to apply impartially and consistently throughout the world. They did nevertheless develop a major shift in attitudes towards the principle of non-intervention as the international community, albeit in the shape of the victorious powers, became involved with the rights of the individual within another nation-state. For the first time there were international moves verbally to denounce and expose human rights abuses (see Zalman and Siegel 1997). Human rights initiatives however, developed prior to this historic decision and therefore, before moving on to investigate human rights in the European context, there needs to be some brief discussion of wider global developments.

Global human rights

In 1919 after the end of the First World War, the League of Nations was established. Although having no direct human rights provision it was based on the assumption that its members would respect human rights: respect what lawyers term an 'international standard of justice' (Vincent 1988: 44). The fact that the United States refused to join and that the League had no power to enforce decisions meant that it was largely ineffective. Despite the setting up of this supranational body, human rights remained firmly in the domain of the nation-state and its legislature.

One of the first charters

Developed in 1215 the Magna Carta, while not applying to the 'common' people, was one of the first political documents to secure certain rudimentary rights and liberties on the part of subjects. Under pressure from the Barons, King John was forced to secure certain 'liberties', the most notable among these being freedom from imprisonment, exile or from dispossession of his property, 'unless by the lawful judgement of his peers or by the law of the land' and a crude form of a right to fair trial in the words, 'To none will we sell, deny or delay right of justice'.

While conferring only local and particular freedoms, the Charter was to play an important role in the development of subsequent rights documents. Various rulers reissued it at least thirty-eight times in the centuries that followed. The Petition of Rights (1628), the Habeas Corpus Acts (1679) and The Bill of Rights (1689) all refer directly to the Charter, as do the national and state constitutions of the United States.

Eleanor Roosevelt, in her famous address to the UN at the launch of the Universal Declaration on Human Rights stated, 'This Universal Declaration of Human Rights may well become the International Magna Carta of all men everywhere.'

The setting up of the United Nations in 1945 saw a growing acknowledgement that countries were becoming more interconnected and interdependent. The UN Charter (drawn up at the San Francisco conference of 1945) forms the constituent statute of the UN as an intergovernmental organisation and proposed to promote 'respect for human rights and fundamental freedoms'. Article 56 states that 'all members pledge to take joint and separate action' to achieve this purpose. An ambiguity arises however because, while recognising that states are 'jealously sovereign' (Article 2 of the Charter espouses the principle of state sovereignty and prohibits interference in the domestic affairs of nation-states) they are at the same time placed 'under pressure to resolve disagreements by peaceful means and according to legal criteria . . . and constrained to observe certain standards' (Cassese 1991: 265). This is further complicated by the fact that the Charter does not specify what *are* the human rights and fundamental freedoms to be protected. It was within this framework that the Universal Declaration of Human Rights (UDHR) was developed.

The UDHR (1948) set out in its Articles the fundamental freedoms that are to be promoted: the civil, political and economic rights. The UDHR is however a 'declaration' of rights which has considerable moral force but is *not* a treaty and therefore is *not* a legally binding document. There was therefore a need to transform the Declaration into a legal document; this was accomplished by the adoption of the International Covenants on Human Rights (1966). These Covenants are legally binding only on those states that ratify them. Ratification was a slow process. It was some ten years before the required thirty-five states ratified both of them. This was largely because states, recognising that the Declaration was not legally binding, argued that democratic countries by their very nature conform to human rights standards and that any differences in how they measure up to those standards could be attributed to differences in ideology (see Falk 1995). Even today some states have signed only 'with reservations'.

These global initiatives paved the way towards the formation of the European Convention for the Protection of Human Rights and Fundamental Freedoms (1950) and ensuing European developments, which are outlined below.

European initiatives

The European Convention for the Protection of Human Rights and Fundamental Freedoms and the Court of Human Rights

Foreign ministers of the member states of the Council of Europe met on 4 November 1950 to sign the European Convention for the Protection of Human Rights and Fundamental Freedoms (ECHR), 'an organisation within the Council of Europe to ensure the collective guarantee of human rights' (see Teitgen *et al.* 1949). The Council of Europe is an intergovernmental organisation that has, as one of its aims, the protection of human rights. Any European state can become a member of the Council of Europe subject to their acceptance of the principle of the rule of law and the guarantee to uphold human rights. All the member states of the EU are members of the Council of Europe.

When drawing up the Convention the members of the Council were able to refer to the statement of rights as outlined in the UDHR. The European Convention came into force in September 1953. At first the Council was concerned with the upholding of civil and political rights, but recognised that social rights would be addressed at some future date (Teitgen, Official Report 7 September 1949). This was to be remedied with the adoption of the Social Charter in 1961, which came into force in 1965 although not all states signed up to it. It is worth noting at this point that there have been a number of other treaties sponsored by the Council of Europe that impact on human rights such as the 1987 European Convention for the Prevention of Torture and the 1995 Convention for the Protection of Minorities (European Treaty Series nos 126 and 157 respectively).

The Statute of the Council of Europe specifies that the preservation of human rights is not just an objective of the Council but a 'condition of membership', the violation of which can lead to suspension or expulsion from the Council (see Articles 1, 3 and 8 of the Statute). The Convention deals with a wide range of issues, including the right to life, the right not to suffer torture or inhumane treatment, the right to a fair trial and many others. This does not mean that these rights are guaranteed without limit. Some are, but others take into consideration such things as national security, public safety, the prevention of crime and so forth. It has been suggested that the ECHR has proven to be the 'most fully developed and best observed of all regional human rights treaties' (Robertson and Merrills 1993: 286). The Convention was, however, primarily concerned with the rights of individuals rather than bringing states to task for breaching human rights norms. The focus is on encouraging states to respect rights rather than putting governments in the dock.

In an effort to implement the collective enforcement of human rights, the Convention created two main institutions: the European Commission of Human Rights (1954) and the European Court of Human Rights (1959). These institutions along with the Committee of Ministers of the Council of Europe (the latter comprising the ministers of foreign affairs of the member states or their representatives) were to ensure the collective enforcement of human rights obligations of contracting member states.

Member states or individuals (the right of individual petition came into being in 1955 and has been described as the 'cornerstone of the Convention' (Robertson and Merrills 1996: 13)) could bring any alleged violation of the Convention to the attention of the Commission. The Commission, consisting of an expert elected from every state that had signed up to the Convention, had a filtering role, investigating the alleged breach of the Convention and if possible arranging a friendly settlement. If the Commission found that a breach of human rights had occurred, this decision of itself was not legally binding on states. If conciliation failed, a three-month period elapsed during which a report was sent to the Committee of Ministers. The Commission or a State, but not in this case the complainant, could refer the matter to the Court; if the Court ruled that a breach of the convention had been made the matter was passed back to the Committee of Ministers of the Council of Europe for 'appropriate action'. In this way the Court was not able to decide which cases to hear and was therefore at the mercy of the Commission or the state concerned. This was to change with the adoption of the 9th Protocol that came into force in 1994 amending Article 44, giving individuals the right to bring a case before the Court. Individuals and associations had first to try to settle the matter through the domestic courts; only after this had been exhausted could a matter be brought to the attention of the Commission. An individual could only make a complaint 'if the respondent country had recognised the right of individual petition' (Ewing 1999: 83). There was no provision for the Court to demand that states take remedial action or to force them to repeal their acts. The Court could, however, award damages to the injured party/parties.

The Committee of Ministers (set up before the Convention), like the Court, had no power to invalidate or overrule a national decision or to specify what remedial action should be taken on the part of the violators of rights (see Article 32 of the Convention). It was, and still is, the responsibility of the individual government concerned to decide what measures should be taken. The Committee could, however, prescribe a time period in which these measures should take place, and impose 'sanctions' if this was not done. These 'sanctions' took the form of published reports on the abuse, the states and/or the individuals involved. This was an unusual and effective device at the time, as reports would not normally have been published. In practice however, changes in implementation of the Convention on the part of a state could be prolonged and it was only necessary for the Committee to 'take note' of remedial matters and there was no comment on the adequacy of any measures taken. The inadequacy of the Committee of Ministers' involvement in this matter reflects the fact that the contracting states of the Council of Europe wanted to have a political organ rather than a judicial one as the ultimate decision-maker.

The Committee nevertheless has the powers to suspend or expel a member state from the Council of Europe if Article 3 of the Statute of the Council of Europe is seriously violated. This Article makes respect for the law and the 'enjoyment of all persons within its jurisdiction of human rights and fundamental freedoms' a condition of membership. To date this has never been used (see Robertson and Merrills 1996). The European Convention unlike the International Covenants allows a state party to denounce them; that is, to announce to other state parties that they will no longer be bound by them. This has happened once: Greece withdrew from the Council of Europe before it was effectively expelled in 1969, after a *coup d'état* in 1967. Democracy was restored in 1974 when Greece rejoined the Council and ratified the Convention.

Through the 1980s and 1990s the number of cases brought before the European institutions rose significantly (registered applications rose from 404 in 1981 to 4750 in 1997), in part due to the accession of new contracting states (to date some forty-three states have ratified the Convention and various optional Protocols, including most of the states of central and eastern Europe) (http://www.echr.coe.int). The increased workload and pressure on the various institutions meant that reform of the human rights mechanisms was needed.

The new European Court of Human Rights

On 1 November 1998 the new European Court of Human Rights came into being in line with Protocol 11 (a decision taken at the Vienna Summit in 1993 and confirmed at the Strasbourg Summit in 1997). This Protocol, concerned with the restructuring of the human rights machinery, was initially opposed by the UK which objected to the fact that the right to petition by the individual should be allowed to remain open for periodic review. The UK finally agreed only after it was made clear that the whole procedure could not go ahead without unanimous support (see Spencer 1995).

The Court, under a revised Convention, comprises a number of judges equal to the number of parties to the Convention (Article 20) and not as previously the Council of Europe (although in practice acceptance of the ECHR is mandatory on states wanting to become part of the Council of Europe). Judges sit as individuals and not as representatives of their country. The Court is divided into four Sections. Each Section has a Committee of three judges that carry out the filtering work previously carried out by the Commission and a Chamber of seven members. A Grand Chamber of seventeen judges presides over difficult cases or cases where there is no previous set precedent.

States or individuals who claim to be a victim of a breach of a Convention right can now lodge complaints directly with the Court; in the case of individuals, after they have exhausted all domestic means of remedy (Article 35). Each application is assigned to a Section, and after some investigation a decision is made as to whether a settlement can be made, or if not, to determine the appropriate level at which the complaint should be dealt with (Committee, Chamber or in exceptional cases Grand Chamber). Proceedings, except in exceptional cases, are public (Article 40). The Convention itself does not specify whether the Court has the power to order remedial measures; however, the Rules of the Court (31 and 32) state that the Court's decisions are binding on respondent states. The Court does have the power to award damages (Article 47). Convention Article 46 provides for the Committee of Ministers of the Council of Europe to monitor the execution of judgments and decide whether states have taken 'adequate' remedial measures to apply the Court's recommendations. The Committee no longer has a role to play in deciding whether a violation of the Convention has occurred but otherwise its role is essentially the same as under the old Court system.

There is little doubt that the European Court of Human Rights is a powerful force for challenging the authority of an individual state. It has the 'broadest application' of any rights document: applying to 'all persons within the jurisdiction of the signatory states' (Bhabha 1999: 117). Judgments of the Court are binding on signatory states. An analysis of the system, however, does raise some concerns. Previously, the Commission was responsible for admissibility, securing an early friendly settlement, drafting a final report to the Court and acting as an assistant to the Court, while the Court made the final judgment, now the Court has taken on the work of the Commission. The Court engages in its own 'fact-finding' both of the alleged events and of the individual national law of the states involved. This has led some commentators to question whether the Court system will become too bureaucratic and officious and whether ultimately this will have an effect on the timing of proceedings and their ability to function smoothly (see March Hunnings 1996).

Although individuals can make an application directly to the Court, they can only do so after having 'tried all remedies in the State concerned' making 'correct use of the available remedies' (ECHR 22 May 2000:1) and having fulfilled a number of other criteria (see Betten and Grief 1998). This means that individuals are for the most part involved in an often time-consuming, complex legal process at an international level that is largely out of their control. Many of the cases coming before the Court are declared inadmissible because they do not fulfil procedural requirements. This is not surprising because, as Betten and Grief argue (1998: 37), 'many of the complaints sent to the ECHR are made by individuals who have not consulted a lawyer'.

The UK, terrorism and the ECHR

The UK government has introduced new legislation to combat terrorism. As part of this legislation the government has decided to derogate (opt out of) Article 5(1) of the ECHR.

The new legislation allows the government to hold indefinitely without charge or trial 'suspected international terrorists'. Without the safeguards of the formal legal system an individual can be imprisoned on the basis of suspicion, not proof. The basis for that suspicion is to be kept secret.

This clearly contravenes one of the most basic human rights, namely the right to a fair trial, and highlights that the European Convention only partially limits state action.

Another area of concern relates to the enforcement of individuals' rights at the nation-state level. While it is true that many of the Court's judgments are adhered to, the doctrine of 'the margin of appreciation' developed by the ECHR means that in practice 'states are accorded considerable discretion and leeway, particularly in "sensitive" areas' (for example, public security and immigration) (Bhabha 1999: 117). Consequently, it is clear that the European Court of Human Rights only partially limits the role of the state and for the most part the state is still the main forum for the implementation of rights. This is evidenced by the fact that states can derogate or opt out of the Convention at any time.

While the Convention and Court are the main mechanism by which human rights are protected and promoted within Europe, they are by no means the only way. It is worth therefore widening the approach to encompass some of these other initiatives.

The Conference on Security and Cooperation in Europe (CSCE/OCSE) 1973

The CSCE, now known as the Organisation for Security and Cooperation in Europe (OCSE), initially convened in Helsinki on 3 July 1973. The thirty-five participating states (now fifty-five) included all the sovereign states of eastern and western Europe (with the exception of Albania, which became a member in 1991), the USA and Canada. This was a means of further integrating the countries of Europe by means of 'soft security' and diplomatic co-operation (Bromley 2001). For the western participants, however, one of its primary purposes was to put pressure on the USSR. It was decided that one of the most effective ways to accomplish this was to try and secure political commitment from the USSR to act on human rights issues. It thus, at that time, became fashionable and politically expedient for politicians to speak about human rights issues in a way they had not done before.

Although the CSCE was primarily concerned with international security and relations between states, there were within the Helsinki Accords signed on 1 August 1975 (otherwise known as the Final Act) a number of Principles specifying human rights issues. Principle VII, for example, states that participating states will 'respect human rights and fundamental freedoms' and that they will 'fulfil their obligations as set forth in the international declarations and agreements in this field . . . by which they may be bound'. In practice, however, when a participating state accuses another of failing to comply with Principle VII the other can invoke Principle VI – 'The participating states will refrain from *any* intervention . . . in the internal or external affairs falling within the domestic jurisdiction of another participating state' (OSCE docs 2000) – again the invoking of the principle of national sovereignty. In this way the Final Accords may be viewed as a bundle of sometimes conflicting Principles.

The 'Helsinki Agreement' is not legally binding. Nonetheless the CSCE process did, in 1989 at the Vienna Conference, feature a number of key human rights features, including an agreement to develop law in the area of human rights, a commitment to freedom of religion and also provisions for dealing with national minorities. A monitoring procedure was also set up, which has become known as the Human Dimension mechanism (for a full discussion see Bloed *et al.* 1991: 74). This monitoring procedure is not a legal procedure but rather a political one. It consists mainly of naming and shaming states involved in human rights abuses. Reading through the proceedings of one of the review meetings one might be forgiven for thinking that this mechanism is used as a 'tit for tat' exercise with states condemning each other in such a way as to negate the whole procedure (Pentikainen 1997). This is not to suggest that it has not been used effectively; for example, the UK used the procedure against Czechoslovakia and this ultimately contributed to the release of the playwright Vaclav Havel. It is therefore ultimately a politically subjective process leading to inconsistencies in the issues raised and responses to those issues. For example, Yugoslavia was suspended as a member because of human rights abuses, while Bosnia and Herzegovina have been admitted despite findings of human rights abuses by Council of Europe monitors (see Nowak 1999).

It could be argued that one of the most significant challenges to state sovereignty came about in the 1992 Declaration of the Helsinki Conference. The Declaration addresses the need for states to become increasingly accountable to one another with regard to human rights issues. It states in part, 'the [human rights] commitments undertaken . . . are matters of direct and legitimate concern to all participating states and do not belong exclusively to the internal affairs to the state concerned. The protection and promotion of human rights . . . continue to be a vital basis for our . . . security' (CSCE 1992: 2 para 8).

This Declaration signals a new approach to the concept of legitimate political power within an international context (see Held 1995a). It is necessary to keep in mind that the Declaration is a statement of intent and not a legally binding document, and as such is open to misuse and abuse. It can justifiably be argued that many CSCE/OSCE states are themselves guilty of human rights abuses: ex-Yugoslavian states have been guilty of hampering the movement of refugees; Turkey in its treatment of minority groups; Albania, Bulgaria, Slovakia, the Czech Republic and Romania for their treatment of the Roma.

The EU and human rights

This section will look at the impact which the setting up of the EC/EU has had on the human rights agenda. In 1957 The Treaty of Rome (TOR) establishing the European Community was primarily used as a means of promoting closer economic integration within Europe. Earlier in the 1950s the drawing up of a bill of rights was proposed but 'none of the subsequent treaties contained such a bill or a list of enumerated rights' (Steiner and Alston 2000: 790). The TOR was more concerned with the protection of the rights of states from EC interference than with the rights of the individual. Protections for individual rights were deemed to be the domain of the nation-state. The preamble to the TOR did, however, outline the need for the EC to function in 'accordance with the principles of the Charter of the United Nations' (recall at this point that the Charter indicates one of its aims as the promotion of the 'respect for human rights and fundamental freedoms'). No codification of human rights was provided, however, which in effect nullified the statement.

The 1992 Treaty on European Union however did make provision for human rights. Article F (s) states, 'The Union shall respect fundamental rights, as guaranteed by the European Convention for the Protection of Human Rights and Fundamental Freedoms signed in Rome on 4 November 1950 and as they resulted from the constitutional traditions common to the member states, as general principles of Community law' (EU 1992).

The use of the word 'respect', however, does not carry any enforcement mechanism. These words were reiterated later in the amendment to the TEU (which was provided for by the Treaty of Amsterdam signed in 1997). Article 6 (1 and 2) provides that:

1   The Union is founded on the principles of liberty, democracy, respect for human rights and fundamental freedoms . . . principles which are common to the member states.
2   The Union shall respect fundamental rights as guaranteed by the [ECHR].

Article 7 does, however, allow for the suspension of membership rights in the EU if a 'serious and persistent breach' of human rights is considered to have occurred within a member state.

The approach to human rights taken by the EU has been criticised for being 'splintered . . . [without necessary] leadership and profile . . . and marginalised in policy-making' (EC Report 1999). In 1996 Amnesty International in a proposal put forward to the IGC suggested that greater 'respect' would be shown to human rights if the EU itself were to accede to the ECHR. Five years on this still has not been done. So the dichotomous arrangement exists whereby nation-states within the EU are bound by the ECHR whereas the EU itself is not.

The European Court of Justice

Based in Luxembourg, the judicial arm of the EU, the Court of Justice (ECJ) is primarily concerned with 'ensuring that the law is observed in the interpretation and applications of the Treaties establishing the European Communities' (Europa downloaded 28 September 00). Way back in 1969, however, the ECJ (in the Stauder case no. 61969J0029) used the consideration of human rights within its deliberations. For the most part, however, human rights within the ECJ have been applied to the actions of the European Community itself and not to the actions of specific nation-states. The Amsterdam Treaty did increase the Court's jurisdiction within Articles 6 (1 and 2). The involvement of the ECJ in the human rights domain in a limited way (concerns for the implementation of EU legislation in a human rights 'friendly' way) has meant that in some cases there is an overlapping of roles between the ECJ and the European Court of Human Rights. The ECJ being part of the EU has not acceded to the ECHR and, although there are arrangements to facilitate consultation and co-ordination between the various organs of the EU and Council of Europe, they are separate entities with separate concerns and operating in different arenas.

The Charter of Fundamental Rights

The fiftieth anniversary of the European Convention on Human Rights in 1998 saw the beginnings of calls to embed human rights within the European Community itself by means of an EU Charter or Bill of Rights that would then come under the auspices of the Court of Justice. The Helsinki European Council in December 1999 allowed for the setting up of a working group that would draw up a draft Charter. The Charter was adopted at the Nice Treaty in December 2000, and incorporates elements from existing charters and international rights declarations and treaties, especially the European Convention on Human Rights as well as the 'constitutional traditions' that are common to all member states (see preamble to Charter). It consists of fifty-four Articles spanning differing areas of rights and freedoms: Dignity; Freedoms; Equality; Solidarity; Citizens' Rights, and Justice. It is not a legally binding document but rather as the British Prime Minister Tony Blair stated, 'simply a statement of policy . . . [not] something of a binding nature' (Blair speech, 14 November 2000).

There have been various reasons put forward for the drawing up of the Charter. It has been suggested (see Miller 2000) that the inclusion of new states into Europe especially from central and eastern Europe necessitates the inclusion of stronger human rights guarantees within the EU legal system and the Charter is a means by which this may be accomplished. It is difficult to agree with this view, however, in view of the non-binding nature of the document. Others suggest that the Charter is little more than a 'consciousness-raising public relations exercise leading to no binding instrument' (de Burca 2001: 127). Indeed it would seem that others too hold this view; the Cologne Conclusions state that 'There appears to be a need . . . to establish a Charter of fundamental rights in order to make their overriding importance and relevance *more visible* to the Union's citizens' (Cologne European Council 1999).

There are however a number of concerns raised about the Charter and its application. It is not clear whether the Charter and the rights set out within it are to be relevant to the member states or only to EU institutions. Indeed a close reading of the Charter and the statements surrounding its development would seem to suggest that there is little need for member states to be concerned with the norms specified within the Charter apart from in cases linked to the EU – in the actual implementation of EU legislation (see Article 51 of the Charter).

One area of concern is in regard to the rights included in the Charter itself. While the fact that the Charter includes rights found in various national constitutions is commendable, Besselink (2001) has shown that the drafting process diverged significantly from the strict definition of constitutional traditions 'common to all Member States'. This may mean that there is state variation in an understanding of 'fundamental' rights and will give rise to the question as to which fundamental rights, namely those proffered by the EU or by the state, should be adhered to.

Another question is raised concerning where exactly an individual now takes a complaint regarding the violation of human rights. The Charter targets a range of differing individuals – sometimes protection is given to EU citizens, sometimes to third-country nationals, sometimes to both groups and other rights are said to be 'universal', applying to all (see e.g. Article 15). How these individuals go about securing redress for any violation is not clear however; it seems to be left in the hands of the lawyers as to which level and to which court appropriate action should be taken. The question concerning which court (the ECHR or the ECJ) will take precedence is not fully answered. There are serious concerns with problems of having two courts ruling on similar issues, or if we take into account the national state legislature, three court systems and the controversy over the exercise of powers at different levels (see Canor 2000: 3). It may therefore be the case that while there are differing rights regulations and codes there is the possibility that states can strategically manipulate the system so as to move the conflict to the forum whose rights seem to be more in their favour (see Engel 2001). This is linked to a concern raised by Weiler (1996: 79–81), who suggests that increasing the number of rights mechanisms actually leads to 'rights saturation rather than rights deprivation'. Looking practically at these issues the potential extra work involved for whichever Court takes responsibility for them within the context of the EU might lead to a slowing down of procedures and the necessity of setting up of yet more institutions for filtering and admissibility considerations.

Many of these questions remain unanswered. Time will tell what effect the Charter will have in practice. There is little doubt that the Charter makes fundamental rights more 'visible' to the citizens of the Union and, if this was the main reasoning behind its drawing up, then it can be said to have fulfilled its purpose. If, however, the purpose was to secure human rights in a more fundamental way than before, it has failed. As de Burca notes, 'The political *desire* to draw up [the Charter] is in contrast with the political *will* . . . to constrain and keep within clear limits the human rights role of the European Union' (2001: 128; italics added). The political will is lacking. If the EU and indeed its member states were serious regarding the coupling of human rights to the EU institutions, they could have chosen long ago to amend treaties so as to accede to the European Convention. Discussions have been ongoing as to whether this should be done but this possibility has never been taken up. In the meantime we are left with a document which outlines a number of fundamental rights but which ultimately lacks teeth.

Discussion

Human rights agreements can reinforce democracy but they cannot guarantee freedom from abuse when powerful forces violate democracy, as in the case of Greece in 1967. A survey of the Democratic Audit (a project based at the Human Rights Centre at the University of Essex) investigating the United Kingdom's 'compliance of British law with [the country's] international human rights obligations' identifies forty-two separate violations of international human rights standards (Klug *et al.* 1996). So even when conventions and treaties are in place these do not necessarily ensure that rights will be respected. This may be due in part to the view that seems to dominate many major states, including the UK, that '[ratified] human rights treaties are instruments of foreign policy rather than domestic' (Falk and Szentes 1997: 179). Falk goes on to suggest that this may be why the Foreign Office in the UK is the main department with responsibility for overseeing the UK's obligations under the ECHR and the United Nations International Covenants (UNIC). Where monitoring procedures *are* put in place, action is not standard but arbitrary.

It has become evident through this analysis that over time a dichotomy has arisen between nation-state sovereignty, with its non-interventionist approach, and movements to internationalise human rights. Gradually, incremental gains *have* been made, gains that often cannot be recognised without the benefit of hindsight. A plethora of treaties, covenants and declarations have developed throughout the years since the first attempts at defining human rights. The European Convention and the two UN International Covenants have been hailed as landmarks in the human rights process (Robertson and Merrills 1993: 287).

The criterion for success, however, must *not* be based on how many of such documents can be drawn up but rather the extent to which they are ratified and implemented. If the treaties already established were accepted and acted upon, then human rights legislation would become stronger. Where the implementation of human rights procedures are optional, however, states often do not incorporate them. While the nation-state, for the most part, is still the focal point for implementing human rights legislation it is still where most violations take place.

Recent years have seen the founding of the new European Court of Human Rights and the EU Charter of Fundamental Rights. The conflict between national, international and supranational legal systems has not diminished however – it still remains. It might even be suggested that the conflict has been heightened by some of these changes. One thing has become apparent through this work, however; adding yet more 'patches' through the drawing up of new charters, treaties and declarations does not provide a clear solution to this problem.

Further reading

Beddard, R. (1993) *Human Rights and Europe*. Cambridge: Grotius (3rd edn).

Janis, M., Kay, R. and Bradley, A. (2000) *European Human Rights Law: Text and Materials*. Milton Keynes: Open University Press (2nd edn).

Merrills, J. and Robertson, A. (2001) *Human Rights in Europe: A Study of the European Convention on Human Rights* . Manchester: Manchester University Press (4th edn).

Special Issue of *Maastricht Journal of European and Comparative Law*, Vol. 8, No. 1.

Weiler, J. (1999) *The Constitution of Europe*. Cambridge: Cambridge University Press.

'Europe' and European identity

Key concepts

- Council of Europe
- *Eurobarometer*
- European identity
- People's Europe

In the 2001 EU White Paper on *European Governance* (CEC 2001a), which sets out the EU's vision of how democracy in the EU is to be advanced, there are some statements that, while almost slipping by unnoticed, nevertheless require further thought. The statements in question relate to 'Europe' and 'European'. The White Paper begins by commenting that people 'do not necessarily feel less European' (CEC 2001: 5); it concludes by stating that the goal of integration remains the desire to 'integrate the people of Europe'. The terms 'Europe' and 'European' are used unproblematically; there is no attempt to explain what is understood by these terms. It would be quite erroneous, however, to assume that this means the substance of these terms is somehow clear and beyond debate. As this chapter will argue, 'Europe' and 'European' are *ideas*, and as such the manner in which they have been defined has altered since the Middle Ages, when, as we will show, interest began to grow in them. How these ideas have been given form has always held important implications for both those who have been defined as belonging to 'Europe' and those defined as non-'European', and have been informed by changing political currents.

In exploring the idea of 'Europe' and, more particularly, 'European identity', this chapter addresses three main issues. First, it considers the development of the idea of 'Europe' in order to demonstrate how the borders of this entity, and the cultural substance it supposedly embodies, have altered since the Middle Ages. Second, it examines the efforts of the EU, and the European Commission in particular, to give form to the idea of European identity. The final concern of the chapter is to point to the diversity within 'Europe'.

Europe: a brief history of an idea

In Greek mythology, Europe, or Europa, was the daughter of Agenor, King of Tyre. She was admired and subsequently abducted by Zeus who, in the shape of a bull, swam with her on his back to the island of Crete. Since Europeans have for centuries looked for an appropriate version of their past in the 'classical' period of Greece and Rome, this may be fairly taken as the origin of the term. In ancient Greece the term 'European' was at first applied only to the central area, Athens and Sparta, but later it was used for the whole of the Greek mainland.

In Christian teaching Europeans are seen as the descendants of one of the three sons of Noah, the other two being the progenitors of Arabs and Africans. But throughout history any possible identity for Europe has changed with circumstances. The Greeks of classical times are well known for referring to all outsiders as barbarians, but the Macedonians of Alexander the Great superimposed upon Greece an empire which famously extended through the Middle East to India where its descendants can still be identified by their blue eyes. Subsequently the Roman Empire covered all the lands around the Mediterranean, utilising their peoples as soldiers in the legions or as slaves. The identity of recognised citizens was Roman, based upon the city itself, but the cosmopolitan nature of the empire makes it Mediterranean rather than European despite its conquests in western Europe. At the height of its power the empire stretched from Scotland to the Sahara and from Gibraltar to the Euphrates and, however much Europeans like to associate their past with classical Rome, if anything it was the term 'Romania' that designated the empire as a whole. Even that did not appear until the fourth century AD when the western empire was declining.

Nevertheless it was the acceptance of Christianity by the Roman Empire, after initial persecutions, that played a large part in spreading the religion in Europe and, as we shall see, the link between Christianity and Europe is vital in terms of the historical development of a European identity. It was the Emperor Constantine who officially embraced Christianity after winning the battle of Milvian Bridge in AD 312, when apparently he had given the Christian god a try by applying a suitable monogram to his soldiers' shields. On the other hand, however, it was he who moved the focus of the Roman Empire away from western Europe. Given the administrative division of the Empire into two halves by the Emperor Diocletian in AD 284, Constantine preferred the eastern half and built his new capital Constantinople, 'the new Rome', on the site of a Greek city 'Byzantium' (modern-day Istanbul). The split ultimately produced two versions of Christianity: the 'Roman' church of the West and the 'Orthodox' church of the East. With the collapse of the western Roman empire (Rome was sacked for the first time in AD 410), the confusingly named 'Byzantine' empire endured in considerable opulence for another thousand years – until its demise at the hands of the Ottoman Turks in 1244.

The sack of Rome was not however the complete end of the western empire. It tended to accommodate its conquerors rather successfully. The conquerors tended not to be the barbarians they are usually portrayed as, since their proximity to the Roman Empire had resulted in some of its culture rubbing off. Consequently the two halves of the Empire co-existed for some time in a rather uncomfortable relationship with the pope in Rome subordinate to the Byzantine emperor, who was styled 'equal of the apostles', whereas the patriarch of the church in Constantinople, technically at least, was subordinate to the pope. Not until 1054 did the two churches finally separate and these curious relationships end. Even then the Byzantines maintained a presence in Italy, mainly at Ravenna, and under emperors such as Basil II actually conquered Italy and restored, in part and temporarily at least, the old Roman Empire. One very important consequence of the schism, however, was that eastern Christianity experienced a different history to that of the West, with no Renaissance, Reformation or Counter-Reformation, and this in itself provides one definition of what is European and what is not.

The important development for the present purpose, however, came at the end of the eighth century when Charlemagne, King of the Franks, conquered most of the old western empire and on Christmas Day 800 was crowned emperor in the West by Pope Leo III in Rome. This was significant in the detachment of the western empire from the eastern but also in the creation of a European identity because Charlemagne became known subsequently as 'Europae Pater', Father of Europe. Charlemagne was the only such emperor truly to rule the old western half of the Roman Empire, but he nevertheless had many successors and by the twelfth century their territories had become known as the Holy Roman Empire. The extent of its possessions was dependent upon conquests and royal marriages, but under the Habsburg dynasty they held much of central Europe, part of southern Italy, Mediterranean islands and, for a period, Spain. The succession was eventually brought to an end by another emperor, Napoleon Bonaparte.

Despite the way that he himself has been remembered, the Europe defined by Charlemagne would subsequently have been commonly referred to, if indeed it was referred to at all, as 'Christendom'. Even this usage has not been identified before the eleventh century because, despite the presence of the pope in Rome, the spread of Christianity in the West still generally lagged behind that in the East. At this point the Christian identity became important in the conflict with Islam and the launching of the Crusades to reclaim Jerusalem and the Holy Land. This Christianity was emphatically western Christianity; however, the Crusades consistently threatened Byzantium and in the end contributed to its downfall at the hands of Islamic forces. Europe was at this time known as Christendom but to the exclusion of the Orthodox Christianity of Byzantium and those parts of eastern Europe which the latter had influenced, and this must be seen as significant in the development of contemporary problems in defining exactly what is and what is not Europe.

The term 'Christendom' lasted in the popular parlance until at least the fifteenth century when the first evidence is found of significant use of the term 'Europe'. Even then, people would not have thought of themselves as European. Indeed, it was not until the time of Louis XIV in the late sixteenth century that his subjects began to think of themselves as French (instead of Normands, Bretons, Languedociens, Gascons, Burgundians, Basques, for example) let alone contemplate a European identity and the situation would have been similar throughout the European states. The Holy Roman Empire was relatively unimportant in the long term because the Europe that expanded to create a global culture was a Europe of independent sovereign states. They were in fact in competition with each other and this was probably one of the most important factors. It was so significant that the nation-state system of Europe virtually unchanged in principle became the global system of the United Nations in modern times.

By the nineteenth century the civilisation of western Europe was seen simply as civilisation itself and Europe as the bountiful donor of this to the rest of the world. This may be seen in the development of academic disciplines. Most were simply the study of Europe, its history, its institutions and its knowledge. Then there was orientalism, the study of other civilisations, while anthropology was the study of 'primitive' peoples. By the early twentieth century there was a perceptible 'standard of civilisation' against which all cultures could be measured. This was of course the standard of European (or western) civilisation and when Sun Yat-Sen introduced modernisation into China in 1911 it was very much with this in mind. Even in 1917 Lenin was forced reluctantly to take this into account in his establishment of the state structure and foreign policy of the Soviet Union.

Europe: change and integration

According to Immanuel Wallerstein, from the sixteenth century onwards European capitalism gave rise to what he refers to as a 'modern world-system'. This differs from the comparable economic systems of previous civilisations in that it has never come to be dominated by a military empire as they did. Rome, Byzantium, Persia, China, for example, all had economies dominated by the emperor and enforced by his armies. Furthermore, Wallerstein's claim is that in Europe's case major wars have prevented this. Thus during the seventeenth century the Thirty Years' War prevented the Habsburg Holy Roman Empire from dominating a European economy expanded by the influx of silver from the Spanish American colonies, and spices and silks from Portuguese trading enclaves in the East. Two centuries later the Napoleonic Wars, ending with Waterloo in 1815, prevented Napoleon from taking over a European economy in which the Industrial Revolution was already in progress. During the twentieth century, two European conflicts that became world wars prevented Germany from taking over a fully industrialised 'modern world-system'. Wallerstein has been criticised for an overly economistic analysis of world history and, in any case, the outcome would seem to be an American dominated world since the USA came out of the Second World War with 40 per cent of the world's manufacturing capacity and 70 per cent of its gold and hard currency reserves. However, the USA did not create a post-war military empire in the old sense, despite criticism of its military-industrial complex.

At the heart of the two World Wars were, if Europe is to be considered an entity in its own right, two European 'civil wars'. The outcome of these was decisive for Europe over a period of almost fifty years. The First World War left a kind of impasse which was not to be resolved until after the Second World War – and then unsatisfactorily. Russia had extricated itself from the First World War after the October Revolution of 1917, allowing Germany to expand itself eastwards and presaging later aspirations. Defeat, however, took away this advantage and the reparations demanded by the victors, particularly France, placed it in an impossible economic situation. The resulting Second World War could not have been won as it was by the Allies without Stalin's USSR – which in fact bore the brunt of the struggle in Europe, and at Yalta, with Roosevelt manifestly recognising the Soviet contribution, Churchill could only protect Greece from the USSR's 'sphere of interest'. As Churchill put it in 1946, 'from Stettin in the Baltic to Trieste in the Adriatic an iron curtain . . . descended upon Europe'. The Cold War period in fact crystallised an older division between the western Europe of Wallerstein's 'modern world-system' and the eastern Europe of relative economic backwardness and peripherality. This definition of Europe with a west and an east shading off into Russia lasted until the 1990s.

Meanwhile, the desire to prevent once and for all the Franco–German conflict that had been a major part of all the wars referred to by Wallerstein led to the establishment of the European Economic Community in 1957. Four decades later the transition to European Union roughly coincided with the collapse of the Soviet Union and the delayed 'liberation' of the eastern European countries – which were soon queuing up for entry to the European Union. In the twentieth century therefore the identity of Europe tended to be confined to western Europe and by the 1990s the membership of the European Union coincided with this, except for Norway and Switzerland which had declined to join. At the time of writing, even the most advanced of the countries of central-east Europe still await membership.

Being 'European'

Like the concept of 'Europe', the notion of being 'European' is difficult to pin down. Yet, just as Anderson (1991) suggests that when we position ourselves as belonging to nations we imagine limits beyond which lie other nations, so, too, when we invoke the label 'European' we must imagine that there is a line beyond which live non-Europeans. As the previous sections made clear, this line has ebbed and flowed over the past 500 years. Most recently it has been the drawing back of the 'Iron Curtain' since the late 1980s and the moves on the part of many countries of central-east Europe, including some of the westerly territories of the former Soviet Union, to join the EU (and, in some cases, to have joined NATO) that is driving the most recent redefinition of 'Europe'. As Norman Davies comments in the last lines of his widely acclaimed *Europe – A History*, 'somewhere between the depths of Russia and the heart of Europe a new dividing line will have to be established' (1997: 1136). What, then, symbolises the imagined limits of the 'European' experience? When we speak of 'Europe' as an imagined community what are the characteristics shared by those inhabiting this space?

For any collective identity an essential ingredient is an historical narrative that locates 'our' origins and progress. If we are to speak of a 'European' identity, what are its historic roots? Many commentators on this issue refer to the classical Graeco-Roman origins of Europe. Huntingdon, for example, refers to a 'classical civilisation' – the features of which include 'Greek philosophy and rationalism, Roman law, Latin, and Christianity' (1997: 69) – which informed a later 'European civilisation', and which, in turn, underpinned the rise of 'Western civilisation'. More recently, Viviane Reding (2000), EU Commissioner for Education and Culture, underscored the centrality of the classical legacy, telling an audience in Greece in 2000 that 'Greek heritage . . . is an integrative part of the European cultural identity', adding that it is 'impossible to understand our European civilisation without taking into consideration the Greek heritage.' Christianity, too, is often cited as one of the defining features of a European civilisation. As Smith remarks, there is a 'clear sense, going back at least to the Crusades . . . in which Europeans see themselves as not-Muslim or as not-Jews' (1992: 69). Delanty (1995), too, comments that from about the seventh century onwards 'Europe' as an idea embodying certain values was increasingly defined in opposition to Islam.

To what extent may we regard these phenomena as essential elements of what it means to be 'European'? The legacies of classical civilisation and Christianity have certainly played central roles in the narrative of 'Europe' as it has been developed by some scholars and artists since the fifteenth century, when the idea of 'Europe' began to flourish during the Renaissance. This narrative continues to be expounded by modern observers. In a speech to the European Parliament in 1994 Vaclav Havel, President of the Czech Republic, remarked that the EU is founded on a 'large set of values, with roots in antiquity and in Christianity which over 2000 years evolved into what we recognise today as the foundations of modern democracy, the rule of law and civil society' (Havel 1994). Christianity has indeed played a major role in the development of 'Europe' as an idea, and, in turn, of *a* European identity. These developments cannot be understood, however, without considering them in opposition to Islam and the conflict between Christians and Muslims, such as during the Crusades between the eleventh and thirteenth centuries AD, and in the face of the rise of the Ottoman empire from the fourteenth century onwards. The identity of 'Europe' during the Middle Ages was thus increasingly defined through its association with western Christendom.

Despite the dominance of Christianity, however, it cannot be described as an integrating force among 'Europeans'. Although sharing a broad belief system, the history of European Christianity highlights the legacy of division and conflict among Europeans, as first it split into its Latin and Orthodox churches and, later, as western Christendom was ruptured by the Reformation into Catholicism and Protestantism. Thus, while Christianity has undoubtedly played a powerful role in European history, its divisions raise questions about its suitability as a broad base for a modern European identity. Parts of what would now be included, with little dispute, within the geographical notion of 'Europe', such as Albania, Hungary, and, indeed, Greece, were once territories of the vast Ottoman Empire. As we shall touch on below, if these territories are to be included within our definition of 'Europe', then Islam has also had a direct hand in shaping the identity of 'Europe'. Indeed, Huntingdon's (1997) definition of 'Europe' – for which we should read 'western Christendom' – leaves Greece, as part of eastern Orthodoxy, outside of historic 'Europe'.

What of the other institutions and experiences, such as the rule of law, democracy (both supposedly part of the Graeco-Roman heritage) and the Renaissance, that are often regarded as being at the core of the European identity? The Renaissance, for example, a period generally accepted as spanning the fifteenth and sixteenth centuries, had a considerable impact on post-Medieval Europe. At the core of the Renaissance (the term itself was not coined until the nineteenth century) lay the application of the science and philosophy of Graeco-Roman civilisation to the contemporary era, such as in the practice of art or architecture, as well as in the spheres of education and, more controversially, theology. It is often held to be one of the defining markers between the European mind and the ways of thinking among non-European peoples. The impact of the Renaissance was indeed widespread, but again its impact was largely limited to the areas where the Catholic faith was dominant; indeed, one of the primary forces behind the Renaissance was a reaction against the Catholic Church.

The point, therefore, as with our comments on the place of Christianity, is that the Renaissance fits with one particular narrative of 'Europe', and one version of what it means to be 'European'. If the construction of a European identity is selective with regard to what is included as part of a 'European spirit', it is similarly partial in terms of what is ignored. For example, if 'democracy' is at the core of a European identity, how are we to explain the forms of government across Europe that, even during the course of the twentieth century, have been anything but democratic? Moreover, the idea of what it means to be 'European' is further problematised once we begin to take account of the impact of 'non-European' influences on 'Europe'. We have already noted, for example, the historic impact of Islam in territories that are, today, being considered for membership of the EU. Davies (1997) makes the point that Greece's formative modern experiences occurred under the rule of the Ottomans. Nederveen Pieterse (1994), in an interesting essay, traces the historic multiple non-European influences on the development of 'Europe', ranging from the import of ideas and commodities that had important effects to the way in which knowledge of non-European cultures acted as models for the social development of European societies. Indeed, Pieterse makes a convincing case for seeing the supposedly foundational aspects of European identity – Greece, Rome, Christianity and the Renaissance – as moments of 'cultural mixing' (1994: 146). A more recent example of such 'cultural mixing' is exemplified by the non-European influences on the development of art nouveau in the late nineteenth and early twentieth centuries. Often recognised as a movement that sought to 'change the character of European civilisation' (Greenhalgh 2000: 15), and which was embraced across Europe – from Glasgow to Moscow – art nouveau borrowed from a number of non-European cultures, including China and Japan, as well as from classicism. The greatest external influence, arguably, came from Islamic art however (Vanke 2000). Today, the influences come in different forms, but their 'non-European' sources are equally as diverse. As Shore argues, 'American television, Japanese electronics and computer games, Indian and Chinese cuisine, clothes manufactured in South-East Asia and Afro-Caribbean music are all now aspects of everyday European culture' (2000: 64).

With this diversity is it still possible to demarcate a European identity? Some have sought to squeeze this diversity into a broad framework which, while recognising the limitations of speaking of a common European identity, nevertheless holds that there are what may be described as shared cultural foundations. Smith (1992), for example, suggests that a 'family of cultures' underpins a European identity. Not all of the phenomena that are often declared to be distinctively European may have touched every part of Europe, but there is sufficient 'cross-fertilisation of cultural traditions' to speak of a shared 'European experience' (Smith 1992: 70–71). Perhaps the most high-profile effort in this sense has been the EU notion of 'unity in diversity' as the basis of European identity. Diversity in the European context does not equate with unity, however, for the very phenomena that encourage Europeans to identify with their respective nations – such as war, historical narratives, ideas of homeland – are more often than not sources of tension between nations. As the next section will show, such obstacles have not prevented EU policy-makers from seeking to generate a popular sense of Europeanness to underpin the EU.

Integration and 'European' identity

In the post-war era what 'Europe' means has become increasingly bound up with the process of European integration. Indeed, over the past thirty years, during which the architects of integration have become increasingly concerned with (and about) public attitudes to the Union, 'Europe' has come to be used as shorthand for the EU. Each year, for example, *Eurobarometer*, the European Commission's statistical device for measuring public opinion in the EU, records the way in which being 'European' is balanced against 'nationality'. Moreover, throughout the *Eurobarometer* reports one finds references to 'European institutions' (referring to the governing institutions of the EU), 'European enlargement' (instead of the expansion of the EU), and, most recently, to a 'European constitution' (for which we should read 'constitution of the EU'). These points may seem like academic pedantry, but they must be viewed alongside the process through which 'European institutions', especially the European Commission, have sought to give form to a pan-European identity among the peoples of the EU.

Since the early 1970s there has been growing support within the main EU institutions to give 'Europe' a larger presence in the hearts and minds of the citizens

Attitudes towards 'Europe': the *Eurobarometer*

In order to gauge public attitudes to the EU, the European Commission carries out a number of different types of opinion surveys that inform the work of the Commission's Directorate Generales. Of these, two in particular provide interesting data with which to compare not only differences in attitudes across the EU and the Applicant Countries, but also variation over time: the 'standard *Eurobarometer* surveys' and, from 2001, the 'Applicant Countries *Eurobarometer*' (this was preceded, between 1990 and 1998, by the *Central and East European Eurobarometer*). The 'standard *Eurobarometer* surveys', or *Eurobarometer* as it is more commonly known, has been in operation since 1973, providing snapshots of attitudes of citizens, aged 15 and over, in the member states of the European Union. The *Eurobarometer* is conducted by face-to-face interviews, between two and five times each year (reports appear twice a year), with a sample of 1000 people drawn from most EU member states (although 1300 people are sampled in the UK and 600 people interviewed in Luxembourg). Some questions are permanent fixtures in the surveys, such as those asking about attitudes towards support for their country's membership of the EU and, since the late 1990s, attitudes towards the single currency. Other issues addressed by the *Eurobarometer* reflect the concerns of the various DG or particular initiatives sponsored by the EU, such as the European Year Against Racism in 1997. The results of the *Eurobarometer* are an undoubtedly valuable source of information for social scientists, but it is sometimes necessary to look beyond how the findings are interpreted in the reports.

of the member states. The European Commission, as the supranational driving force of integration, has taken a particular interest in this project (see Shore (1996, 2000) for some very interesting analyses of the role of the Commission). Our discussion of EU citizenship explores how this changing mood manifests itself in the promotion of citizenship of the EU. This process has not, however, been limited to a concern with the legal and political issues conventionally associated with citizenship. Rather, the wider goal has been to promote a sense of common identity among member state nationals. The 1975 *Tindemans Report*, produced by the Belgian Prime Minister Leo Tindemans, is broadly recognised as one of the first significant statements on the importance of promoting a European identity. Subsequent years have seen other notable statements on this theme, such as in the 1985 *Adonnino Reports* and the 1993 *De Clercq Report* (which focused on the necessity of more effective communication of 'Europe' to EU citizens).

Since the mid-1980s the efforts to foster a European identity have been assisted by the often directly linked campaigns to give the EU a public persona. The *Adonnino* reports are especially significant in that, as part of a 'People's Europe' campaign intended to engender a popular sense of being 'European', they recommended the bold move of adopting Community symbols. To this end, a number of pan-EU icons and symbols were introduced. In 1985, for example, the European Community adopted a standardised European passport. During the same period 'Ode to Joy' from Beethoven's *Ninth Symphony* assumed the role of unofficial anthem of the

Community. Perhaps most significantly in 1985 the Community adopted its official flag. Positioned all over the EU, the flag has now become one of the symbols most readily associated with the EU. Indeed, in the *Central and East European Eurobarometer*, one of the main ways of testing awareness of EU affairs is the extent to which those polled are able to correctly identify the EU flag.

Today, arguably the most significant symbols of unification, especially, but not exclusively, in the 'eurozone' (the area formed by the countries participating in the European Monetary Union) are the new notes of the euro. Launched in August 2001 (and becoming legal tender on 1 January 2002) these notes are the most pervasive symbols of the EU, and they are the most concrete manifestation of the desire to bring 'Europe close to its citizens' as expressed in the 1975 *Tindemans Report* which first marked the Community's interest in European identity. As with the other EU symbols, the euro notes have been designed to appeal to a pan-EU audience; each of the seven notes bears an image of a bridge intended to represent different European architectural styles. Great care has been taken to distance the images on the notes from actual European places; the designer took photographs of real bridges, such as the Rialto Bridge in Venice and the Neuilly Bridge outside Paris, and then proceeded to remove any features that might betray their original location.

These icons are perhaps the most readily identifiable symbols of the integration process and of the EU as a political entity. The publicity campaigns that bring these symbols to our attention not only seek to communicate what they symbolise as 'European' icons, they also generate a sense of 'us' – those to whom the messages are directed – as an imagined European community. In the case of the euro, for example, the European Central Bank, the institution responsible for the management of the currency, had spent €80 million by the end of 2001 on advertising campaigns to increase public awareness of *The Euro, Our Money*, as the campaign's slogan declared. Similarly, when the euro was floated on the world's financial markets on 1 January 2000 the event was marked by elaborate public ceremonies across the eurozone. The public campaigns associated with these phenomena can therefore be viewed as helping to give form to the idea of what it means to be 'European'.

In this respect these high-profile campaigns are buttressed by many other 'Europeanisation' policies. The 1992 Maastricht Treaty formally enabled the EU to intervene in some aspects of policy-making in the fields of education, youth and culture. Of particular importance are the Treaty's references to the necessity of 'developing the European dimension in education' (Article 126) and of 'bringing the common cultural heritage to the fore' (Article 128) in EU policy. Since this time EU policy-makers have responded to this challenge by promoting awareness of European integration through its education and training programmes, such as *Erasmus*, *Leonardo*, *Socrates* and *Tempus*. The effect has been not so much to 'bring' a 'common cultural heritage to the fore' in Europe; rather the upshot has been actively to create this 'heritage'. By the mid-1990s '[t]hings European' had, 'to use a Foucauldian phrase, become "inscribed" in educational discourse' (Sultana 1995: 130). Other researchers have explored the many ways in which a European dimension has been actively cultivated through the activities of different groups. Shore, for example, turns his attention to those working within the European Commission who, from the mid-1980s, have sought to promote what one Commission official describes as 'some sort of supra-nationality' (2000: 51).

Why has so much energy been dedicated to fostering this European 'su
nationality'? It is an issue that generates considerable emotion in some quarters
former British prime minister, Margaret Thatcher, in what has become known
'Bruges speech' (the speech was delivered to the College of Europe, Bruges, 1988),
famously spoke out against what she saw as the efforts of some to create 'some sort
of identikit European personality'. Answers to this question can thus hinge on one's
political persuasion on the issue of 'Europe'. Overall, however, we can say that the
principal driving force has been the need to strengthen the popular base of support
for integration. The importance of a 'European identity' is recognised by EU policy-
makers. In a working paper on the issue of European identity produced by the
Forward Studies Unit of the European Commission, one Commission official remarks
that the 'Union's very ability to survive, grow, act and succeed in its endeavours' rests
with whether or not EU citizens actively 'espouse the spirit of the Union' (Jansen
1999: 29).

The task of encouraging popular identification with 'Europe' and the EU
therefore remains a concern for EU policy-makers today, although in some quarters
it is possible to detect a slightly different approach to this matter. The 2001 White
Paper on *European Governance*, for example, remarks that, despite the EU's
successes, 'many Europeans feel alienated from the Union's work', yet whereas the
Adonnino Reports advocate strengthening European identity, in the *Governance*
White Paper the accent is on rebuilding 'trust' in the EU to deliver effective policies.
As the White Paper states: 'People do not necessarily feel less European. They still
expect Europe-wide action in many domains, but they no longer trust the complex
system to deliver what they want' (CEC 2001a). The concerns at the heart of the
Governance White Paper are in many respects side effects of the advance in the
integration process. Declining levels of public trust in government, especially at
the national level, are evident in many countries across the world in the late twentieth
and early twenty-first centuries. In the case of the EU, however, this problem is
compounded by charges that decision-making in the EU is not accountable to EU
citizens and that a 'democratic deficit' exists between citizens and EU policy-makers.
As more powers are transferred to the EU so this notion of a 'democratic deficit' has
been subject to increasing debate.

There is, then, much at stake. For critics of the EU, and in particular of
its efforts to forge a European identity, this project is portrayed as a threat to
national cultures and identities. For the EU the need to establish strong lines of
communication with EU citizens and to generate identification with the EU are
becoming of greater importance to the progress of integration. While a widely held
European consciousness has not prevented the EU from speaking on behalf of
'Europe' in its foreign policy, and certainly has not derailed the integration process,
a stronger popular declaration of loyalty to the EU would undoubtedly bolster
integration. To what extent therefore has the EU been successful in its efforts to
generate an attachment to 'Europe' among EU citizens?

Studies undertaken by the European Commission show mixed findings. On the
one hand, there is evidence of an underlying sense of Europeanness, although this
is not necessarily associated with the EU. A 2001 study of attitudes towards the EU
on the part of citizens in the fifteen member states and nine candidate countries
claims that among those interviewed there is 'more or less spontaneous empathy

for other Europeans' (CEC 2001b: 5), and an awareness of discernible differences between 'Europe' and the USA. The report nevertheless reveals considerable variation, and some worrying divisions between member states. For example, citizens in some north European member states, such as Denmark, the Netherlands, the UK and Sweden, are less likely to consider themselves as Europeans, and perceive themselves to have a different 'mentality' to southern Europeans. These divisions are borne out in attitudes among EU citizens towards their putative common cultural bonds. A 2000 *Eurobarometer* poll shows that the majority of EU citizens do not believe they share a common cultural identity: nearly 50 per cent of EU citizens 'slightly or completely disagree' with the idea that they share a common European culture (CEC 2000).

The *Eurobarometer* polls also provide us with interesting data on the subject of relative attachments to nation and 'Europe'. These polls show that around 50 per cent of citizens of the EU profess some degree of attachment to a European identity, although over 40 per cent regularly profess an attachment only to their nation. For example, in 1997 45 per cent of those interviewed identified themselves only by their nationality (given a choice between their nation and 'Europe'), and a similar figure was registered in 2000, while by 2001 only 34 per cent of those interviewed felt an attachment only to their nation (CEC 1997, 2000, 2001c). Judging by other figures, however, it would be incorrect to view this latter statistic as suggesting a diminution in attachment to national identity. The 2001 *Eurobarometer* shows that nearly 60 per cent of EU citizens have an attachment to 'Europe', but this figure is 25 per cent less than their attachment to their town/village and nearly 30 per cent less than their attachment to their nation (CEC 2001b). Moreover, elsewhere in the report we find that national pride still runs very high in almost all EU member states. Germans emerge as having the weakest recorded sense of national pride, although even here 68 per cent of the population declare themselves proud to be German. In eleven member states above 85 per cent of the population were proud to belong to their nation.

Clearly, then, among EU citizens identification with 'Europe' lags considerably behind attachments to their respective national states. Data gathered from EU surveys show that the EU has yet to emerge as contender for the loyalties of EU citizens. The prospects of the latter situation changing dramatically do not look good. A 2001 *Eurobarometer* Special Edition shows that the majority of citizens in each of the member states do not feel they have enough knowledge about the EU to take part in a public discussion of its future (CEC 2001d). For example, in Sweden 75 per cent of those interviewed did not feel sufficiently well informed about the EU to want to take part in public discussions, while nearly two-thirds were not interested in taking part in such discussions. Even in Luxembourg, the population of which is generally regarded as having among the strongest attachments to the EU, 73 per cent of Luxembourgeois did not wish to take part in any discussions on the future of the EU. Across the EU as a whole, 79 per cent of those interviewed did not believe they were sufficiently well informed about EU affairs, while 62 per cent did not want to participate in the debate. Whether or not the notion of a 'democratic deficit' influences people's perceptions of the EU is not clear, but EU citizens are more likely to be satisfied with democracy at the national level than with democracy as practised by the EU. The 2001 *Eurobarometer* finds that levels of support for EU democracy are nearly 20 per cent lower than for national democracy (CEC 2001c).

It seems unlikely that a European identity, with the EU as its political foundation, will generate the sorts of passions and loyalty that people feel towards their nations. Even the EU's own indicators find that 'Europe' is distant from the everyday lives of the overwhelming majority of EU citizens, and most have little desire to see this situation change. 'Europe' nevertheless *is* part of our everyday environment. EU legislation, for example, though we may not be consciously aware of it, exerts an influence over a growing number of areas, although most notably in relation to economic affairs. Perhaps most significantly, adapting Billig's (1995) idea of 'banal nationalism', the EU flag, dotted on everything from bridges to buildings in all member states, and the euro, in the pockets of millions of EU citizens, represent the 'forgotten reminders' (Billig 1995: 38) of the EU. That for most of the time we do not consciously register these symbols (or, in the case of the euro, will, in all likelihood, not notice after the currency has been in circulation for some time) is evidence of how the EU has become part of national societies. The problem for the EU, however, is that for most EU citizens this 'banal' Europeanism does not translate into consciousness of a European identity.

Patchwork Europe: European identities

In *Rediscovering Europe*, Leonard remarks that the principal concern for EU policy-makers should be with 'creating a common space in which diversity can flourish' (1998: 61). Despite championing the notion of 'unity in diversity' the EU does not show signs of taking on board Leonard's view (shared by most commentators on this matter) that Europe is a 'patchwork of different cultures, religions, languages, and views' (1998: 60). The extent of the social and cultural diversity within this 'patchwork' Europe presents a challenge to any effort to speak of a common European experience. As Borneman and Fowler note, the 'people in Europe currently identify with 32 different European nations and speak 67 languages (not counting dialects)' (1998: 487).

With such diversity it is perhaps not surprising that 'Europe' itself can mean many things. We have already reported that among some citizens of Denmark, the Netherlands, the UK, and, less strongly, Sweden, there is a 'weak empathy' with other Europeans, while citizens of south European countries are, the European Commission reports, 'even quite overtly despised (for not being responsible, hard-working, orderly, etc.)' (CEC 2001b: 5). The same survey finds also finds that 'some Estonians, and also some Czechs have a similar stance, restricting the Europe for which they have an affinity to the most highly developed, most organised countries of the Northwest of the continent' (CEC 2001b: 5). Other divisions are apparent with regard to the enlargement of the EU, sometimes referred to as a move 'back to Europe' on the part of the countries of central-east Europe. For example, at a general level a majority (61 per cent) of EU citizens feel that 'Europe will be culturally richer' as a consequence of enlargement, yet less than one-third (30 per cent) are willing for the EU to assist applicant countries financially in order that this cultural enrichment should proceed smoothly. Moreover, despite feeling that 'Europe' will be culturally enriched by enlargement, the 1996 *Eurobarometer* found that EU citizens trusted Americans and Japanese more than they trusted many other Europeans. For example, 59 per cent had a 'lot or some trust' in Americans and 50 per cent had similar feelings towards Japanese, while Hungarians (37 per cent), Czechs (34 per cent), Russians (24 per cent) and Turks (21 per cent) were trusted considerably less. Below the surface, EU member states evidently have different views as to which countries are more compatible with their vision of 'Europe'. Nearly 90 per cent of Greek citizens wish for Cyprus to join the EU (not a surprising result given the ethnic ties between Greek Cypriots and Greek nationals) while less than 20 per cent of Austrians are in favour of Bulgaria and Romania joining the EU (perhaps due to the geographic proximity of these countries to Austria).

One of the clearest illustrations of 'patchwork' Europe is the extent of the differences between nationals of EU member states. As we explain elsewhere in our discussion of nationalism, 'nations' are no more natural than 'Europe'; as with 'Europe', national ideas of common culture, shared memories, and even attachments to territory are forged over time. The idea of the 'nation' nevertheless has stronger roots among the populations of Europe than the notion of 'Europe'. Many areas of everyday experience, such as the media, sport and even humour, help to reproduce awareness of 'us' as a nation. We have already noted that attachment to national identities remains strong in the EU, but *Eurobarometer* surveys reveal some interesting findings with regard to attitudes *between* nations. The 1996 *Eurobarometer*, for example, found that while EU citizens do not have complete trust in their fellow nationals, their levels of trust are significantly higher than the trust in those of other countries, both inside and outside the EU. Thus while 69 per cent of Italians had trust in other Italians – the lowest level of trust in a fellow national among EU member states – only 50 per cent of EU citizens had a 'lot or some trust' in Italians. Such findings arguably highlight the relative lack of a sense of shared experiences between nations. Building on Anderson's (1991) idea of the 'imagined community', we can say that while individuals will never personally know all their fellow nationals, the fact that they trust them over 'foreigners' suggests an intuitive belief that members of a nation share a common bond.

The notion of *l'Europe des états*, a phrase first employed by Charles de Gaulle, a former president of France, arguably remains the preferred vision of 'Europe' for most Europeans. The diversity resulting from attachments to nation-states is, however, only one level of patchwork Europe. Many European countries face challenges from minority nationalist movements, and countries such as Spain and the UK, for example, contain a number of self-declared 'nations'. Since the beginning of the 1990s the notion of a 'Europe of the regions' has also been promoted by a variety of actors, from political parties to business organisations. The creation of the Committee of the Regions by the 1992 Maastricht Treaty is recognition of this dimension of political life in the EU.

Attachments to national or regional identities do not, however, mean that Europeans are necessarily hostile to those whom they perceive as belonging to other such groups. The 2000 *Eurobarometer* finds that EU citizens are largely tolerant of citizens of other countries and of religious groups other than their own. In only three countries (Belgium, Denmark and Greece) did more then 20 per cent of those interviewed state that they found the presence of people of other religions 'disturbing', and in only three countries – again, Belgium, Denmark and Greece – were more than 20 per cent 'disturbed' by the presence of people of a different nationality (CEC 2000). EU citizens are also largely tolerant of the movement of third-country nationals to the EU for work, with over 70 per cent in favour of the ability of people from countries south of the Mediterranean to work in the EU (although 60 per cent wanted some kind of restriction on movement) (CEC 1997). As debates on immigration often reveal, opinions can be sharply divided over this issue. Thus, while 35 per cent of Spaniards are happy for people from south of the Mediterranean to move to the EU to work without any restrictions, in ten member states over one-fifth of the population would not be willing to accept such movement at all (CEC 1997).

Concerns about 'foreigners' are nevertheless evident. The 1997 *Eurobarometer* highlights that 45 per cent of EU citizens believe that there are 'too many' foreigners living in their country, and in five member states this figure climbs to 50 per cent and above (CEC 1997). The same survey finds that 33 per cent of those interviewed declared themselves to be 'quite racist' or 'very racist' (CEC 1997). It was findings such as these that moved the EU to to establish the Monitoring Centre on Racism and Xenophobia in 1997 and launch a European Year against Racism in 1997. In 2000 the Commission recorded that in four EU member states more than 20 per cent of those interviewed stated that they were 'disturbed' by the presence of members of another 'race'. Some commentators suggest that the EU itself has contributed to the racialisation of 'Europe' through its vision of a European identity discussed in the previous section. Shore, for example, argues that by 'pitting Europe competitively and hierarchically against its supposed rivals, commercial (as with American and Japan) or conceptual (as with Africa, Asia and Islam), the EU also fuels xenophobia and makes racism more respectable' (1996: 487). Even if the EU has contributed to this situation, problems of racism, both in the EU and in other European countries, also have local forms, as our discussion of racism elsewhere highlights.

Attitudes towards 'race' and nation across Europe highlight the diversity of European experiences, and point to the difficulties of forging a meaningful European identity that does not exclude or offend many who also believe themselves to be Europeans. Even if difference does not lead to hostility, Europe's patchwork cultural and political fabric militates against an imposed, top-down uniform identity. If some Europeans are to come to identify with a limited vision of 'Europe', in the form of the EU, then this idea of 'Europe' will need to be broad enough to accommodate a diverse range of cultural experiences.

Summary

This chapter has contended that any effort to define the parameters of 'Europe', and to give form to the idea of what it means to be 'European', must be treated with caution. Since 'Europe' began to be used in the Middle Ages to refer to a Christian world in opposition to Islam, and the Ottoman Empire in particular, the term has been inseparable from political developments. As has been argued, the validity of this idea of Europe may be questioned from a number of perspectives. To speak of certain *core* aspects of a European identity, such as Christianity or the Graeco-Roman heritage, is to miss the fact that these do not reflect the experiences of *all* Europeans.

Today, the Council of Europe and the EU are both engaged in considering what are the core elements of a shared European culture. While, as we highlighted above, there are still references to ethnically specific characteristics, such as Christianity (as Vaclav Havel's comments illustrate), there are signs that the political leaders of the CoE and the EU are conscious of the dangers of culturally specific definitions of 'Europe' and 'European'. While both the CoE and the EU speak of a 'cultural heritage', they are both vague as to what this term means, preferring instead to proclaim universal concepts, such as tolerance, the rule of law and respect for human rights as the basis of a modern European identity. As multinational and multicultural organisations, the CoE and the EU are understandably careful not to offend elements of their membership by creating a European identity that is not sufficiently all-embracing. It is for this reason that the concept of European citizenship, discussed at the outset of this book, represents an interesting development in EU politics.

'Greater Europe': The Council of Europe

The Council of Europe (CoE) was established by the *Statute of the Council of Europe*, signed in London on 5 May 1949. At this time the membership comprised ten states: Belgium, Denmark, France, the Republic of Ireland, Italy, Luxembourg, the Netherlands, Norway, Sweden and the United Kingdom. From this beginning the CoE has expanded to forty-three member states, and now stretches from Iceland (1950) and the Republic of Ireland in the West to the Russian Federation (1996) and Azerbaijan (2001) in the East. The largest expansion of the CoE came in the 1990s, when seventeen new members joined from central and eastern Europe. The CoE emerged from the immediate aftermath of the Second World War with the aim of forging closer co-operation between European states. In contrast to the EU, the CoE is a firmly intergovernmental body; while members agree to work towards common aims, membership of the CoE does not necessitate any pooling of sovereign powers. Indeed, some of the initial founding members of the CoE also went on to create the European Coal and Steel Community in 1951, the first stage in the building of what we now recognise as the EU, in order to advance the idea of economic and political integration. The role of the CoE is to prepare opinions and resolutions on issues relating generally to the functioning of democracy, the 'cultural identity' of Europe and the rule of law, and to ensure that member states abide by the agreements reached. Two principal institutions guide the CoE in its work: the Committee of Ministers (which brings together the foreign ministers of member states twice a year) and the Parliamentary Assembly (comprising 301 representatives appointed by national parliaments). While the CoE may not have the broad public profile of the EU, it has nevertheless made some important contributions to social and political life in Europe. Arguably the CoE's most significant contribution was the *European Convention on Human Rights*, signed in Rome on 4 November 1950, which paved the way for the establishment of the European Court of Human Rights, based in Strasbourg, in 1959.

In the case of the EU the substance of European identity has not been the major concern; the main concern has been to foster identification with the EU as a political entity. There is no doubt that in the post-war period those people living within the expanding European Union have come to share aspects of a common existence in a way which has not happened hitherto. Although the 2001 *Governance* White Paper (CEC 2001a) acknowledges that, half a century after the Treaty of Paris formally launched the integration process, many EU citizens do not know the difference between EU institutions, these institutions are nevertheless arguably establishing a *trans*national space. EMU is undoubtedly the most concrete manifestation of the existence of this transnational community, but in other areas too, such as environment and public health, the EU has played a very public role. Thus, while most European citizens may not feel they share a common European culture, as noted above, there is a possibility that as more people become aware of the significance of EU policy the EU will become more of a focus for their concerns and aspirations. The 2001 *Governance* White Paper places considerable emphasis on the need for the EU to connect with organisations outside the formal political sphere in order to give the EU a greater presence in the everyday lives of its citizens. Whether or not the EU will succeed in making stronger connections to the lives of its citizens remains to be seen, but the emphasis on institutions and citizenship at least lays the foundations for a more inclusive idea of 'Europe'.

Further reading

Davies, N. (1997) *Europe. A History*. London: Pimlico.

Delanty, G. (1995) *Inventing Europe*. London: Macmillan.

Leonard, M. (1998) *Making Europe Popular: The Search for a European Identity*. London: Demos.

Shore, C. (2000) *Building Europe. The Cultural Politics of European Integration*. London: Routledge.

Chapter 9

European nation-states

Institutions and integration

Key concepts

- The European model of the nation-state
- The institutions of the European state
- The Common Market develops into the European Union
- European political integration

The nation-state with all its constituent features is itself a European institution, or more accurately a set of institutions. That is, the nation-state emerged from the political development of Europe and, as part of Europe's influence on the rest of the world, became adopted globally. The contemporary world is a world of nation-states, as confirmed by the existence of the United Nations Organisation with its membership comprising virtually all the nation-states of the world, numbering 188 at the time of writing.

Currently we may perceive that Europe's nation-states, each with its own government and administration, are well advanced in the process of coming to terms with the European Union which is an overarching constitutional entity developing its own state-like forms of organisation. Fifteen European states are already members of the European Union and there is what amounts to a queue of prospective members striving to qualify for entry. These are mainly derived from the breakup of Yugoslavia and eastern European states formerly dominated by the Soviet Union.

In view of the history of the European states and the more recent emergence of the European Union, we must look at the development of those long-standing European institutions (i.e. government, administration, law, police, armed forces, etc.) which gave us the Europe of the nation-states. From there we must go on to see how all this is affected by the emergence of pan-European institutions.

The Treaty of Rome in 1957 put European integration into motion with the foundation of the European Economic Community (EEC) which, with greater emphasis on political co-operation, developed during the 1980s into the European Community (EC). Since the early 1990s, however, the concept of European Union (EU) has come into being with the enactment of the Maastricht Treaty in 1991, the Single Market in 1993 and the moves to introduce a single currency, the euro, since 1998.

Nevertheless, the prior existence of European nation-states has of course provided the background to all subsequent developments in Europe. Equally the globalised world, against which the European Union is intended to provide protection for Europeans, was also created by Europeans or people of European origin. It was Europeans who began the globalisation process with their dominance of international trade from the sixteenth century onwards and it was those Europeans who settled across the Atlantic and established the United States of America who have notably contributed to this globalisation process during the twentieth century. Subsequently, it is those Europeans who are most in favour of European integration who see a future United States of Europe as a politico-economic entity capable of matching in all respects the superpower status of the USA.

Antecedents of the modern European nation-state

The arrangements that societies have made for their government and administration are commonly referred to as the state. This implies permanent or at least enduring institutions of government that originally played a significant part in distinguishing a society with a settled urbanised core from a nomadic or semi-nomadic tribal society. The development of the state is taken to be one of the hallmarks of civilisation.

The earliest states were city-states, that is arrangements for government – and also belief system and trade – located within the walls of the city. The walls served not only for protection but also as a barrier to monitor the movement of people and to tax the passage of goods in trade. These are long-term functions of the state.

In the case of Europe, we like to look back to the city-states of ancient Greece as the origins of our political institutions: the polity, democracy, etc. Moving forward far in time many centuries, the city-states of the Italian Renaissance are often linked with these (apart from politics) because of their patronage in the reproduction of many aspects of the classical arts.

There is of course no example of a perfect society in terms of governance and administration, but the significance of principles of citizenship, liberty and democracy is clear in the governance and administration of European societies especially since the nineteenth century. Furthermore, these have become established principles not only for Europe but also for other parts of the world where European influence has been felt and that virtually amounts to the whole world. This applies even though the principles are often discernible in their denial or misuse.

To move directly from classical city-states to the contemporary world would be to miss out other examples of European state-building. There are the medieval sovereign states and the so-called absolutist states of the Reformation in which state power was much more effectively centralised, although still in the name of the king. Put simply, a king who could diminish the power of his nobles and make sure that all the taxes came to him could afford to be more powerful militarily. Effective centralisation of government and administration makes possible the concentration of revenue collection. This provides for the financing of permanent armed forces which assures the continued existence of the state.

It is a circular process of empowerment. States that were successful in doing this have in general survived. In fact, not only have they survived, they have swallowed up the weaker states. It is estimated that the 500 or so states that existed in Europe in 1500 were reduced to only twenty-five by 1900 (Tilly 1975: 12). For instance, Aragon and Castile became Spain under Ferdinand and Isabella during the late fifteenth and early sixteenth centuries. The Bourbon kings, especially Louis XIV, gave the many provinces of France the common national identity that we recognise today. Scotland joined England and Wales as Great Britain by the Act of Union in 1707. These are significant examples but there are of course numerous others involving the subsuming of small kingdoms, principalities, independent cities and other parcels of territory into the borders of nation-states. Not that these borders were necessarily permanent even then, but modern borders are a great deal more permanent than they were in earlier times.

The European state and the onset of modernity

The principles of centralisation in state administration, with its attendant advantages in the concentration of fiscal revenues, are evident in the modern nation-state that with modern bureaucracy has much greater administrative capabilities. The absolutist monarchs used the concentration of revenue to equip their armies and navies with the latest military technology, principally in the form of artillery that enabled their adversaries' defences to be literally blown away. The modern nation-state gained an accepted monopoly of much greater armed force with the industrialisation of weapons production and the application of advanced technology. Moreover, the armed forces of the modern state are accepted as legitimate, while the existence of any other armed force is regarded as criminal or terrorist.

With the transition to modernity the power of the king was removed, to be replaced by that of democratic government, and with this European institutions became transformed into more or less what we see today. Arguably the first really significant and influential example was the English Civil War and the later Glorious Revolution during the seventeenth century. The Civil War was between royalists and parliamentarians and the victory of Parliament was followed by the trial and execution of the king. Nevertheless, after the death of the parliamentary leader Oliver Cromwell, the crown was restored with the reinstatement of the king's son, Charles II. In the longer term this turned out to be only a partial restoration because, with the replacement of the Stuart dynasty by the House of Orange in the Glorious Revolution, the power of Parliament over the king was firmly established by the Bill of Rights in 1689. Even then, though, it was more than a century before a long process of reform began to bring forth the rights of citizenship in law, elections and social welfare which are taken for granted today.

A much more dramatic and even more influential example of the onset of modernity was the American Revolution with the Declaration of Independence in 1776, when those Europeans who had settled in North America decided they had had enough of the rule of kings. These revolutionaries were principally British and they were rebelling against the rule of the Hanoverian dynasty in the person of King George III. The outcome was not just the establishment of the United States of America but of 'the rights of man and the citizen' derived from the writings of Thomas Paine and embodied in the American Constitution. This was the first time that the principles of government of a nation-state had been set out in an all-encompassing legal document. As such it represents the codification of state institutions in a legal-rational form consistent with the spirit of the Enlightenment. Whatever the shortcomings of the American Constitution, full credit has to be given to the attempt to establish government on rational principles, removing permanently government vested in kings, hereditary succession and aristocracy.

A little while after the American Declaration of Independence a similar and just as significant establishment of the rights of the citizen took place with the French Revolution beginning in 1789. In this case not only was the king executed but part of the aristocracy as well and many others connected with them, during the so-called Reign of Terror. The transformation of state institutions was comprehensive, initially to the extent of introducing a new calendar commencing with the Revolution. Even the emergence of Napoleon and his subsequent self-declaration as emperor did not interrupt widespread reform – as, for instance, in a new legal system, the Code Napoléon, and a new education system based upon the state rather than the church.

These three major examples of radical change in European institutions were historically very different and yet all three contributed significantly to the establishment in principle of the familiar organs of the state: elected government, permanent and impartial administration, independent judiciary, backed up by a monopoly of the means of violence embodied in police and armed forces.

It was notably Max Weber who recognised and defined the rational-legal form of authority as it applied to the organisation of the state. He distinguished this from forms of rationality based upon tradition or charismatic leadership. These latter two were of course the characteristics of the state in traditional societies before the onset of modernity. With the Enlightenment had come the desire for explanation based upon science and, in the state, a form of government which avoided both the stasis of tradition and the foibles of rule by kings and their successors. The revolutions described above may therefore be seen as the constitutional equivalents of breakthroughs in scientific explanation of the physical world, as stimulated by the work of Isaac Newton, and of the natural world, by that of Charles Darwin. That is, traditional explanation was giving way to rational explanation. No longer were people content to accept the government they were given. Instead they wanted to play a part in its creation and this was offered by the use of the ballot-box. Along with equality before the law, these are the fundamental principles of citizenship, the recognition of the individual as a legal entity with rights. Only after that comes the pressure for a range of welfare benefits which, writ broadly, encompass health, education and care, especially in old age.

Mass education in particular has been held up as one of the hallmarks of a civilised society, although in fact it is a reciprocal arrangement. The state requires educated citizens in order that they understand what is at stake in elections and government, and that they are able to contribute to the economy of a modern society. Citizens require education in order to be able to participate fully in the institutions of a modern society and to fulfil their duties to the state and to work, including military service when necessary. This is the essence of the social contract as recognised by Jean-Jacques Rousseau. The citizen must contribute to society as well as enjoy its benefits, and education potentiates this. The arrangement is eminently rational in the sense referred to here and in all respects a product of the Enlightenment.

From the perspective of the twenty-first century, the flaws in the contemporary outcome are all too apparent but we should not lose sight of the significance of the state and citizenship in European institutions. Only then can we begin to debate the possibilities for the European Union as it struggles to find a formula for integration, while at the same time to enlarge itself by admitting the growing number of countries which are eager for membership.

Institutions of the modern nation-state

Expressed very simply, the modern nation-state is characterised by a democratically elected government, served by a permanent and impartial administration, upheld by an independent judiciary, backed up by a police force for internal order and armed forces for external defence. In real-life examples there are breaches in the nature of this simple structure of which we are only too aware. The USSR, Nazi Germany and Fascist Italy were all modern states that transgressed into military regimes. In fact, in the late 1930s more European states were authoritarian than liberal democratic. Yet, despite all of this, the remarkable thing is the resilience and ubiquity of the model as an idealised and aspired-to form.

Notional format of the European nation-state

Head of State – an elected president or hereditary monarch.
Government by Elected Assembly – the political party with an outright majority of votes in an election, or else a majority of elected members as in Britain, forms the government. Alternatively a coalition government is formed by arrangement between a number of political parties.
Impartial bureaucracy – a permanent civil service is maintained in the form of a bureaucracy consisting of full-time salaried officials appointed on the basis of aptitude, determined in the first instance by academic qualifications.
Independent judiciary – statutes and laws enacted by the government are upheld and justice is dispensed in courts of law consisting of judges, lawyers and clerks, on the principle that their independence from the other bodies is maintained at all times.
Forces of coercion – the statutes and laws of the state are enforced where necessary by police, while external defence is maintained by armed forces. These two have a 'monopoly of violence' in and for the state and all other use of force is regarded as unlawful.

However, it should not be assumed that there has been a straightforward evolution of the European state from the city-state, through the absolutist state, to the modern nation-state. European institutions developed through centuries of history involving much conflict and struggle, and this means that change did not progress in a neat evolutionary direction. In terms of Enlightenment principles there have been many backward steps. The outcome, however, is the state institutions that we see and recognise today. At present the independent nation-states of Europe are attempting to accommodate these established institutions of government with the emerging political and administrative structure of the European Union. Quite clearly, attitudes towards the progressive development of the European Union vary enormously across Europe and so, in this continuing development, we can expect no simple evolutionary pathway either.

It can be seen that the definition employed here is of state institutions that Europeans have devised for their government and administration, and which are currently in an as yet partial and incomplete process of absorption into the European Union. Moreover, the process may remain incomplete for the foreseeable future. The outcome and the balance of authority between the European Union itself and the nation-states of which it consists is unclear and is likely to remain so. This can only be further complicated by the admission to the EU of those eastern European states that were formerly dominated by the Soviet Union. Given their economic disadvantages, they are now among the most fervent advocates not only of EU membership but of its progressive integration.

The development of European institutions based upon the nation-state is inseparable from the experience of the people who live within Europe. This experience brought forth, as principles, citizenship and citizenship rights and, although even in Europe these have all too often been suppressed in totalitarian states, this only makes the principles more significant. The rights of the individual as citizen should include equality before the law, suffrage and welfare, all vested in the nation-state. Even to exist in the modern world, one needs to be a citizen of a nation-state and, manifestly, the existence of stateless persons is uncomfortable and often hazardous.

For an example of the plight of stateless people we may refer to the Europeans' imposition of their model of the state outside of Europe. This has bestowed uncomplicated citizenship on some people, but others were left out of the process. The Kurds, for instance, now live on the margins of several countries, principally Turkey and Iraq, without state or internationally recognised nationality of their own. The situation came about after the collapse of the Ottoman Empire, at the end of the First World War, when Britain and France took it upon themselves to divide up the so-called 'Arab rectangle' of the Middle East into nation-states based upon the European model. This organised rather amorphous groups of Arabs into nations of Lebanese, Syrians, Iraqis, Jordanians and Palestinians. Ruling dynasties were installed who were sympathetic to the West and its oil interests, but the identity of some groups was conveniently passed over and in particular the Kurds' claim to be a nation in their own right was ignored. As a consequence of this, their very existence has since been at the mercy of the Turkish and Iraqi nation-states which, as recent experience shows, has resulted in their persecution.

The global significance of European state institutions

The division of the Middle East as described above was only a more recent episode in European domination. Much of the world was colonised or else strongly influenced by Europeans during the period after the sixteenth century, with the result that European social, political and economic institutions were implanted. The means used to govern the colonies were the same in principle as those used to govern home societies, but quite clearly colonial citizens of indigenous origin were treated more harshly than home citizens – let alone by comparison with the privileged existence of white settler populations. During the colonial period, despite the inequality and discrimination, European institutions of government became established and reproduced among colonial populations through the medium of education and the use of some indigenous people in colonial administration. The result of this was that these institutions lasted beyond colonialism.

The indigenous political leaders who emerged and strove for constitutional independence in the European colonies during the twentieth century were themselves educated to the European pattern. Many had continued their studies in Europe or North America. They used the familiar forms of political parties and trade unions to further their claims for independence. When independence came the 'emergent nations', as they were at first called, were nations out of the European mould.

They attempted to install democratically elected governments, although many examples subsequently collapsed to be replaced by military coups and dictatorships. Colonial administrations, with the Europeans removed, maintained the role of civil service although many examples became mired in corruption. Legal systems were already modelled on those of the former colonisers, although all too often they broke down in the face of dictatorship and corruption. Police and armed forces were based upon European models but they suffered in the face of the same problems. Expenditure on arms in the former colonies has tended to be greater than on anything else.

The post-colonial state, therefore, has inherited the language, law, education and many other institutions of colonialism. Even countries never actually colonised, such as China, have nevertheless absorbed European institutions. This is the legacy of both the rise and decline of the West. The world now works largely on the basis of European institutions. The United Nations Organisation is, in a sense, the global acceptance of the European model of the nation-state. The World Bank, the International Monetary Fund and the World Trade Organisation are extensions of European banking and trade practices. The International Court of Justice is to all intents and purposes a law court on the European model. It seems that all aspects of international organisation have come to terms with European ways of doing things, but this should not be surprising if we take into account that all were organised by people of European origin and culture.

Ironically, in Europe where this process of nation-state building began, change has come from the need to consolidate in the face of a world that Europe no longer dominates. With the global economy dominated by the USA and Japan, the European nation-states have come to see the advantages of first economic and then, to a lesser extent so far, political union. As a result of this the organisation of a European community of nations, now known as the European Union, has involved to an increasing extent the erosion of the independent, sovereign nation-state. The process of European union, which begins with the move to a coal and steel community in 1951, will be described below.

The emergence of the European Union

Two Frenchmen, Jean Monnet and Robert Schuman, are recognised as setting in motion the concrete proposal for European union. The driving force came with the end of the Second World War when, understandably given the previous six years of destruction, there was a belief that the only reliable guarantee of future peace lay in combining the interests of France and Germany. The original European Coal and Steel Community dated from 1951 and included Belgium, Italy, the Netherlands and Luxembourg as well as France and Germany (then West Germany of course). These same six countries went on to sign the Treaty of Rome in 1957 so forming a customs union, the European Economic Community (EEC). This was often referred to as the Common Market.

The saga of Britain's role is well known. The Conservative governments of the 1950s were against joining and in favour of Imperial Preference, the trading system of the British Empire. However, the Empire was fast transforming itself into the Commonwealth, but the British applications of the 1960s were vetoed by President Charles de Gaulle of France who, it is sometimes suggested, was merely getting revenge for what he perceived as his shabby treatment during the Second World War (although he claimed that it was because Britain would be a disruptive member). It therefore fell to Conservative Prime Minister Edward Heath, a fervent pro-European, to negotiate Britain's admission to the EEC in January 1973, at which point Denmark and Ireland joined too.

The poorer countries of southern Europe took longer to prepare and first had to shed extreme right-wing governments. Greece was admitted in January 1981 and Spain and Portugal in January 1986. Much later, in January 1995, the richer but at first reluctant countries of Austria, Finland and Sweden joined. This left only Norway and Switzerland in western Europe as non-members.

At the beginning of the twenty-first century there is a long list of would-be member countries in the Mediterranean, the Balkans and eastern Europe. They await admission and participation (while Britain still agonises over its membership of a progressively integrating Union). The implications of this impending substantial increase in membership are enormous, and yet the institutions of the present European Union are to date the same in principle as they were when the European Economic Community was formed in 1957.

It is useful to distinguish between 'intergovernmental institutions' – those made up of people from the governments and administrations of member states – and 'supranational institutions' – those made up of people employed by the European Union. This distinction in itself shows up the inherent tension within the European Union as it simultaneously encompasses integration and association.

The intergovernmental institutions

The intergovernmental institutions are councils of ministers of member governments not, it should be made clear, of the European Union itself. Not surprisingly, the most important issues are taken up by a council of prime ministers or their equivalents – this is the *European Council*. It meets twice a year, amidst great preparation in a different European city, and often takes the form of a milestone in the development of union, such as the meeting in Maastricht in 1991. The purpose is to discuss broad issues and form strategic policy, including of course the future form of the European Union itself.

In the case of more specialised issues, other ministers from member state governments meet under the aegis of a *Council of Ministers*. For instance, agricultural issues will be dealt with by a meeting of agriculture ministers, foreign issues by foreign ministers, etc. The most important of these have assumed a permanent existence and there is the Agricultural Council, the Economic and Financial Council and the Foreign Affairs Council, each of which meets monthly.

The ground is prepared for these councils by civil servants and diplomats from member states who meet twice weekly to plan the meetings and prepare agenda and other papers. The councils form the medium by which member state governments maintain their overall control over the European Union. To date the balance of power has remained firmly in favour of member states, with the supranational institutions, described below, maintaining the European Union rather than giving shape to it. The European Council and to a lesser extent the councils of ministers have absolute power within the Union. The principle for this is that, notwithstanding the existence of the European Parliament, the main democratic institutions of Europe at present reside essentially in the electorates of member states and in the existence of member state governments. These therefore maintain precedence over decision-making within the European Union. This will remain so until such a time as the European Parliament assumes a role similar or even equivalent to that of the parliaments of member states.

The supranational institutions

The foremost of the supranational institutions is the *European Commission*. This is a permanent body charged with a largely bureaucratic or civil service type of role but also, significantly, with responsibility for upholding the constituted principles of the European Union as established in the Treaty of Rome and the subsequent treaties of extension and amendment.

The European Commission is made up of commissioners who are appointed by the governments of member states. Every member state has at least one commissioner, and the larger states of France, Italy, Germany, Spain and the UK each has two, although at the time of writing this advantage is under review – especially in the face of enlargement.

The Commission has a president who is selected through a process of bargaining in the European Council. The president then has to work with the appointed commissioners and an important factor here is that it is the prerogative of member states to maintain or replace their commissioners at any time, without any reference necessarily to the president. This is another facet of the tension between supranational and intergovernmental influences. However, the president does have the responsibility for assigning roles to the commissioners.

An indicator of the practical role played by commissioners is provided in those occasions when the governments of member states have come to regard 'their' commissioners, the commissioners appointed by them, as 'going native'. That is, commissioners have appeared to be operating in the interests of the EU rather than those of the member state. There have been several instances of this and it demonstrates yet another aspect of EU–member state conflict.

The history and status of the European Commission has been mixed, and this has most often depended upon the personality and capabilities of its president. The political leaders of member states have sometimes worked strongly against the Commission, particularly in the face of progressive European integration. The first president of the original High Commission of the European Coal and Steel Community was Jean Monnet, truly a visionary of European union. His term (1952 to 1955) was, as might be expected, extremely influential and he left it only to establish the Action Committee for the United States of Europe. Later, during the 1960s, President Charles de Gaulle of France worked strongly against the power of the president of, by then, the Commission of the European Economic Community. Later on, during the 1980s, there was a series of strong presidents, but in 1988 Margaret Thatcher made her Bruges speech in which she retaliated against the integrative tendencies of one such progressive, Jacques Delors.

More damaging still, during the 1990s and particularly the latter part of that decade, the Commission became mired in corruption scandals to the extent that in the end almost the entire Commission was made to resign *en masse*. Significantly, however, it was the European Parliament rather than member states that brought this about, and this has therefore to be recognised as an important indicator of its increasing role. There is now an anti-corruption commissioner! This nevertheless harmed the cause of European integration immeasurably and yet the reconstituted Commission is still charged with implementing the principles of the Treaty of Rome and successive treaties and declarations, principally the Single European Act of 1985 and the Treaty on European Union of 1992.

The second supranational institution is the *European Parliament*. Initially, this was merely an assembly comprising parliamentary representatives of political parties in member states. Direct elections did not come until as late as 1979, and even now there are different methods of election in different countries – although convergence is planned. As with the Commission, the larger countries have more representation, and since reunification Germany has more than any other in recognition of its larger population. The precise numbers of MEPs in relation to the different sizes of member country populations have become almost a permanent item on the political agenda of the European Union.

Since the establishment of direct elections the European Parliament has been able to establish itself more powerfully as a component of EU government. It can now more convincingly claim to have influenced decision-making and policy formation when before there was really little evidence of this. It has produced two major party groupings: the Socialist Group, which has been consistently the largest, and the centre-right European People's Party (Christian Democrat/Conservative). These are derived from the political alignments of member states but it can also be claimed that a European party system is developing with transnational policies and programmes – not only astride the traditional left–right divide but also in the form of the 'Rainbow Alliance' which consists of 'green' and other alternative positions.

During 2001 the German government put forward proposals for a properly constituted and empowered European Parliament to take over the role of the European Council. This was widely interpreted as a potentially significant step in the direction of an at least partially federal Europe, with a properly functioning democratic government drawn from across member states. The proposal was immediately opposed by Britain and a little later by France, but there can be no doubt that it remains upon the agenda.

The third supranational institution is the *European Court of Justice*. This is a court operating along familiar lines whose judges are appointed from member states, one from each state for a term of six years. There is also a smaller number of advocates general who have a subsidiary role. It is a constitutional court in that it upholds the principles of those treaties that have formed the European Union and also the laws which have been enacted by it. Its business is largely focused on transgressions of treaties and laws and may take a number of forms including actions by the Commission against member states or by one member state against another. Individual citizens or groups of citizens may apply to the court, especially under the terms of the European Convention on Human Rights, although this is being gradually absorbed into the legal systems of member states, leaving the European Court as the ultimate court of appeal.

In some ways the current weakness of the European Parliament and the strength of the Council only reflects the imbalances of the cabinet–assembly relationship in the governments of member states. However, one thing which must be emphasised is that the European Parliament and the parliaments of member states are quite separate entities, as are the European Commission and the civil services of member states, while by contrast it is the ministers of member state governments who make up the European Council. This may be illustrated thus:

Member state governments		*European Union*
Prime ministers	$\longrightarrow$	European Council
Ministers	$\longrightarrow$	Councils of ministers
Parliament	$\longleftrightarrow$	European Parliament
Civil service	$\longleftrightarrow$	European Commission

The strategic decision-making of the European Union is currently carried out by ministers of member state governments and this is taken to reflect the democracies of those member states. Decisions are then drawn up into policy documents by the Commission that must put detailed proposals before the European Parliament for approval. These are the basic principles, although, of course, in practice the system is more complicated and it is the less visible or even invisible workings that tend to cause suspicions about the so-called 'rule from Brussels'. However, far from the 'alien bureaucracy' often portrayed, especially by the British, the EU administration is in fact drawn from all member states and, at the highest level, Britain has two commissioners.

European integration

With the Maastricht Treaty of 1992, the Single Market of 1993 and foundation of the single currency in 2002, there can be no doubt that the intention of the most pro-European politicians is political as well as economic union. The outcome of existing developments will take the European Union of the nation-states towards a European federation. Allowing for variation in the use of terms, this may be seen as a 'federated Europe' with the nation-states merely further integrated or else a 'federal Europe' which to all intents and purposes would be a single political entity. The goal of some is an outright United States of Europe, a politico-economic state that would be larger and potentially more powerful than the United States of America.

The European Union is often taken to be a threat to the integrity of the nation-state. Indeed it is, but that is not necessarily the same thing as a threat to the rights and freedoms of the people who make up the nation-state. When all is said and done the nation-state is merely a contrived arrangement for the government of the people who inhabit a bounded territory. It was the development of the nation-state that brought fixed territorial boundaries – state borders – in contrast to previous political arrangements, notably military empires, that had frontiers which fluctuated with the success or failure of virtually constant military campaigns. It is not unknown for the borders of nation-states to change, but this is not the norm.

Borders between states set apart specific populations but these may or may not have in common straightforward ethnic identity or cultural heritage. This is because the nation-state is essentially an administrative device and in few cases does it coincide with a single undisputed nation. Once fixed, the border contains the people who live within it and they are encouraged, and in some cases enforced, to recognise a particular nationality – that of the nation-state. On the other hand, the many political struggles over split nationality, as in Belgium or Northern Ireland, or over peripheral nationality, as in the Basque region of Spain or Northern Ireland again, serve to draw our attention to the contrived nature of the nation-state and the particular form of nationality which it propagates.

In contrast to the singular nature of the unitary nation-state, the federal form can produce tiers of government and administration which may bring decision-making over many matters closer to the people. In the case of the USA, as well as the federal government there are the state governments with different approaches to many issues. The more sensational instances of these differences are those states that have retained or revived the death penalty for murder, or the few with restrictions over the consumption or even the prohibition of alcohol. These are examples which come immediately to mind but there are many other distinctions which have appeal to the people who live in particular states within the federation. In the European Union there is the case of the German *Länder* and their differing approaches, for instance, to agriculture, which have emerged in relation to the Common Agricultural Policy or, more recently, to the prohibition of British beef in the face of BSE ('mad cow disease').

There is another factor in relation to peripherality in the nation-state that has a bearing on the probable future of the European Union. There are those instances in which the European Union, as an overarching political entity, has offered finance to peripheral regions of Europe over and above that already provided by their governments. The EU symbol is exhibited on many civil engineering and other developments which it has financed in part if not in total. In effect, therefore, the European Union has already demonstrated that it can offer benefits at a number of levels across Europe regardless of nation-states or their governments.

In fact, if national sovereignty is considered to be largely an emotive issue, the real benefits which the European Union may be able to confer could be considered as much more important. In the case of Britain and the possible introduction of the euro, for instance, the significance which is attached to retaining the Queen's head on sterling currency banknotes may prove to be quite shallow when considered in the context of what precise advantages an independent pound may provide in the future for the people who use it and depend upon it. In fact the strong pound, at the time of writing, has serious disadvantages because the price of exports is too high and jobs are being lost as a result of British industry's inability to compete in international markets. If the living standards of people rather than a form of national pride are taken to be paramount, then support for the pound may be swept away in favour of the euro. The Queen's head may be a potent national symbol but it does little for Britain's GDP per capita, which over the second half of the twentieth century declined in relation to that of its European partners.

In many respects there can be little doubt that the size and strength of a fully integrated Europe, in whatever form that takes, would protect the interests of the people of Europe and their standard of living in a progressively globalising world with a highly competitive global economy. The European Union is one part of what has been described as the 'global triad', the other two parts being North America and Japan. In terms of trade, North America is now NAFTA – the North American Free Trade Area that already includes Canada and Mexico and may admit some

South American countries in the near future. In East Asia there is ASEAN, the Association of South East Asian Nations, but a future trade alliance may contain or, according to some observers, even be led by China. Already there are many cross-national commercial and industrial partnerships within China's 'special development areas' and even beyond. Alternatively, there is the projected Asia-Pacific or Pacific Rim grouping that could link East Asian countries with Australasia and the West Coast of the USA. Already there are annual conferences that are considered important enough to be attended in person by the President of the United States.

In this scheme of things the existing European Union, plus those several countries from the Mediterranean and eastern Europe which are regarded as the next wave of entrants, would become the largest economic entity for the foreseeable future, although of course China would still make any East Asian alliance the largest conglomeration of people. In fact China would, if translated into consumer society on the scale of the West, be the largest market in the world with all that this implies for economic expansion and the balance of economic power. It is this kind of scenario that lends much weight to the argument for an integrated European Union.

Summary

- The modern nation-state is a development of European (Western) civilisation which contrasts with the imperial hierarchies of the other major civilisations.
- With the onset of modernity, revolutions within European nation-states (including the American Declaration of Independence) gave rise to the familiar modern form of state involving elected government, permanent administration, independent judiciary and a 'monopoly of violence' on the part of police and armed forces.
- Through colonialism and associated cultural influences the European state system was carried virtually unchanged into the global arena, as confirmed by the existence of the United Nations Organisation.
- The European Union is a unique attempt at transcending the interests of individual nation-states in favour of collective interests.
- European integration involves the development of political community alongside existing economic community.

Further reading

Arter, D. (1993) *The Politics of European Integration in the Twentieth Century.* Aldershot: Dartmouth.

Holland, M. (1993) *European Integration. From Community to Union.* London: Pinter.

Smith, D. and Wright, S. (eds) (1999) *Whose Europe? The Turn Towards Democracy.* Oxford: Blackwell/The Sociological Review.

Wistrich, E. (1994) *The United States of Europe.* London: Routledge.

The enlargement of the European Union

Key concepts

- Candidate countries
- Common Agricultural Policy
- Structural funds
- Treaty of Nice

Introduction

The enlargement of the European Union (EU) from its present fifteen members has a certain populist ideology in terms of 'back to Europe' or a 'return to Europe' for many of those states that were either satellites or actually part of the former Soviet Union. The dramatic events in eastern Europe over a decade ago almost immediately made many of the newly independent states cast their gaze westwards and to the EU in particular, since the EU represented all that these states hoped to achieve with their new-found liberty – stable democracy, economic prosperity, a powerful international voice – and so the long process of seeking membership of the EU commenced with the latter itself welcoming the advances.

This chapter traces this process of application and the EU's responses and subsequent negotiations to the present day and beyond. It also examines the EU itself, already institutionally creaking from the last enlargement in 1995, and identifies the key problem areas where reform of present arrangements would appear essential in order to accommodate to the new candidate states. These states are, of course, different in many respects from former new members, particularly in terms of their low economic base. The likely impact of this on present budgetary and political policies is also detailed. Coupled with this has to be an explanation of how national identity and self-interest among existing EU members has influenced and might in future influence attitudes and practices towards enlargement.

Enlargement to date

Since the original Treaty of Rome in 1957 enlargement has been a constant theme of European politics and economics. The possibility, indeed the expectation, of enlargement was there from the beginning and that position has been reiterated ever since. The Treaty on European Union in 1992, for example, clearly states that 'Any European State may apply to become a member of the Union'. The 1957 Treaty created a union of six member countries and since then there have been four successive waves of enlargement:

1   1973 – the entry of the UK, Ireland and Denmark;
2   1981 – the accession of Greece;
3   1986 – the joining of Portugal and Spain;
4   1995 – the accession of Austria, Finland and Sweden.

Other negotiations took place over that period resulting, for example, in the acceptance of Norway in 1975 and in 1995 – on both occasions the electorate rejected membership. Similarly, the negotiations started with Switzerland in 1992 were halted following a referendum, and Iceland abandoned its negotiations after an approach in 1973 on the grounds that its economic interests in particular were best served outside the Union.[1]

There has thus been no shortage of applicants to join, even from the early days, though this is not reflected in the long period between 1957 and the first enlargement wave in 1973. As Croft *et al.* (1999: 58) point out, 'the process of economic integration within the EU had barely begun before it was being courted by prospective new members'. In spite of its reputation as a reluctant European, even the UK was one of these prospective new members when it formally applied for membership in 1961. It was clear to the UK and other prospective members as far back as the early 1960s that membership brought with it a range of improved economic prospects. This perception became even clearer as the decade moved on, as can be seen from the UK's second attempt to accede in 1967. Economically, the original six members seemed to be forging ahead of other European countries outside of the Treaty. Arguably, because the applicants that were successful in 1973 themselves had strong economic ties between themselves, for one to join it became almost necessary for all three to join simultaneously. This was particularly the case with Ireland. In other words, the idea of a grand vision of a united Europe could well have been secondary to the obvious economic benefits of not lagging behind.

While economics were the main driving force of the first wave, politics came much more to the fore in the second and third waves involving the Mediterranean countries. Each of the countries were recent democracies after periods of fascist or authoritarian rule. The Nine, as they were then, were very sympathetic to these countries, recognising the periods of stagnation and repression each had experienced, and demonstrating a genuine desire to help them on the road to democracy. In this sense, there was a political will rather than a desire to embrace the countries for the added-value economic strength their membership would bring. Clearly it would not and did not. Within member countries there was strong resistance, especially from the farming lobbies which recognised the economic cost of the potential Mediterranean membership. This actually explains the five-year gap between Greece's accession and that of both Portugal and Spain. The latter two countries' membership was strongly objected to by Italian and French farmers in a vociferous and highly active way.

In the most recent wave of enlargement, the actual negotiation period was much shorter but no less difficult than previous waves. Switzerland did not proceed with its negotiations after a referendum demonstrated rejection of membership of the European Economic Area (EEA), and, as indicated above, the Norwegian population rejected membership.

In terms of national identity this brief history of previous enlargements shows that the EU itself has little interest in individual identities. Identity has been an eligibility deliberation in cases where there has been some question of whether or not a country is European (e.g. Turkey and Morocco). The EU's own identity and its economic and political interests come into play during pre-accession negotiations. Yet individual members can be highly protective of their own national interests and identity as, for example, in the attitude of France to the UK's application when the former's veto effectively prevented the UK application going forward for further consideration.

Equally, the first forty years after the original Treaty have shown that national economic policies have been highly influential in determining whether a member does advance economically according to the original intention of membership. Ireland, for example, has forged ahead as a result of the EU economic aid *and* its domestic economic policies whereas Greece has not.

All new members have imposed on them the 80,000 pages and thirty-one chapters of the *acquis communautaire* which is, in effect, a set of principles that members are expected to abide by. They include the laws, policies and practices of the EU together with laid-down objectives and obligations. Furthermore, all the Treaties, laws and judgments of the European Court of Justice and all the ultimate goals (*finalités politiques*) have to be adopted by all member countries. In this sense the EU imposes these upon new members even though they have not been party to their enactment.

Present enlargement proposals

Membership negotiations took place with Turkey from 1987 and Cyprus and Malta since 1990 with varying degrees of success. Malta froze its membership application in 1996 but reopened it in 1998. The major post-1994 negotiations have been with a number of former Soviet bloc central and east European countries (CEECs). During 1994/1995 applications for membership were received from Bulgaria, the Czech Republic, Estonia, Hungary, Latvia, Lithuania, Poland, Romania, Slovakia and Slovenia. This was an unprecedented number of applications for membership that, if successful, would increase the size of the EU from fifteen to twenty-five, would increase the geographical area of the Union by 34 per cent, and would generate a population increase of 105 million. While this in itself is unique, it needs to be recognised that previous accessions have meant that new members had to adapt to the EU by adopting and accepting the entire *acquis communautaire*; the post-1995 applications suggest a change in emphasis with the EU itself having to adapt in order to accommodate to the countries likely to gain admission. A much larger Union would necessarily involve the EU having to prepare itself for this expansion in the same way that individual applicants have themselves to prepare and adapt both in the past and today. There is, of course, no question of all the above ten countries joining the EU at the same time; indeed, the process could take anything up to twenty years for full accession, as discussed below.

Following the initial approaches from the ten countries, in 1997 the Commission published its 'Opinions' (*avis*) on each CEEC country alongside a statement on policy intentions entitled *Agenda 2000*. The latter is a major policy statement because it covers not only the enlargement process but also how reforms might take place affecting the Common Agricultural Policy (CAP), the Structural and Cohesion Funds and the whole way in which the EU might be financed in the future; in other words, evidence of the EU adapting in ways it has never previously countenanced.

Agenda 2000 recommended that only five of the ten CEEC applicants should go forward for accession negotiations in the first instance. These were Hungary, Poland, the Czech Republic, Slovenia and Estonia. The other five's applications were not ruled out completely but they were told that membership might eventually be considered after satisfying certain conditions on both economic and political matters. The five 'first wave' candidates from the CEECs were also joined by Cyprus and Malta. The actual statement in *Agenda 2000* reads as follows:

> Concerning the countries of Central and Eastern Europe . . . The Commission considers that none of them fully satisfy all the criteria at the present time. However, nine countries satisfy the political conditions,[2] while certain countries

have made sufficient progress towards satisfying the economic conditions and those related to the other obligations of membership.

In the light of its analysis, and in accordance with their respective merits, the Commission considers that Hungary, Poland, Estonia, the Czech Republic and Slovenia could be in a position to satisfy all the conditions of membership in the medium term if they maintain and strongly sustain their efforts of preparation.

(EC Cons Doc 9984/97, Vol 1, Part Two (VII))

The recommendations were adopted in December 1997 by the Luxembourg European Council. At this time the Council also reaffirmed Turkey's eligibility for membership at some point in the future but its deficient economic and political indices ruled it out of the two waves of membership envisaged for the ten CEECs.

The position changed, however, as a result of the deliberations of the EU Helsinki Summit in December 1999. The rather dramatic diplomatic manoeuvring at the Summit led to Turkey achieving candidate status for membership, even though talks will not start for some years because of the poor Turkish record on political and human rights behaviour coupled with the territorial disputes with Greece in the Aegean and, of course, the unresolved problem over Cyprus. The December 1999 Summit also agreed to invite six new countries – Bulgaria, Latvia, Lithuania, Malta, Romania and Slovakia – to start accession negotiations in 2000.

It can now be seen what a lengthy, and at times a tortuous, process has to be undergone. Even if the Council of Ministers accepts an application in *prima facie* form, the Council may later reject an application (the case of Morocco comes to mind) and in the case of the CEECs an *avis* has been sought from the Commission on each application. The *avis* is clearly crucial since the Council normally accepts the Commission's advice.

The criteria for membership that have been identified by the European Council are those concluded at the European Council Meetings in Copenhagen in June 1993. The Copenhagen criteria actually go beyond the *acquis communautaire* and, indeed, the actual *acquis* has expanded since the last wave of enlargement in 1995 since it now includes the Maastricht Treaty (the Treaty on European Union or TEU) covering, *inter alia*, a wide raft of security policies and co-operation in matters of justice and home affairs. Furthermore, new objectives have been added relating to economic, political and monetary union. More recently, as discussed below, the Treaty of Nice has introduced further changes. Clearly, the conditions for joining have become more stringent with an obvious increase in the number and the size of the hurdles to overcome.

Agenda 2000 put forward a 'Reinforced Pre-Accession Strategy' (SPAR) directed to all the CEECs which had made application, regardless of whether they were deemed ready for the 'first wave' or not. The Strategy seeks to work in partnership with the CEECs in developing a clear programme for satisfying the Commission's demands. Thus, the individual *avis* on each of the applications identified specific problems, and SPAR seeks ways to overcome these problems. There is also some financial assistance in the pre-accession period, largely disbursed through the PHARE programme. *Agenda 2000* recommended a PHARE budget of €1.5 billion a year (at 1997 prices). In addition, the intention was to provide agricultural development aid

Presidency Conclusions, Copenhagen European Council, June 1993

Accession will take place as soon as an associated country is able to assume the obligations of membership by satisfying the economic and political conditions required. Membership requires:

- that the candidate country has achieved stability of institutions guaranteeing democracy, the rule of law, human rights and respect for and protection of minorities;
- the existence of a functioning market economy, as well as the capacity to cope with competitive pressure and market forces within the Union;
- membership presupposes the candidate's ability to take on the obligations of membership including adherence to the aims of political, economic and monetary union.

The Union's capacity to absorb new members, while maintaining the momentum of European integration, is also an important consideration in the general interest of both the Union and the candidate countries.

(€500 million a year) and structural aid of €1 billion. Other financial assistance for the CEECs includes the opportunities for them to participate in certain education, training and research programmes, help in harmonising their legislation in line with Community law, and assistance with 'institution-building' in areas such as law, customs, public accounts, environment, telecommunications and energy.

Taking 1999 prices, the Commission has now agreed to provide a total of €79.9 billion for the CEECs between 2000 and 2006. 'This amount represents about 11% of the total payments throughout the period 2000 to 2006 or just over twice the amount that the Commission expects to spend on administration. Of this €79.9 billion, €61.8 billion will be transferred to the new members, leaving €18.1 billion to the other applicants' (House of Commons 1998: 5).

The economics of enlargement

At the time of writing the most significant differences between the present EU membership of fifteen and the ten CEECs being considered for membership are between GDP per capita and the proportional size of the agricultural workforce. Thus, if the EU15 GDP per capita is rated at 100 then the equivalent for CEEC10 is a mere 30. Indeed, even if the poorest four EU countries' GDP per capita is taken this is nevertheless double that of CEEC10. 'The problems of absorbing the CEEC10 into the EU can be indicated by considering that even with an average growth of 2.5% among the EU15 and 4% among applicant countries, it would take about 25 years for the latter to achieve 50% of the 15's average GDP per head' (House of Commons 1998: 9).

Taking only the five CEECs selected for the first wave of future enlargement there would be dramatic effects on geographical area, population and GDP as

Table 10.1 Impact of successive enlargements of the EU

1995 data	Increase in area (%)	Increase in population (%)	Increase in total GDP (%)	Change in per capita GDP (%)	Average per capita GDP (EUR6=100)
EU9/EU6	31	32	29	−3	97
EU12/EU9	48	22	15	−6	91
EU15/EU12	43	11	8	−3	89
EU20/EU15	**17**	**17**	**6**	**−9**	**81**
EU26/EU15	34	29	9	−16	75

Source: Agenda 2000, COM(97) Volume II

indicated in Table 10.1. Clearly, the effects of the five first wave candidates are considerably less than if all ten CEECs were to be admitted simultaneously.

In spite of the obvious difficulties indicated by the above, the Commission remains fairly optimistic about the position. The Impact Study produced as part of the *Agenda 2000* report certainly suggests this:

> Economic benefits from enlargement are expected to follow from the expansion of the Single Market, from the overall integration process, as well as from the strengthening of the Union's position in global markets. The Union's human potential will be considerably enriched, not least in qualified and highly qualified labour. Acceding countries have significant natural resources (agricultural land, some minerals, biodiversity, etc). Their geographic position will be an asset with respect to transport, energy transit and communications. The integration of these countries into the Union will be a powerful stimulus to their economic development. Major investments related to the radical modernisation of the acceding countries' economies and their catching up with EU living standards will boost demand across the Union and strengthen competitiveness.
>
> (Impact Study (COM (97) 2000 Vol II: 97))

Such optimism is, however, not universally felt across the EU largely because the effect of the accession of the CEECs will be differentially felt from one country to another. *Agenda 2000* makes the assumption that the increased spending which would be required would come, in part, from growth within the EU and from revenue from the newly admitted countries themselves. The question is whether the predicted growth rate of 2.5 per cent p.a. for existing members and 4 per cent for new members is realistic. The other source of extra money would come from reforms of the Common Agricultural Policy (CAP) and of the Cohesion and Structural Funds (CSF). The latter are addressed below. The worry for many countries is that if the predicted growth rate fails to materialise then existing members may be called upon to find the extra funding.

In a sense, the problem is not a new one. The UK complained, as long ago as 1984, about its net contribution to the EU budget, and has secured an annual rebate based upon a complicated formula. More recently, the disquiet has spread to Germany, France, the Netherlands, Sweden and Italy. The case of Germany is particularly interesting since it is the largest net contributor to the EU budget – providing a staggering 60 per cent of net contributions. In each case, the main concern lies with the operation of the CAP and in each case there have been calls for the reform of the policy.

As might be expected, of course, those countries benefiting most from the present financial arrangements are the ones least wanting any kind of reform. Greece, Portugal and Spain are thus the most vocal in this respect alongside Ireland and Belgium. The opposition took a dramatic turn in the debate over the 1997 budget where proposals were made to reduce the budgets of both the CAP and CSF. Greece, Portugal, Ireland and Spain were vehemently opposed to cuts in the Objective 1 budget and Italy joined the opposition because of its objections to cuts in agricultural subsidies. This blocking minority won the day with the outcome that Objective 1 funds were not cut.

The importance of the CAP and CSF to the debate over enlargement may be seen from the fact that they consume 46 per cent and 35 per cent respectively of the total EU budget – over 80 per cent of the total. It is to these two core features that the chapter now turns.

The Common Agricultural Policy

The financial implications of extending the CAP to the new CEEC members cannot be emphasised enough, given as indicated above that the Policy consumes nearly half of the Union's budget and cost almost €40 billion in 1999. As Table 10.2 shows,

Table 10.2 Relative importance of agriculture in CEEC10 and EU15, 1995

	Agricultural production (as % of GDP)	Employment in agriculture (as % of total)
Czech Republic	5.2	6.3
Hungary	6.2	8.0
Poland	7.6	26.9
Slovakia	6.3	9.7
Slovenia	5.0	7.1
Bulgaria	13.9	23.2
Romania	20.5	34.4
Estonia	8.1	13.1
Latvia	9.9	18.5
Lithuania	9.3	23.8
CEEC10 total	8.6	22.5
EU15 total	2.4	5.3

Source: CEC (1997, Vol. II: 68)

agriculture is a far more significant feature of the economies of the CEECs and is certainly less efficient than is found in EU countries.

Within the CEECs, as shown in Table 10.2, there are major differences in the importance of agriculture, with Poland and Romania having very large agricultural sectors compared to the *relatively* smaller proportions to be found in the Czech Republic and Slovenia.

Another key fact not shown by the above figures is that the market conditions in the CEECs are very different from those prevailing in EU15. For example, prices are between 40 and 80 per cent of those in EU countries, partly because of the high support prices in the EU and partly because of lower quality in the CEECs. Furthermore, efficiency levels are considerably lower and all CEECs (with the exception of Hungary) are net importers of EU food.

> The Common Agricultural Policy has been moderately successful in its aims of protecting European agriculture as well as developing it. The set prices and subsidies do appear to engage with deficiencies in the market as well as overcoming instability. But alongside this are the problems of the CAP's increasing cost, the fact that it distorts the market and the contentious issue of over-production. Attempts at reform have been made over the years (for example, in 1970 the CAP consumed over 80 per cent of the community budget) but over the past thirty years the costs of the CAP have grown over eightfold. It is estimated that if the five 'first wave' countries were to accede to the EU with no change in the current CAP then double the present amount would have to be spent on the CAP. The actual annual figure is probably about €30–35 billion. The Commission has suggested, in the first instance, that there should be a reduction in basic support prices for beef, milk and cereals. This would be followed by other products such as olive oil and wine.

What should not be forgotten is the strength of the farming lobby in all EU15 countries. For example, although Germany is expressing increased concern over its net contribution to the EU budget, the German agricultural lobby argues that no reform of the CAP should take place. In this sense, when (not if) change does occur it will not be overnight and is most likely to come about as a consequence of external factors such as the need to reduce export subsidies as a result of pressure from the World Trade Organisation (WTO).

Cohesion and Structural Funds

The basic aim of the CSF has been to try to produce a degree of economic harmonisation across EU member states. In this sense, the less developed countries have always benefited at the expense of the more economically prosperous. The budget of the Cohesion Fund stands at around €2 billion, while that of the structural funds is about €11 billion. The latter cover a broad range of projects including halting industrial decline, high unemployment, education and training, rural areas and the like. The Structural Funds are separated into regional policy objectives (the most recent, covering areas of low population density, having been introduced as an inducement for Sweden and Finland) with Objective 1 (regions having per capita GDP below 75 per cent of the EU average) swallowing up 70 per cent of the total allocation. In this way, the allocation of funds is highly selective and generally favours poorer and smaller countries. The Cohesion Fund is far more selective in that to qualify under existing arrangements member countries need to have a GDP per head of less than 90 per cent of the EU average, which has tended to restrict its allocation to Greece, Portugal, Spain and Ireland.

As far as enlargement is concerned, *Agenda 2000* suggested that only a small addition to the CSF would be needed (though with the proposal that there should be a ceiling of 4 per cent of GNP on Structural Funds receipts). If that were to be the case then the allocations would be spread much more thinly than at present with EU15 since the CEECs – under existing arrangements – would all qualify for Objective 1 and Cohesion Fund money. In this way many of those regions and, indeed, countries presently benefiting from CSF would lose a considerable amount of their entitlement. In all probability regions such as Northern Ireland, eastern Germany and the whole of Belgium would lose out completely. In these circumstances there is every reason to suspect that any proposed reforms of the current CSF system would be likely to meet with considerable opposition. The effect, then, on fundamental European principles such as solidarity and cohesion is likely to be immense and very divisive.

Institutional reform

Much of the above suggests that if enlargement does go ahead – even if with only five new members – the EU's institutions will themselves have to change. The last enlargement to fifteen members produced strains in the EU's institutions; the peculiar problems that the CEECs would bring with them could strain the institutions to breaking-point. This is not a new observation. There is widespread acceptance that things need to change, that reforms have to be made and that there must be a willingness on the part of existing member countries to expedite change. Where there is not acceptance is in deciding what kinds of changes need to be made, how fundamental they should be and when they should be introduced. The Amsterdam IGC of 1997 opened the debate on such matters but resolved nothing. It was left to the culmination of the IGC at the Nice Summit in December 2000 to arrive at resolutions.

The Treaty of Nice

Discussions in Nice and the consequent Treaty of Nice were very much concentrated on ways in which the enlargement of the EU could be accommodated. Indeed, the IGC was primarily confronted with the problem of how to make improvements to the institutional framework in order to ensure that an almost doubling of member states did not cause the administrative apparatus to grind to a halt. At the end of the negotiations the host – President Chirac – talked of the Summit and the Treaty being a huge success. Similarly, the Commissioner for Enlargement – Günter Verheugen

– referred in a speech in Brussels (January 2001) to the previous year having been 'an excellent year for the whole enlargement project . . . we have achieved every one of the ambitious goals that we set for ourselves'. Yet there is increasing evidence that such jubilation was possibly hyperbole. The debate was not so much about the principle of enlargement as about the consequences of enlargement for power relations within Europe and the relative influence each country might have.

The actual Treaty was agreed at the Nice Summit in December 2000 and formally signed by the Heads of State or Government in February 2001. Following the signing, a lengthy period involving ratification by each member state has to follow. In all but one case ratification is undertaken by national parliaments but in the case of Ireland ratification has to be by popular referendum. The ratification referendum in Ireland took place in June 2001 with the unexpected rejection of the Treaty by a clear majority, albeit on a low turnout of 34 per cent. This result generated confusion in Brussels since the Treaty can only become law if all fifteen member states ratify it. Thus, for the Treaty to become law there will need to be a second referendum. In the meantime, negotiations with candidate countries continue in the expectation that the original Irish vote will eventually be overturned.

The main changes in the Treaty

1   The issue of *majority voting* and the avoidance of national vetoes was central. Until now smaller countries had more votes than their populations would suggest at the Council of Ministers. Following Nice, the weighting of votes has shifted to the advantage of the larger countries (and to the chagrin of the smaller countries) as shown in Table 10.3. The actual system agreed upon is, however, extremely complex and applies to decision-making on thirty articles that currently require unanimity. As from January 2005, different countries will have different numbers of votes; in order for there to be a 'qualified majority' 74.6 per cent of the total must be achieved. Thus, three of the larger countries along with one of the smaller ones could actually block a qualified majority. In addition, in the enlarged EU, a decision will only be accepted if it has the support from countries totalling at least 62 per cent of the total population. A blocking minority could be easily established, especially if Germany were to be involved with any other two countries. The voting arrangements in the Treaty of Nice clearly represent a power shift towards the larger states and to Germany in particular.

2   *The role of the Commission* had to be addressed by the Treaty because it would have increased almost fourfold under current arrangements with the accession of the twelve countries seeking membership. The Treaty lays down that the Commission will, from 2005, comprise simply one member from each member state up to a maximum size of twenty-seven member states. Should there be more than twenty-seven member states then a rotation system will operate in the interests of fairness.

3   For the *European Parliament*, the Treaty of Nice decrees a maximum of 732 MEPs and has determined the seat allocation based on a population formula so that, for example, the largest country (Germany) will have ninety-nine seats and the smallest (Malta) just five seats.

Table 10.3 Existing and proposed voting allocation in the Council of Ministers

| | Council of Ministers voting allocation | | |
	Current	New	Population (million)
Germany	10	29	82.0
UK	10	29	59.2
France	10	29	59.0
Italy	10	29	57.6
Spain	8	27	39.4
Netherlands	5	13	15.8
Greece	5	12	10.5
Belgium	5	12	10.2
Portugal	5	12	10.0
Sweden	4	10	8.9
Austria	4	10	8.1
Denmark	3	7	5.3
Finland	3	7	5.2
Ireland	3	7	3.7
Luxembourg	2	4	0.4
Total	**87**	**237**	**375.3**
Candidate countries*			
Poland	8	27	38.7
Romania	6	14	22.5
Czech Republic	5	12	10.3
Hungary	5	12	10.1
Bulgaria	4	10	8.2
Slovakia	3	7	5.4
Lithuania	3	7	3.7
Latvia	3	4	2.4
Slovenia	3	4	2.0
Estonia	3	4	1.4
Cyprus	2	4	0.8
Malta	2	3	0.4
Total	**134**	**345**	**481.2**

Note: *Figures presented as if the country were an EU member

Source: Council of the European Union 2001

4 Other changes relate to the Court of Justice (maintaining one judge per country but allowing the Grand Chamber to meet with just thirteen judges rather than all), the Court of Auditors (qualified majority voting rather than unanimous decision-making as at present), the Economic and Social Committee and the Committee of the Regions (in both these latter cases membership will be

limited to 350 members). In addition, with regard to respect for fundamental rights, the Treaty of Nice enables the Council with a four-fifths majority to address and penalise a member state where violation of rights and/or freedoms occurs.

The Treaty of Nice therefore does address many of the issues that the IGC was charged with addressing, and does offer some opportunities for smoother administrative arrangements should enlargement occur. Although supporting statements were made about the dates when the first wave of new members might be admitted (repeated at the Gothenberg Summit in June 2001), the statements have all been rather vague. Although serious negotiations have been continuing since 1998, there is still no firm date by which accession may occur, although entry for the first 'wave' could be by early 2003. However, target dates almost invariably slip, perhaps making 2004 more realistic. Interestingly, the Gothenberg Summit expressed a wish to see the first 'wave' enter in time to participate in the next European elections in June 2004, a view reiterated more recently by Romano Prodi in November 2001.

As indicated above, all thirty-one chapters of the *acquis communautaire* have to be closed before a candidate country may be admitted. The strategy has been for the simplest chapters to be addressed first. By June 2001 Cyprus, Estonia and Slovenia had completed eighteen chapters, Hungary seventeen, Poland fifteen, down to Romania which had closed only six chapters. Given that the earlier chapters are the least controversial, it may be expected that later ones will take more time to close. In particular, agriculture and regional aid have yet to be addressed and are not due to be tackled until well into 2002. It is also worth pointing out that the Treaty of Nice did not address the reform of agricultural and regional policies. Nor did it arrive at a solution to the vexed question of the movement of labour from the poorer countries of eastern Europe to the richer countries of western Europe. The issue of labour mobility is coming more to the fore as negotiations continue, especially since Germany and Austria have proposed a transition period of up to seven years during which there would not be free movement of labour from East to West (in fact, such a period would not be unique since an even longer one was imposed on Spain and Portugal when they joined).

It also needs to be borne in mind that, even when all the chapters are closed and the formal invitation to join the Union is made, there then has to be ratification by the parliaments of the existing members, and most of the aspirant member states will hold referendums (recall the case of Norway where all conditions were satisfied but accession was rejected by the people via a referendum).

External relations

The discussion so far has concentrated on the internal implications of enlargement to the EU itself and how it might cope with the extra member states from central and eastern Europe. It must be stressed, however, that the EU does not operate as if it were an island; events in recent years (e.g. Kosova) have shown the (growing) importance of the EU as an international player. Clearly if the enlargement with the CEECs does take place then the Union, at a stroke, becomes a more powerful and influential player on the world stage. Furthermore, it will have different eastern borders from those existing now and will be cheek-by-jowl alongside Russia, Ukraine and Turkey. There will be a particular problem once Poland and Lithuania become members because the Russian enclave of Kaliningrad will be entirely within the borders of the EU. In this sense there will be a redrawing of the geo-political map of Europe with the ensuing questions of European security.

Beyond Europe, there is little doubt that the USA would expect European states and the EU itself to be less dependent on American security support. At the same time the USA would, in all probability, expect the EU to provide greater assistance in global security matters. It is the case, however, that the USA strongly supports an enlarged EU. It is, of course, NATO that the USA uses as the conduit for its influence in Europe and, again, there is strong support for NATO enlarging the number of member states beyond the CEECs that have already joined. It should be noted that Turkey is a keen supporter of NATO as well as being a close ally of the United States – facts that did not go unrecognised in the Helsinki overtures to Turkey in December 1999.

The problem with all this is that the EU has yet to formulate a clear and realistic foreign or external policy. In the same way, as argued above, that enlargement could prove to be divisive rather than integrative for the EU's institutions, so too could the very differences between member states and their very heterogeneity prove to be a major barrier to producing any credible external policy.

As far as the new borders are concerned, there have been no objections from Russia or any of the newly independent states (NIS) about the accessions of the CEECs. Some concern has been expressed about trade balances. Geographically, it is worth pointing out that Ukraine could be the most significant of EU20's neighbours given that it could have three of the new member states on its borders – Poland, Hungary and Slovakia.

Discussion

The road to the next wave of EU enlargement was never going to be smooth and this chapter has briefly discussed the main, though by no means all, difficulties to be overcome before the CEECs and others accede. It is clear that the process is going to take considerable time given all the institutional, political and financial problems that have been identified. The process is likely to be divisive for the Union itself as the interests of individual member states come to the fore. The enthusiasm with which enlargement was originally greeted has declined. Each of the problem areas discussed are interdependent, and until each has been solved to the satisfaction of all, the problems will remain. Yet, in all likelihood, the problems will continue to be faced in a piecemeal fashion. These problems could so easily lead to a slowing down of the enlargement process and certainly a slowing down of the process of European integration.

The proposed fast-track entry of the 'first wave' of candidate states is, in fact, proving divisive and exposing current weaknesses within the EU itself. Unless a systematic programme of institutional and financial reform takes place the enlargement process will become even more complicated and liable to stall. To an extent, the institutional problems have been addressed by the Treaty of Nice. However, it is perfectly understandable why certain member states are objecting to any reform of the current financial system since the benefits to them are enormous. Perceived national interests, rather than the grand European federal vision, become paramount for a member state likely to lose the economic advantages it has enjoyed in recent years.

It should also not be forgotten that the enthusiasm for membership among the general populations of the CEECs appears to have dampened as the years have dragged on. This is largely a result of the long drawn-out process of negotiation but also an increasing recognition that whatever budgetary reforms are made within the EU, the CEECs are unlikely to receive the same positive financial discrimination that the Mediterranean states and Ireland have received in the past. There is also a growing awareness among those CEECs in the 'second wave' that they could receive fewer economic benefits than those in the 'first wave' as successive reforms of the EU's budgetary policies take effect. Rather than an integrated Europe, the future could be a multi-layered Europe with a range of internal conflicts and strains embedded within it.

Further reading

Avery, G. and Cameron, F. (1998) *The Enlargement of the European Union*. Sheffield: Sheffield Academic Press.

Croft, S., Redmond, J., Rees, G. and Webber, M. (1999) *The Enlargement of Europe*. Manchester: Manchester University Press.

Curzon-Price, V., Landau, A. and Whitman, R. (eds) (1999) *The Enlargement of the European Union: Issues and Strategies*. London: Routledge.

Falkner, G. and Nentwich, M. (2001) 'Enlarging the European Union', in J. Richardson (ed.) *European Union: Power and Policy-making*. London: Routledge, pp. 259–282.

Grabbe, H. and Hughes, K. (1998) *Enlarging the European Union Eastwards*. London: Royal Institution for International Affairs.

Henderson, K. (ed.) (1999) *Back to Europe – Central and Eastern Europe and the European Union*. London: UCL Press.

Lewis, P. (2001) 'The enlargement of the European Union', in S. Bromley (ed.) *Governing Europe*. London: Sage, pp. 221–254.

Preston, C. (1997) *Enlargement and Integration in the European Union*. London: Routledge.

Tiersky, R. (ed.) (1999) *Europe Today*. Oxford: Rowman & Littlefield.

European nation-states and globalisation

Key concepts

- the nation-state
- the nation-state system
- the modern world system
- the capitalist world economy
- globalisation

The origins of a state system and the beginnings of globalisation

After the collapse of the Roman Empire and the period sometimes referred to as the Dark Ages, European civilisation developed not in the form of a single imperial hierarchy but instead as a number of independent states. This distinguishes it from other major civilisations, particularly the Chinese or the Ottoman empires. European civilisation came to be known as Western civilisation since Europeans crossed the Atlantic to inhabit the Americas and went on to dominate much of the rest of the world too. Part of that domination has taken the form of a pervasive culture, the world's first truly global culture. The development of the European model of the state and the pervasiveness of Western culture are both dimensions to the process now popularly known as globalisation. Stated very simply, the European state system has provided the model for the global state system and Western culture has become the predominant global culture.

We can divide our view of the globalisation process into four dimensions if we adopt the model from Anthony Giddens' work on structuration theory and the concept of inter-societal systems:

1 Global communications (the global communication system)

The media by which Western culture became so pervasive but also a significant part of the globalisation process in their own right.

In conceptual terms it is the means by which the global culture is signified.

2 The nation-state system (the global polity)

From the sixteenth century onwards Europe developed as a set of independent states competing for politico-military power. Out of this process emerged the model for the modern nation-state, and the system of nation-states became adopted as the form of organisation for the global polity.

In conceptual terms it is the means by which global power is legitimated as authority.

3 The global economy (the capitalist world economy)

At the same time, by a process of colonial exploitation and the extension of its trade, Europe drew a significant proportion of global economic transactions into its own market system operating on the principles of capitalist economics. The capitalist market system became adopted as the form of organisation for the global economy.

In conceptual terms it is the means by which the global allocation of resources is legitimated.

4 The world order (the global military order)

Colonialism was a process by which the world outside of Europe was largely divided up between the European states on the basis of their military power. Other areas, such as China, were coerced into dealings with Europeans on their terms. The European notion of the balance of power became adopted as the world order.

In conceptual terms it is the means by which sanctions (to enforce the world order) are legitimated.

(after Giddens 1985: 277)

The way in which the situation referred to above came about is a significant part of the history of the world over the past six centuries, and here we may emphasise some significant features of that process in order to understand the development of the European state and the pervasiveness of cultural domination in the form of globalisation.

The emergence of European states and the establishment of oceanic navigation

Most historians agree that the sixteenth century was the time when, significantly in terms of world history, European states began to make their presence felt upon the rest of the world. During the period before that time Christian Europe had been effectively contained by the civilisation of the rival Islamic religion which occupied the whole of the land area to the east (the Middle East) and to the south (North Africa). The Crusades represented broadly the attempts of Christian knights, their armies and camp followers to regain the Holy Land from Islam, but their successes were only temporary. The population of Europe was small at the time and European armies were unable to make a lasting impression upon those of the more powerful Arab Islamic civilisation. Instead, success for Europeans came not on land but by sea and yet, as emphasised above, the subsequent territorial expansion did not involve the creation of a single hierarchical European empire. Instead adventurers representing the crowns of different European states competed to seize overseas colonies and trading enclaves in the name of their royal patrons.

The pioneering voyages from Portugal and Spain were in the first place continuations of the Crusades. There were red crosses on the ships' sails, larger versions of those which had been displayed on the crusading knights' tunics, and sailors who died on the voyages were deemed to have died as crusaders. To circumvent the flanks of Islam was regarded as a worthy Christian purpose in its own right but the more earthly goal was to gain direct access to trade with India and China. The spices, silks and other desirable goods sought by the increasing numbers of Europeans who could afford them had to be obtained via the territories of the Islamic

Caliphate in the Middle East whose merchants took considerable profits in the trade. In addition, the powerful city-state of Venice, as heir to the Byzantine Empire, controlled the sea lanes of the eastern Mediterranean and added a mark-up of its own. Its many trading enclaves were protected by armed galleys and armies of *Condottieri* mercenaries to maintain an effective monopoly of trade in goods from India and China obtained exclusively through the Islamic territories.

There were therefore huge potential gains to be made for anyone who could break these arrangements and supply the goods directly to western Europe without the intercession of merchants of Islam and the Venetian Republic. This is more than anything else what spurred on Christopher Columbus and Vasco da Gama in their establishment of ocean routes at a time when navigation was primitive and voyages almost always along the coastline with plenty of overnight pauses where safe havens were available.

> As the circumstances of the time dictated, those adventurers who might be considered to be the European instigators of globalisation nevertheless required royal patronage in order to be able to achieve anything legitimate and enduring. European expansion when it came was a combination of individual initiative and the backing and protection of the increasingly more powerful European states.

We shall look now at three episodes in the process of European states entering the global arena since this adds interest to the story, but more importantly it provides an informative commentary on the initial European expansionism against the background of the development of more powerful European states. The characters themselves, the developing states and the discovery of opportunities unimagined and unanticipated, as well as some failures, add colour to the rather blank concepts of European state development and globalisation.

Illustration 1: Portugal

The first of these expansionary European states was Portugal, a small country but one established early in the development of medieval Europe. Throughout the fifteenth century Portuguese ships pressed southwards down the west coast of Africa in search of a trade route into the Indian Ocean at a time when it was not known for sure that there was a passage around the southern cape of the continent. This was an enterprise begun by one of its princes, Dom Enrique, who is known in English as 'Henry the Navigator'.

Henry was third in line to the Portuguese throne and therefore unlikely to accede, but he had at his disposal considerable resources in the form of a religious foundation, the Order of Christ. Indulging his own interests in astronomy, he established what would be seen today as a centre for the study of navigation. This was at Sagres on Portugal's Atlantic coast, literally looking out from Europe to the wider world. From 1418 onwards, maritime expeditions representing the Portuguese state set out from Lisbon in search of a route around Africa to India. In the process

The progression from the Middle Ages to modernity is important for understanding the origins of both the European state system and globalisation. Henry was an intensely medieval figure, a crusader knighted on the battlefield at Ceuta in North Africa. Yet, whereas the crusades were affairs of the Mediterranean, the oceanic exploration which he sponsored was to take Europeans out into the wider world and on towards the global culture which we see today.

the mariners mastered the wind ellipses of the Atlantic and some believe that they probably became aware of lands to the west. However, they sailed out into the Atlantic in order to complete their round trip more easily but in so doing they developed oceanic navigation in practice. Without this, global trade was impossible. It was a long-term enterprise and it did not find its goal until long after the death of Henry when in 1498 four 'caravels' under the command of Vasco da Gama finally reached India.

It is indicative of the European ability to maximise the use of existing knowledge that these ships used the compass and the centre post rudder from China, the astrolabe from Islamic science and the so-called 'Jacob's staff' from Jewry. On the final leg of the voyage the expedition even enlisted the help of a pilot, Ahmad ibn-Majid, a Gujerati Muslim from India. They picked him up at Malindi, one of a string of African cities along the east coast. The Swahili people had been converted to Islam and their cities become wealthy through the trading of goods from the African interior with the Arab Islamic civilisation further north. This was part of the long-established Indian Ocean trade that Europeans wanted to break into and it is one of the curiosities of such developments that a Muslim should have helped a European state to finally overcome the land blockade effectively imposed by the Islamic Empire's occupation of North Africa and the Middle East.

The Portuguese expedition landed at Calicut to find a vigorous trading port in which they were not welcome. Subsequently the use of cannon by larger fleets would overcome any objections, but the immediate result in any case was a cargo of pepper and other spices landed at Lisbon. This undercut in price the existing supplies that hitherto came to Europe mostly via the Islamic port of Alexandria, from where they were carried to European ports by the Venetian galleys.

The pepper brought back by the Portuguese was in fact traded in a thoroughly modern fashion, that is in competition through an existing commodity market at one-fifth of the price of the Venetian pepper. The centre of this activity was the Flemish city of Antwerp, cradle of the northern Renaissance and focus of European banking and finance at the time. The state exchequers of European kings as well as the merchants went to Antwerp for loans. This is an important factor because the pioneering ocean voyages by European states such as Portugal have to be set against the background not only of a developing European state system but also of a developing and overarching European capitalist economy.

Illustration 2: Spain

During the Portuguese pursuit of an eastern route to India, the Genoese adventurer Cristoforo Colombo, known in English as Christopher Columbus, arrived on the scene. Italy was not to develop as a nation-state until the nineteenth century and Genoa was one of many city-states, but Venice's chief rival in the Mediterranean trade. Each owed its existence to trade but Genoa was less powerful, continually embattled and therefore more piratical in its endeavours. This was Columbus' background and, although an experienced seaman already, he was nevertheless shipwrecked off the Portuguese coast in 1476. His unscheduled arrival was however aided considerably by the fact that his brother Bartolomeo lived in Lisbon, a member of a Genoese chart-making fraternity. Columbus stayed there for some time, subsequently sailing to England and probably Iceland, but more importantly to the Portuguese possessions of the Azores (lost to Castile in 1479) and the fort of La Mina on the west coast of Africa. The Azores were strategically placed off the coast with a developing trade in sugar and African slaves from La Mina working on plantations, in effect a prototype for the later colonisation of the Americas.

Columbus lived for a while with his Portuguese wife and daughter on the small island of Porto Santo, close to another Portuguese Atlantic possession, Madeira, and it was during this period that he developed his plan for a western route to China across the Atlantic. Unfortunately this was in competition with the existing Portuguese plan for an eastern route to India and China. It was therefore rejected, although apparently not without some investigation, by King John II, who considered himself the spiritual heir to his uncle, Prince Henry.

Undaunted, Columbus subsequently took his scheme to neighbouring Castile. There he suffered further rejections, including that from the Duke of Medina Sidonia whose successor was later to command the Spanish Armada against the English. But with the support of a sympathetic astronomer-priest, Fray Antonio de Marchena, he eventually gained access to the royal court where the counsel of other enlightened clerics subsequently convinced the pious Queen Isabella of the advantages for Christendom of circumventing the territories of Islam and obtaining Christian converts. This was precisely the time of the expulsion from Granada of any remaining Muslims. Another factor was the chance of overtaking, in one fell swoop, Portugal's existing lead in the exploration of ocean routes to the Orient. There was nevertheless more frustration and delay, but finally in 1492 Columbus' small flotilla of three ships sailed. Even then they had to pause for a while in the Canaries to repair a broken rudder.

The flotilla set off under a specially made banner representing jointly Isabella of Castile and Ferdinand of Aragon. The marriage of these two was to be instrumental in the creation of a new and powerful state, Spain, although at the time of the voyage the two parts still had separate constitutions. Clearly state-building and the creation of overseas links, such as in these examples, were a feature of the development of Europe and its global culture.

Columbus of course reached neither China nor India and his voyages failed to provide the immediate commercial gains that Vasco da Gama had achieved. Yet it opened up to the Spanish and subsequently to other European states the potential of America, a continent named after Columbus' Florentine contemporary, Amerigo Vespucci, who worked with Columbus on his second and third voyages before sailing on his own account as a surveyor of the American coastline for the Spanish government. Not only did he give his name to the continent, he is also credited with the original usage of the term 'New World' with all that this implies.

> The Italian city-states, such as Columbus' home, Genoa, and Vespucci's, Florence, had been the economic centres of existing Mediterranean trade, whereas Portugal and Spain were embryonic nation-states extending European trade out into the world. Yet for several centuries the rulers of European nation-states were dependent for finance and banking upon mercantile city-states, subsequently not those of the Mediterranean but the Flemish cities of Antwerp and Amsterdam in Protestant north-western Europe.

Illustration 3: The Treaty of Tordesillas

Portugal and Spain are the earliest examples of European states entering the global arena for politico-economic reasons. They struck out against Islamic military power. The Portuguese broke into the Indian Ocean trade that had existed for centuries and some time later the Spanish began to take African slaves to their American colonies to replace the labour of the indigenous civilisations which they destroyed.

In 1494, only two years after Columbus' first voyage, Portugal and Spain sealed the Treaty of Tordesillas. This sought to divide the world's potential trade and conquest between the two countries. It was an agreement that had been mooted for some time, supported by the papacy which was keen to see Catholic countries extend their power and influence in the world. The idea was to create a north–south line in the Atlantic that would divide Portugal's sphere of influence to the east from Spain's to the West. King John II of Portugal successfully negotiated a line further to the West than at first envisaged and this bisected Latin America longitudinally to give Portugal the colony of Brazil. To this day Brazilians speak Portuguese whereas the rest of Latin America speaks Spanish, such are the long-term consequences of even these first global steps by Europeans.

The Treaty of Tordesillas was of course a huge piece of European arrogance but it does vividly illustrate the global outlook of Europeans which at the time was unmatched by any other civilisation. Islamic teaching regarded ocean navigation as impossible, and although the Chinese admiral Cheng Huo had reached East Africa several times almost a century before the Portuguese and with much larger fleets, there was no desire in the Chinese imperial court to develop the route.

The earlier Crusaders had encountered a superior Islamic culture in the Middle East, one that they were pleased to emulate in many ways, but in later centuries

> Nevertheless, it was unrealistic for the Portuguese and Spanish to think that they could maintain their Treaty because the Dutch, the French and the English, all seafaring powers themselves, were soon to be in search of their own colonial empires. From the sixteenth century onwards the progress of the European states outside of Europe and the Mediterranean was barely impeded by any other power.

European culture eclipsed that of Islam in economic wealth, technical developments and political influence. The Ottoman Empire was the final incarnation of the Islamic Caliphate and it survived, albeit in a long decline, until the early twentieth century. It then made the mistake of taking the German side in the First World War, and this gave Britain and France the excuse to divide up the Middle East for themselves mainly in the interest of securing the rights to oilfields. They established, as separate states, the Lebanon, Syria, Iraq, Palestine and Jordan, installing influential Arab families as their rulers. The 1922 Cairo Conference, where these decisions were ratified, was a major milestone in the formation of the modern Middle East and the subject since of much resentment among Islamic people. Recent manifestations of Islamism or, as Europeans like to call it, Islamic Fundamentalism, are partly the legacy of this.

However, the realisation of the European global view has irrevocably turned the world into a state system based upon the European model. This is the fundamental link between the European nation-states and globalisation.

The modern world-system

One way of conceptualising the development of global connections by people representing the European states is through the work of the French historian, Fernand Braudel, and the American sociologist, Immanuel Wallerstein. Both have interpreted the events described in the previous sections as the beginnings of what Wallerstein refers to as 'the modern world-system'. Both interpret the trade that followed from the pioneering ocean voyages as the spread of European capitalism. In the case of Vasco da Gama's voyage to India, the shipping of pepper began immediately with the return of the three surviving ships. Subsequently, there was investment by speculators in such voyages and the commodities acquired could be traded on existing European markets, notably the network centred on the mercantile city of Antwerp during the sixteenth century.

The location of Antwerp in north-west Europe is significant because Wallerstein sees the *modern world-system* as developing a *core* in north-west Europe and a *periphery* in the areas exploited by Europeans. Spain's American colonies of course came to form part of the periphery; but also central Europe, lacking a trading sector, entered what he describes as a 'second serfdom'. Its landowners were content to live from their feudal tithes supplemented with revenue from the German and Dutch merchants who shipped the grain, but it was the latter who gained most from the arrangement leaving central Europe to stagnate economically.

Of even greater significance, Portugal and Spain lacked the commercial infrastructure to exploit their overseas colonies to greatest advantage and so in

Wallerstein's terms they became a *semi-periphery* of the world system, set between the north-west European core and the colonial periphery. Some of the wealth shipped back from Spanish America, mainly in the form of silver, was used up in maintaining the lavish courts of its monarchs. The financial dealings involved were to a great extent brokered by the merchants and bankers of Antwerp. This is the substance of Wallerstein's emphasis on the developing *capitalist world-economy* as the wealth creator of this *modern world-system*.

Wallerstein's modern world-system represents a particular approach to the creation of globalisation and a globalised world. His work has often been criticised as economistic, since the world-system is based upon the capitalist world-economy rather than any political or cultural factors. For Wallerstein, capitalism transcended even the borders of those European states which created it and rendered their rulers dependent upon the dealings of merchants and bankers for the taxation potential of enhanced trade. This meant that mercantile activity enjoyed a great deal of freedom so long as it contributed to the royal exchequer. As a state's power grew so did the cost of maintaining a standing army and navy for defence. The maintenance of an effective bureaucracy for collecting taxes and administering expenditure was not cheap either.

The combination of powerful states and vigorous mercantile sectors points significantly to the separation of polity and economy in the spread of European civilisation. This is another defining characteristic of European development and one that has been carried into the contemporary globalised world. We speak of 'the public sector' meaning the arena of government and politics and 'the private sector' meaning the arena of business and economic activity. By contrast the imperial systems which surrounded Europe during its period of growth and expansion, such as Islam and China, tended to have one hierarchy embracing polity and economy, and this constrained the kind of vigorous and independent mercantile activity which gave rise to European capitalism.

Wallerstein argues that there have been several examples of 'world-economies' in the history of the world. By this he means systems of economic exchange which have embraced large geographical areas, such as the long-standing Indian Ocean trade into which Vasco da Gama forced entry. In all cases other than Europe, however, a 'world-economy' was taken over by a 'world-empire' and this politico-military control constrained economic expansion. The sole exception, according to him, is the 'modern world-system' or 'capitalist world-economy' created by Europeans which has never been overshadowed by the political organisation of Europe. This arrangement has been so successful that the whole world has adopted the combination of politically independent nation-states and an interdependent world economy.

International relations

If the approach of Wallerstein is overly economistic, another approach with emphasis on politics and the nation-state may be derived from the academic study of international relations. This is usually taken to be a subdiscipline of the study of politics and it is based upon the development of the European state system and what emerged from that, on the global scale.

Formal relations between European states are seen as increasingly significant after the Treaty of Westphalia which ended the Thirty Years' War in 1648. The aftermath of this war was a heightened definition of the division between northern Protestant Europe and central-southern Catholic Europe. The European state system is often referred to as the Westphalian system since the treaty was a milestone in the development of the modern map of Europe and therefore the definition of European states and their borders. But that is not all: there is also the codification of the protocols of diplomacy. The separation of these formal interstate links from trading links is another aspect of the separation of polity from economy, the public sector from the private sector. All of this has been carried from Europe to the world virtually intact. At the beginning of the twentieth century there was reference to a 'standard of civilisation' which in fact consisted simply of the adoption of the European state form and diplomacy by all the nations and would-be nations of the world. This was apparent in Sun Yat-Sen's modernisation of China and even Lenin's creation of the Soviet Union.

International relations therefore represents a politically oriented approach to global development to complement the economistic approach of Immanuel Wallerstein.

Globalisation

Around 1990 the so-called 'cultural turn' in the social sciences began to include the appearance of the term 'globalisation' as an alternative to the world-system of Immanuel Wallerstein or the study of international relations. As stated above, the spread of European culture, especially with the input of twentieth-century American culture, has meant that Western culture has become the world's first truly global culture. The difference between the concept of globalisation and world-system or international relations is culture itself – and communication. The means of spreading the culture is an important part of that culture.

The development of the media of communication has proceeded:

* from sailing-ships through all the developments that have led to air travel;
* from the electric telegraph through all the developments that have led to fibre-optic cabling and the Internet or World Wide Web;
* from radio through all the developments that have led to television and satellite broadcasting;
* from recording cylinders to tapes and CDs and all the developments in sound reproduction that are available today.

These are all significant parts of the global culture.

The appearance of the term 'globalisation' came at a time when electronic technology in communication had already been developed to a very high degree. The pervasiveness of television and the growing use of computers with e-mail and Internet links created a situation significantly different from any that had existed before. This is the view of several observers (see e.g. Giddens 1990; Robertson 1992). The consequences of this constitute a qualitative change in the process of modernity that has been referred to as 'reflexive modernisation' (see e.g. Beck *et al.* 1994).

The 'electronic revolution' has produced a plethora of communications and a dramatic expansion of access to knowledge of all kinds. The impact of this has caused people to be more reflexive about their situation and their relationships with others. Communication is information and information tends to cause questions to be asked. In turn this contributes to the undermining of traditional forms of authority. In Europe and the West, globalisation has been associated with the decline of the state and state authority. In the former communist countries of eastern Europe the impossibility of restricting or censoring the electronic media was associated with the demise of the Soviet Union and the pulling down of the Berlin Wall.

The consequences of globalisation

According to Robertson (1992: 62), globalisation produces outcomes that are 'up for grabs'. Europe may have begun the process of globalisation with its intercessions into other parts of the world and the implanting of European institutions. European culture has proved attractive to most of the people who have come into contact with it. However, having begun the process, having created a global culture, neither Europeans nor their cousins in North America necessarily continue to dominate globalisation. If it means anything, globalisation means that the whole world participates. This cannot occur on such a scale without continuous changes in the process as the result of the sheer extent of participation.

Another of Robertson's principles is that globalisation consists of a process of interpenetration between the global and the local. He states this in the rather difficult language of Talcott Parsons' structural functionalism: 'we are, in the late twentieth century, witnesses to – and participants in – a massive, twofold process involving the interpenetration of the universalisation of particularism and the particularisation of universalism' (Robertson 1992: 100).

The most important point here is that this is a principle of the continuing globalisation process. It is the way in which the global culture is reproduced. The local is as much a part of the process as the global. In fact, in order for globalisation to exist at all it must by definition be reproduced in all the localities that exist. Expressed this way, the conclusion is unavoidable that the reproduction of globalisation in local milieux must have significant effects on the continuing process.

The case of Japan is significant here. This is a society that kept itself closed from Europeans until the second half of the nineteenth century. Then during the twentieth century the Japanese began to devour European institutions while at the same time retaining a strong culture of their own. Progress was brought to a halt with defeat after the disastrous militaristic imperialism of the Second World War, but with rehabilitation at the hands of the US occupying forces after the war the process was intensified. The result was a Japanese version of industrialism with all its attendant institutions drawing from Japanese culture. By now industrialisation was becoming global and so there emerged a strong Japanese contribution to the continuing globalisation process.

An obvious example is the motor industry that really began with Henry Ford's development of assembly-line production during the first decades of the twentieth century. So-called 'Fordist' manufacturing was the hallmark of successful industry for any country during the twentieth century. The Japanese reproduced the organisation of the motor industry but added some of their own cultural traits. *Kanban*, or 'just-in-time' stock control, characterises the broader organisation of Japanese industry and its component supplies. *Kaizen*, or 'quality circles', characterises Japanese workers' approach to their work and the importation of 'groupism' into the workplace. Each of these has been associated with the principles of Confucianism which form a strong and consistent part of the socialisation process in Japanese family life and education. 'Groupism' in Japanese society is held to have its origins in the Samurai period when peasants organised themselves into groups for their own protection. The Samurai are of course considered to have evolved into thrusting Japanese managers of today, and all of these characteristics may be seen as local inputs into the global institutions of motor manufacturing and its management. The outcome of this has been that motor manufacturers in Europe and North America have all seen the advantage of bringing facets of Japanese manufacturing into their organisations. This is often referred to as 'post-Fordism'.

Globalisation and the nation-state

As already stated, globalisation tends to undermine the authority of the nation-state. Global communication brings to the attention of the citizens of the nation-state alternative focuses of authority. On a grand scale the United Nations Organisation dates back to the end of the Second World War in 1945 and regional groupings like the European Union are referred to below as part of a process of 'triadisation'. On a different scale there have appeared non-governmental organisations (NGOs) such as, for example, Greenpeace. This campaigning organisation works globally and in its sphere of interest, environmentalism, its opinions are often listened to with more authority than the governments of nation-states.

Some writers believe that the nation-state is too large to engage the trust of the individual but too small to play much of a part in the global arena. In response to the latter, the European states have combined as the European Union in order that they may have more influence. In this respect the Japanese writer, Kenichi Ohmae, has referred to a process of 'triadisation'. The triad that he is referring to consists of three focuses of politico-economic power that have appeared in the world towards the end of the twentieth century. They are North America, Europe and East Asia and may be expressed more extensively as follows:

- The USA has combined with Canada and Mexico to form the North American Free Trade Association (NAFTA).
- Europe has taken the form of the European Union (EU), and all western European countries are now members with the exception of Norway and Switzerland. Further entrants from eastern Europe are expected in the foreseeable future.

- There is no such formal association in East Asia but where Japan took the lead, Hong Kong, Singapore, South Korea and Taiwan followed as Newly Industrialised Countries (NICs). Since then Indonesia, Malaysia, the Philippines, Thailand and other countries in the area have achieved considerable industrialisation. In practice these form an East Asian economic bloc in which many Western companies have become involved, just as East Asian companies have become involved in the West.

This global triad represents the elite areas of the globalised world and therefore points to new forms of inequality between nations. And yet there is counter-evidence. The systems of fibre-optic cabling which provide the networks for computers and the Internet are expensive and therefore disproportionately represented in North America, Europe and East Asia. But satellite broadcasting, although expensive to set up, operates regardless of distance. Therefore it is used quite widely in the less developed countries. India, one of the poorest countries in the world in terms of per capita income, is also one the largest users of satellite broadcasting in numbers relative to population.

Summary

- European civilisation developed not as an imperial system with a single hierarchy like other civilisations but as a set of independent nation-states.
- From the sixteenth century onwards the Europeans began to implant their institutions throughout the world by the process of colonialism.
- During the same period the economies of the world became influenced by European capitalism to form a capitalist world economy.
- The European model of the nation-state and the nation-state system became adopted by the rest of the world.
- By the second half of the twentieth century through the process of globalisation European (or Western) culture had become the world's first truly global culture.

Further reading

Beynon, J. and Dunkerley, D. (2000) *Globalisation: The Reader*. London: Continuum; New York: Routledge.

Giddens, A. (1985) *The Nation-State and Violence*. Cambridge: Polity Press.

Holton, R.J. (1998) *Globalisation and the Nation-States*. Basingstoke: Macmillan.

Robertson, R. (1992) *Globalisation: Social Theory and Global Culture*. London: Sage.

Spybey, T. (1996) *Globalisation and World Society*. Cambridge: Polity Press.

Wallerstein, I. (1979) *The Capitalist World-Economy*. Cambridge: Cambridge University Press.

Notes

6 Migration and asylum-seeking in Europe

1   These and other figures discussed in this section derive from UNHCR statistics.

10 The enlargement of the European Union

1   Interestingly there is one case of contraction rather than enlargement. When Denmark joined in 1973, Greenland was then a dependency. Following full independence in 1979, Greenland chose to withdraw from the Community in 1985.

2   Slovakia was deemed not to have satisfied the political conditions.

References

Amnesty International (1996) Memorandum to Intergovernmental Conference 1996 available online at: http://europa.eu.int/en/aganda/igc-home/instdoc/ngo/amnen.htm.

Anderson, B. (1991) *Imagined Communities*. London: Verso.

Andrés, M. and Braster, J.F.A. (1999) 'The rebirth of the "Spanish race": the state, nationalism, and education in Spain, 1875–1931', *European History Quarterly*, 29 (1), pp. 75–107.

Anthias, F. and Lazaridis, G. (eds)(1999) *Into the Margins: Migration and Exclusion in Southern Europe*. Aldershot: Ashgate.

Antola, E. and Rosas, A. (eds)(1995) *A Citizens' Europe. In Search of a New Legal Order*. London: Sage.

Armstrong, H.W. (1995) 'The role and evolution of European Community regional policy', in B. Jones and M. Keating (eds) *The European Union and the Regions*. Oxford: Clarendon Press.

Armstrong, H.W. and de Kervenoael, R. (1997) 'Regional economic change in the European Union', in J. Bachtler and I. Turok (eds) *The Coherence of EU Regional Policy. Contrasting Perspectives on the Structural Funds*. London: Jessica Kingsley.

Armstrong, J.A. (1982) *Nations Before Nationalism*. Chapel Hill, NC: University of North Carolina Press.

Armstrong, J.A. (1995) 'Towards a theory of nationalism: consensus and dissensus', in S. Periwal (ed.) *Notions of Nationalism*. London: Central European University Press.

Ashdown, P. (1995) 'Introduction', in P. Harris *Cry Bosnia*. London: Canongate Books.

Avery, G. and Cameron, F. (1998) *The Enlargement of the European Union*. Sheffield: Sheffield Academic Press.

Bache, I. (1998) *The Politics of European Union Regional Policy*. Sheffield: Sheffield University Press.

Bachtler, J. (1998) 'Reforming the Structural Funds: challenges for EU regional policy', *European Planning Studies*, 6 (6), pp. 645–664.

Bachtler, J. and Downes, R. (2000) 'The spatial coverage of regional policy in central and eastern Europe', *European Urban and Regional Studies*, 7 (2), pp. 159–174.

Banton, M. (1999) 'The racialising of the world', in M. Bulmer and J. Solomos (eds) *Racism*. Oxford: Oxford University Press.

Barbalet, J.M. (1988) *Citizenship*. Buckingham: Open University Press.

Batt, J. (1998) 'Introduction: defining central and eastern Europe', in S.White, J. Batt and P.G. Lewis (eds) *Developments in Central and East European Politics*. London: Macmillan.

Bauböck, R. (1997) *Citizenship and National Identities in the European Union*. Jean Monnet Working Papers, Harvard Law School.

Beck, U., Giddens, A. and Lash, S. (1994) *Reflexive Modernization: Politics, Tradition and Aesthetics in the Modern Social Order*. Cambridge: Polity Press.

Beddard, R. (1993) *Human Rights and Europe*. Cambridge: Grotius (3rd edn).

Benz, A. (1998) 'German regions in the European Union: from joint policy-making to multi-level governance', in P. Le Galès and C. Lequesne (eds) *Regions in Europe*. London: Routledge.

Besselink, L. (2001) 'The member states, the national constitutions and the scope of the charter', *Maastricht Journal of European and Comparative Rights Law*, 8 (1). Oxford: Hart, pp. 68–80.

Betten, L. and Grief, N. (1998) *EU Law and Human Rights*. European Law Series. London: Addison Wesley Longman.

Benyon, J. (1994) 'Policing the European Union: the changing basis of co-operation on law enforcement', *International Affairs*, 70 (3), pp. 147–162.

Bhabha, J. (1999) 'Enforcing the human rights of citizens and non-citizens in the era of Maastricht: some reflections on the importance of states', in B. Meyer and P. Geschiere *Globalisation and Identity: Dialects of Flow and Closure*. London: Institute of Social Studies.

Billig, M. (1995) *Banal Nationalism*. London: Sage.

Birnbaum, K. (1976) 'East–West diplomacy in the era of mutilateral negotiations: the case of the Conference on Security and Cooperation in Europe', in N. Andren and K. Birnbaum (eds), *Beyond Détente: Prospects for East–West Co-operation and Security in Europe*. East West Perspectives 3. The Netherlands: Sijthoff-Leyden.

Blair, T. (2000) *Comment* available online at: http://europa.eu.int/comm/justice_home/unit/charte/en/charter03.html.

Bloed, A., Bloed, A. and van Dijk, P. (1991) *The Human Dimension of the Helsinki Process*. The Netherlands: Kluwer.

Borneman, J. and Fowler, N. (1998) 'Europeanization', *Annual Review of Anthropology*, 26, pp. 487–514.

Breuilly, J. (1993) *Nationalism and the State*. Manchester: Manchester University Press.

Bromley, S. (ed.) (2001) *Governing the European Union*. London: Sage.

Brubaker, R. (1996) *Nationalism Reframed*. Cambridge: Cambridge University Press.

Bryson, L. and McCartney, C. (1994) *Clashing Symbols?* Belfast: Institute of Irish Studies.

Budge, I., Newton, K. *et al.* (1997) *The Politics of the New Europe*. London: Longman.

Bullman, U. (1996) 'The politics of the third level', *Regional and Federal Studies*, Special Issue on The Politics of the Third Level, pp. 3–19.

Calhoun, C. (1997) *Nationalism*. Buckingham: Open University Press.

Calleo, D. (1995) 'Reflections on the idea of the nation-state', in C.A. Kupchan (ed.) *Nationalism and Nationalities in the New Europe*. Ithaca, NY: Cornell University Press.

Canor, I. (2000) '*Primus inter pares*. Who is the ultimate guardian of fundamental rights in Europe?', *European Legal Review*. London: Sweet & Maxwell.

Caplan, R. and Feffer, J. (eds) (1996) *Europe's New Nationalism*. Oxford: Oxford University Press.

Carr, F. and Massey, A. (1999) *Public Policy in the New Europe*. Cheltenham: Edward Elgar.

Cassese, A. (1991) 'Violence, war and the rule of war in the international community', in D. Held (ed) (1995) *Political Theory Today*. Cambridge: Polity Press.

Cobban, A. (1969) *The Nation-State and National Self-Determination*. London: Collins.

Colley, L. (1992) *Britons. Forging the Nation 1707–1837*. London: Vintage.

Cologne European Council (1999) *Presidency Conclusions*. Cologne 3/4th June. Available on-line at: http://ue.eu.int/Newsroom/LoadDoc.cfm?MAX=1&DOC=%21%21%21&BID=76&DID=57886&GRP=1799andLANG=1.

Commission of the European Communities (1993) *Legal Instruments to Combat Racism and Xenophobia*. Luxembourg: Office for Official Publications of the European Communities.

Commission of the European Communities (1996) *Eurobarometer, Report No. 45.* Brussels: Commission of the European Communities.

Commission of the European Communities (1997) *Eurobarometer, Report No. 47.* Brussels: Commission of the European Communities.

Commission of the European Communities (2000) *Eurobarometer, Report No. 52.* Brussels: Commission of the European Communities.

Commission of the European Communities (2001) *European Governance* White Paper. Brussels: Commission of the European Communities.

Commission of the European Communities (2001a) *European Governance – A White Paper.* Brussels: Commission of the European Communities.

Commission of the European Communities (2001b) *Perceptions of the European Union.* Brussels: Commission of the European Communities.

Commission of the European Communities (2001c) *Eurobarometer, Report No. 54.* Brussels: Commission of the European Communities.

Commission of the European Communities (2001d) *Eurobarometer 2001 – Special Edition.* Brussels: Commission of the European Communities.

Committee for European Integration (1997) *National Strategy for Integration.* Warsaw: Committee for European Integration.

Cooke, P., Price, A. and Morgan, K. (1995) 'Regulating regional economies: Wales and Baden-Württemberg in transition', in M. Rhodes (ed.) *The Regions and the New Europe. Patterns in Core and Periphery Development.* Manchester: Manchester University Press.

Cowie, L.W. and Wolfson, R. (1985) *Years of Nationalism: European History 1815–1890.* London: Hodder & Stoughton.

Crampton, R.J. (1997) *Eastern Europe in the Twentieth Century – and After.* London: Routledge (2nd edn).

Croft, S., Redmond, J., Rees, G. and Webber, M. (1999) *The Enlargement of Europe.* Manchester: Manchester University Press.

Crouch, C. (1999) *Social Change in Western Europe.* Oxford: Oxford University Press.

CSCE (1992) Conference on Security and Cooperation in Europe. Helsinki.

Curzon-Price, V., Landau, A. and Whitman, R. (eds) (1999) *The Enlargement of the European Union: Issues and Strategies.* London: Routledge.

Davies, N. (1997) *Europe – A History.* London: Pimlico.

de Burca, G. (2001) 'The drafting of the European Union Charter of Fundamental Rights', in *European Law Review,* April. London: Sweet & Maxwell.

Delanty, G. (1995) *Inventing Europe.* London: Macmillan.

Duff, A. (ed.) (1997) *The Treaty of Amsterdam. Text and Commentary.* London: Federal Trust.

Engel, C. (2001) 'The European Charter of Fundamental Rights: a changed political opportunity structure and its normative consequences', *European Law Journal,* 7(2), pp. 151–170. London: Sweet & Maxwell.

EU *Charter of Fundamental Rights* available online at: http://europa.eu.int/comm/justice_home/unit/charte/index_en.html.

EU docs *European Convention for the Prevention of Torture and Inhuman or Degrading Treatment or Punishment,* ETS no.126 available online at: http://conventions.coe.int/Treaty/EN/cadreprincipal.htm.

EU docs *European Convention for the Protection of Human Rights and Fundamental Freedoms* available online at: http://www.echr.coe.int/Convention/webConvenENG.pdf.

EU docs *Framework Convention for the Protection of National Minorities* ETS no.157 available online at: http://conventions.coe.int/Treaty/EN/cadreprincipal.htm.

EU docs *Statute of the Council of Europe* available online at: http://conventions.coe.int/treaty/EN/Treaties/Html/001.htm.

EU docs *Treaty of Amsterdam Guide* available online at: http://europa.eu.int/scadplus/leg/en/s50000.htm.

EU docs *Treaty of European Union* available online at: http://europa.eu.int/en/record/mt/top.html.

Europa (1996) *Intergovernmental Conference* available online at: http://europa.eu.int/en/agenda/igc-home/.

Europa (2000) *What is the European Community?* available online at: http://europa.eu.int/cj/en/pres.comp.htm.

European Commission (1999) *Affirming Fundamental Rights in the European Union: Report of the Expert Group on Fundamental Rights 1999.* Brussels: EC.

European Court of Human Rights http://www.echr.coe.int.

European Court of Justice (1969) Stauder Case no. 61969J0029 http://europa.eu.int/smartapi/cgi/sga_doc?smartapi!celexplus!prod!CELEXnumdocandlg=enandnumdoc=61969J0029.

European Parliament Working Document (1993) A3-0437/93, 21 December.

Evans, A.C. (1995) 'Union citizenship and the equality principle', in A. Rosas (ed.) *A Citizens' Europe. In Search of a New Legal Order.* London: Sage.

Ewing, E.(1999) 'The Human Rights Act and parliamentary democracy', *The Modern Law Review.* 62 (1). Oxford: Blackwell.

Falk, R. (1995) *On Humane Governance Toward a New Global Politics.* Cambridge: Polity Press.

Falk, R. and Szentes, T. (1997) *A New Europe in the Changing Global System.* New York: United Nations University Press.

Falkner, G. and Nentwich, M. (2001) 'Enlarging the European Union', in J. Richardson (ed.) *European Union: Power and Policy-making.* London: Routledge.

Fenton, S. (1999) *Ethnicity: Racism, Class and Culture.* Basingstoke: Macmillan.

Ferro, M. (1999) 'Cultural life in France, 1914–1918', in A. Roshwald and R. Stites (eds) *European Culture in the Great War.* Cambridge: Cambridge University Press.

Ford Report (1991) European Parliament Report drawn up on behalf of the Committee of Inquiry into Racism and Xenophobia on the findings of the Committee of Inquiry. Luxembourg: Office for Official Publications of the European Communities.

Foucault, M. (1965) *Madness and Civilization. A History of Insanity in the Age of Reason*, trans. R. Howard. London: Random House.

Fundamental Rights for the Committee on Institutional Affairs (1993) PE 211.308.

Gaffney, A. (1998) *Aftermath. Remembering the Great War in Wales.* Cardiff: University of Wales Press.

Garmise, S.O. (1995) 'Economic development strategies in Emilia-Romagna', in M. Rhodes (ed.) *The Regions and the New Europe. Patterns in Core and Periphery Development.* Manchester: Manchester University Press.

Geddes, A. (2000) *Immigration and European Integration. Towards Fortress Europe?* Manchester: Manchester University Press.

Gellner, E. (1983) *Nations and Nationalism.* Cambridge: Cambridge University Press.

Gemie, S. (1998) 'France and the Val d'Aran: politics and nationhood on the Pyrenean Border, c. 1800–1825', *European History Quarterly*, 28 (3), pp. 311–345.

Gerstenlauer, H-G. (1995) 'German Länder and the European Community', in B. Jones and M. Keating (eds) *The European Union and the Regions.* Oxford: Clarendon Press.

Geyer, R. (2000) *Exploring European Social Policy.* Cambridge: Polity Press.

Giddens, A. (1985) *The Nation-State and Violence, Vol. 2 of A Contemporary Critique of Historical Materialism.* Cambridge: Polity Press.

Giddens, A. (1990) *The Consequences of Modernity*, Cambridge: Polity Press.

Glenny, M. (1993) *The Revenge of History.* Harmondsworth: Penguin.

Grabbe, H. and Hughes, K. (1998) *Enlarging the European Union Eastwards.* London: Royal Institution for International Affairs.

Greenhalgh, P. (2000) 'The style and the age', in P. Greenhalgh (ed.) *Art Nouveau 1890–1914.* London: V & A Publications.

Gruber, M. (1997) 'Perspectives on EU regional policy from a new Member State: Austria', in J. Bachtler and I. Turok (eds) *The Coherence of EU Regional Policy. Contrasting Perspectives on the Structural Funds*. London: Jessica Kingsley.

Guibernau, M. (1996) *Nationalisms. The Nation-State and Nationalism in the Twentieth Century*. Cambridge: Polity Press.

Gundara, J. and Jacobs, S. (eds) (2000) *Intercultural Europe*. Aldershot: Ashgate.

Habermas, J. (1994) 'Citizenship and national identity', in B. van Steenbergen (ed.) *The Condition of Citizenship*. London: Sage.

Hall, R. and van der Wee, M. (1995) 'The regions in an enlarged Europe', in S. Hardy, M. Hart, L. Albrechts and A. Katos (eds) *An Enlarged Europe. Regions in Competition?* London: Jessica Kingsley.

Havel, V. (1994) 'About European identity', Speech to the European Parliament, Strasbourg, 8 March.

Held, D. (1995a) *Democracy and the Global Order: From the Modern State to Cosmopolitan Governance*. Cambridge: Polity Press.

Held, D. (ed.) (1995b) *Political Theory Today*. Cambridge: Polity Press.

Henderson, K. (ed.) (1999) *Back to Europe – Central and Eastern Europe and the European Union*. London: UCL Press.

Hindess, B. (1994) 'Citizenship in the modern West', in B.S. Turner (ed.) *Citizenship and Social Theory*. London: Sage.

Hobsbawm, E.J. (1990) *Nations and Nationalism Since 1780*. Cambridge: Cambridge University Press.

Holland, M. (1993) *European Integration. From Community to Union*. London: Pinter.

Honauer, J. (1999) 'Federalism in Austria', in P. Wagstaff (ed.) *Regionalism in the European Union*. Exeter: Intellect.

Horsman, M. and Marshall, A. (1995) *After the Nation-State. Citizens, Tribalism, and the New World Order*. London: HarperCollins.

Horváth, G. (1995) 'Economic reforms in east-central Europe', in S. Hardy, M. Hart, L. Albrechts and A. Katos (eds) *An Enlarged Europe. Regions in Competition?* London: Jessica Kingsley.

House of Commons (1998) *Enlargement of the European Union*. London: House of Commons Library, Paper 98/56.

Hroch, M. (2000) *Social Preconditions of National Revival in Europe*. New York: Columbia University Press (2nd edn).

Huntingdon, S. (1997) *The Clash of Civilizations and the Remaking of the World Order*. London: Simon & Schuster.

Janis, M., Kay, R. and Bradley, A. (2000) *European Human Rights Law: Text and Materials*. Milton Keynes: Open University Press (2nd edn).

Jansen, T. (ed.) (1999) *Reflections on European Identity*. Working Paper. Forward Studies Unit, European Commission.

Jáuregui, P. (1999) 'National pride and the meaning of Europe: a comparative study of Britain and Spain', in D. Smith and S. Wright (eds) *Whose Europe? The Turn Towards Democracy*. Oxford: Blackwell.

Joppke, C. (1997) 'Asylum and state sovereignty: a comparison of the United States, Germany and Britain', *Comparative Political Studies*, 30 (3), pp. 259–298.

Joppke, C. (1999) *Immigration and the Nation-State*. Oxford: Oxford University Press.

Keating, M. (1998) 'Is there a regional level of government in Europe?', in P. Le Galès and C. Lequesne (eds) *Regions in Europe*. London: Routledge.

Kedourie, E. (1960) *Nationalism*. London: Hutchinson.

Kennedy, D. (1997) 'The Committee of the Regions: an assessment', *Regional and Federal Studies*, 7 (1), pp. 1–4.

Kennedy, P. (1988) *The Rise and Fall of the Great Powers. Economic Change and Military Conflict from 1500–2000*. London: Unwin and Hyman.

Kerremans, B. and Beyers, J. (1996) 'The Belgian sub-national entities in the European Union: Second or Third Level players?', *Regional and Federal Studies*, Special Issue on The Politics of the Third Level, pp. 41–55.

King, R. (1997) 'Southern Europe in the changing global map and typology of migration'. Paper presented at the conference 'Non-military aspects of security in Southern Europe: migration, employment and labour market', Institute of International Economic Societies, Santorini, Greece.

King, R. and Konjhodzic, I. (1995) *Labour, employment and migration in Southern Europe*. Research papers in geography. Brighton: University of Sussex.

Klug, F., Starmer, K. and Weir, S. (1996) *The Three Pillars of Liberty*. London: Routledge.

Kohn, H. (1967) *The Idea of Nationalism*. New York: Collier-Macmillan (2nd edn).

Konstadinidis, S. (1999) *A People's Europe: Turning a Concept into Content*. Aldershot: Ashgate.

Laursen, F. and Vanhoonacker, S. (eds) (1992) *The Intergovernmental Conference on Political Union*. Maastricht: EIPA.

Layton-Henry, Z. (2001) 'Migrants, refugees and citizenship', in M. Guibernau (ed.) *Governing European Diversity*. London: Sage.

Le Galès, P. and Lequesne, C. (eds) (1998) *Regions in Europe*. London: Routledge.

Lendvai, P. (1991) 'Yugoslavia without Yugoslavs: the roots of the crisis', *International Affairs*, 67 (2), pp. 251–261.

Leonard, M. (1998) *Rediscovering Europe: The Search for a European Identity*. London: Demos.

Lewis, P. (2001) 'The enlargement of the European Union', in S. Bromley (ed.) *Governing Europe*. London: Sage.

Llobera, J. (1994) *The God of Modernity*. Oxford: Berg.

Loughlin, J., Aja, E., Bullman, U., Hendriks, F., Lidstrom, A. and Seiler, D. (1999) *Regional and Local Democracy in the European Union*. Luxembourg: Office for Official Publications of the European Communities.

Lovering, J. (1999) 'Theory led by policy: the inadequacies of the "new regionalism"', *International Journal of Urban and Regional Research*, 23, pp. 379–395.

Luelmo, J. del Rio and Williams, A. (1999) 'Regionalism in Iberia', in P. Wagstaff (ed.) *Regionalism in the European Union*. Exeter: Intellect.

Lynch, P. (1996) *Minority Nationalism and European Integration*. Cardiff: University of Wales Press.

McCrone, D. (1992) *The Sociology of a Stateless Nation*. London: Routledge.

Maastricht Journal of European and Comparative Law (2001) Special Issue on the EU Charter, 8 (1). Oxford: Hart.

Mansell, W. (1999) 'Fundamental human rights premises', in C. Bell, D. Buss and W. Mansell *Teaching Human Rights*. Warwick: National Centre for Legal Education.

March Hunnings, N. (1996) *The European Courts*. London: John Harper.

Marias, E.A. (1994) *European Citizenship*. Maastricht: EIPA.

Marshall, T.H. (1950) *Citizenship and Social Class and Other Essays*. Cambridge: Cambridge University Press.

Martin, S. (1997) 'The effects of EU regional policy on local institutional structures and policies', in J. Bachtler and I. Turok (eds) *The Coherence of EU Regional Policy. Contrasting Perspectives on the Structural Funds*. London: Jessica Kingsley.

Mazey, S. (1995) 'Regional lobbying in the new Europe', in M. Rhodes (ed.) *The Regions and the New Europe. Patterns in Core and Periphery Development*. Manchester: Manchester University Press.

Merrills, J. and Robertson, A. (2001) *Human Rights in Europe: A Study of the European Convention on Human Rights*. Manchester: Manchester University Press (4th edn).

Michie, R. and Fitzgerald, R. (1997) 'The evolution of the Structural Funds', in J. Bachtler and I. Turok (eds) *The Coherence of EU Regional Policy. Contrasting Perspectives on the Structural Funds*. London: Jessica Kingsley.

Miller, D. (1995) *On Nationality.* Oxford: Oxford University Press.

Miller, V. (2000) 'Human rights in the EU: the Charter of Fundamental Rights', *House of Commons Research Paper 00/32.* International Affairs and Defence Section. House of Commons Library. Available online at: http://www.parliament.uk.

Milward, A. (1992) *The European Rescue of the Nation-State.* London: Routledge.

Morata, F. (1995) 'Spanish regions in the European Community', in B. Jones and M. Keating (eds) *The European Union and the Regions.* Oxford: Clarendon Press.

Moretti, M. (1999) 'The search for a "national" history: Italian historiographical trends following unification', in S. Berger, M. Donovan and K. Passmore (eds) *Writing National Histories.* London: Routledge.

Morgan, K. and Price, A. (1998) *The Other Wales. The Case for Objective 1 Funding Post 1999.* Cardiff: Institute of Welsh Affairs.

Navari, C. (1981) 'The origins of the nation-state', in L. Tivey (ed.) *The Nation-State. The Formation of Modern Politics.* Oxford: Robertson.

Nederveen Pieterse, J. (1994) 'Unpacking the West: How European is Europe?', in A. Rattansi and S. Westwood (eds) *Racism, Modernity, Identity: On the Western Front.* Cambridge: Polity Press.

Neunreither, K. (1994) 'The democratic deficit of the European Union: towards closer co-operation between the European Parliament and the National Parliaments', *Government and Opposition*, 29, pp. 300–314.

Newman, M. (1996) *Democracy, Sovereignty and the European Union.* London: Hurst & Company.

Nowak, N. (1999) 'The case of Bosnia Herzegovina', *Human Rights Law Journal*, 20 (7–11). Kehl am Rhein: N.P. Engel.

Ohmae, K. (1996) *The End of the Nation-State.* London: HarperCollins.

O'Leary, S. (1996) *European Union Citizenship. The Options for Reform.* London: IPPR.

Oliver, D. and Heater, D. (1994) *The Foundations of Citizenship.* Hassocks: Harvester Wheatsheaf.

OSCE docs (2000) *Final Act – Helsinki Summit 1975* available online at: http://www/osce.org/docs/english/1990–1999/summits/helfa75e.htm.

Parekh, B. (2000) *The Future of Multi-Ethnic Britain.* London: The Runnymede Trust.

Pentikainen, M. (1997) 'The human dimension of the OSCE in the 1996 Vienna Review Meeting', *Helsinki Monitor*, 8 (1). Netherlands Helsinki Committee and the International Helsinki Federation for Human Rights.

Pereira, A. (1995) 'Regionalism in Portugal', in B. Jones and M. Keating (eds) *The European Union and the Regions.* Oxford: Clarendon Press.

Péteri, G. (2000) 'Between empire and nation-state: comments on the pathology of state formation during the "short twentieth century"', *Contemporary European History*, 9 (3), pp. 367–384.

Preston, C. (1997) *Enlargement and Integration in the European Union.* London: Routledge.

Reding, V. (2000) *European Cultural Policy.* Speech during visit to Greece, October.

Reflection Group (1995) *Report.* Brussels: Secretariat General of the European Council.

Rex, J. (1998) 'Race and ethnicity in Europe', in J. Bailey (ed.) *Social Europe.* Harlow: Longman.

Robertson, A. and Merrills, J. (1993) *Human Rights in the World.* Manchester: Manchester University Press.

Robertson, A. and Merrills, J. (1996) *Human Rights in Europe.* Manchester: Manchester University Press.

Robertson, R. (1992) *Globalisation: Social Theory and Global Culture.* London: Sage.

Schöpflin, G. (1995) 'Nationalism and ethnicity in Europe, East and West', in C.A. Kupchan (ed.) *Nationalism and Nationalities in the New Europe.* Ithaca, NY: Cornell University Press.

Schulze, H. (1996) *States, Nations and Nationalism.* Oxford: Blackwell.

Segel, H.B. (1999) 'Culture in Poland during World War I', in A. Roshwald and R. Stites (eds) *European Culture in the Great War*. Cambridge: Cambridge University Press.

Seton-Watson, H. (1977) *Nations and States*. London: Methuen.

Shafer, B.C. (1972) *Faces of Nationalism*. New York: Harcourt Brace Jovanovich.

Shaw, J. (2000) 'Constitutional settlements and the citizen after the Treaty of Amsterdam', in K. Neunreither and A. Wiener (eds) *European Integration after Amsterdam. Institutional Dynamics and Prospects for Democracy*. Oxford: Oxford University Press.

Shore, C. (1996) 'Transcending the nation-state? The European Commission and the (re)-discovery of Europe', *Journal of Historical Sociology*, 9 (4), pp. 473–496.

Shore, C. (2000) *Building Europe. The Cultural Politics of European Integration*. London: Routledge.

Smith, A. (1998) 'The sub-regional level: key battleground for the Structural Funds?', in P. Le Galès and C. Lequesne (eds) *Regions in Europe*. London: Routledge.

Smith, A.D. (1979) *Nationalism in the Twentieth Century*. Oxford: Martin Robertson.

Smith, A.D. (1986a) *The Ethnic Origins of Nations*. Oxford: Blackwell.

Smith, A.D. (1986b) 'State-making and nation-building', in J.A. Hall (ed.) *States in History*. Oxford: Blackwell.

Smith, A.D. (1991) *National Identity*. Harmondsworth: Penguin.

Smith, A.D. (1992) 'National identity and the idea of European unity', *International Affairs*, 68 (1), pp. 55–76.

Smith, A.D. (1995) *Nations and Nationalism in a Global Era*. Cambridge: Polity Press.

Smith, A.D. (1998) *Nationalism and Modernism*. London: Routledge.

Smith, G. (ed.) (1996) *The Baltic States*. London: Macmillan.

Snyder, L. (1954) *The Meaning of Nationalism*. New Brunswick: Rutgers University Press.

Sorensen, J.M. (1996) *The Exclusive European Citizenship: The Case for Refugees and Immigrants in the European Union*. Aldershot: Ashgate.

Spencer, M. (1995) *States of Injustice: A Guide to Human Rights and Civil Liberties in the EU*. London: Pluto Press.

Steiner, H. and Alston, P. (2000) *International Human Rights in Context: Law, Politics, Morals*. Oxford: Oxford University Press.

Stone, N. (1999) *Europe Transformed 1878–1919*. Oxford: Blackwell (2nd edn).

Sultana, R. (1995) 'A uniting Europe, a dividing education? Euro-centrism and the curriculum', *International Studies in Sociology of Education*, 5 (2), pp. 115–144.

Tamir, Y. (1993) *Liberal Nationalism*. Princeton, NJ: Princeton University Press.

Teitgen, P. (1949) *Doc 77: Establishment of a Collective Guarantee of Essential Freedoms and Fundamental Rights*, 5 September. Dordrecht.

Teitgen, P. and Maxwell Fyfe, D. (1949) *Organisation Within the Council of Europe to Ensure the Collective Guarantee of Human Rights*, 19 August. Dordrecht. September.

Thomas, D. (1996) 'Winner or loser in the new Europe? Regional funding, inward investment and prospects for the Welsh economy', *European Urban and Regional Studies*, 3 (3), pp. 225–240.

Tiersky, R. (ed.) (1999) *Europe Today*. Oxford: Rowman and Littlefield.

Tilly, C. (1975) 'Reflecting on the history of European state-making', in C. Tilly (ed.) *The Formation of the National State in Western Europe*. Princeton, NJ: Princeton University Press.

Tilly, C. (1992) *Coercion, Capital, and European States, AD 990–1992*. Oxford: Blackwell.

United Nations Charter http://www.un.org/aboutun/charter/.

Universal Declaration of Human Rights available online at: http://www.hrweb.org/legal/udhr.html.

van Steenbergen, B. (ed.) (1994) *The Condition of Citizenship*. London: Sage.

Vanke, F. (2000) 'Arabesques: North Africa, Arabia and Europe', in P. Greenhalgh (ed.) *Art Nouveau 1890–1914*. London: V & A Publications.

Vincent, R.J. (1988) *Human Rights and International Relations*. Cambridge: Cambridge University Press.

Wagstaff, P. (ed.) (1999) *Regionalism in the European Union*. Exeter: Intellect.

Warleigh, A. (1997) 'A committee of no importance? Assessing the relevance of the Committee of the Regions', *Politics*, 17 (2), pp. 101–107.

Weber, E. (1978) *Peasants into Frenchmen: The Modernization of Rural France, 1870–1914*. London: Chatto & Windus.

Weiler, J. (1996) 'European citizenship and human rights', in J. Winter, D. Curtin, A. Kellerman and B. de Withe, *Reforming the Treaty on European Union:The Legal Debate*. London: Routledge.

Zalman, N. and Siegel, S. (1997) *Criminal Procedure: Constitution and Society*. St Paul, MN: West (2nd edn).

Index